Piers Plowman Studies X

SIGNES AND SOTHE: LANGUAGE IN
THE *PIERS PLOWMAN* TRADITION

Signes and Sothe examines the literary and historical tradition of poetry inspired by *Piers Plowman*. It explores the relationships of *Richard the Redeless*, *The Crowned King*, *Pierce the Ploughman's Crede* and *Mum and the Sothsegger* to each other, and to *Piers*. The book suggests ways in which these later poets read *Piers*, and how they perpetuated its distinctive compositional temper; it plots the changing significance of quotations from *Piers* when used in these later works; and, more widely, it suggests that the poems of the *Piers* tradition are a rich field for critical exploration – in their own right, and in their relationship to *Piers* and to other contemporary writing, both verse and prose.

The book is based on the premise that language is a social phenomenon, and it draws on a number of critical approaches – from modern linguistics, theories of discourse, manuscript annotation and medieval conceptions of authorship and intention. Throughout, concepts of literary style and poetic diction are considered in relation to the official discourses of Church and State. Analysis of the linguistic positions of the poems reveals their historical and political significance, especially with respect to ecclesiastical and secular allegiances.

The social implications of compositional method are examined in chapters on the use of wordplay, and the employment of distinctive diction, legal and Wycliffite. As in *Piers Plowman*, the use and function of language is an important concern in these poems and is expressly related to their mission to critique excesses and corruption in society. The creative use of 'signes' is a medium of saying 'sothe'.

Piers Plowman Studies

ISSN 0261-9849

Series Editor: James Simpson

Signes and Sothe

Language in the
Piers Plowman
Tradition

HELEN BARR

D. S. BREWER

First published 1994
D. S. Brewer, Cambridge

ISBN 0 85991 419 4

D. S. Brewer is an imprint of Boydell & Brewer Ltd
PO Box 9, Woodbridge, Suffolk IP12 3DF, UK
and of Boydell & Brewer Inc.
PO Box 41026, Rochester, NY 14604-4126, USA

British Library Cataloguing-in-Publication Data
Barr, Helen
    Signes and Sothe: Language in the "Piers Plowman"
    Tradition. – (Piers Plowman Studies, ISSN 0261-9849;
    Vol. 10)
    I. Title   II. Series
    821.1
    ISBN 0-85991-419-4

Library of Congress Catalog Card Number: 94-19105

The paper used in this publication meets the minimum requirements
of American National Standard for Information Sciences -
Permanence of Paper for Printed Library Materials, ANSI Z39.48-1984

Printed in Great Britain by
St Edmundsbury Press Ltd, Bury St Edmunds, Suffolk

Contents

Acknowledgements

I am grateful to Lady Margaret Hall, Oxford, for assistance towards research costs, and for a term's leave from teaching.

I should like to thank James Simpson for commissioning this book, for reading it so meticulously, and for his most generous support during its production. I should also like to thank Anne Hudson for reading the chapters as they were produced, and for her suggestions, and occasionally rescue, when I felt I had reached complete impasse.

Abbreviations

BJRL	*Bulletin of the John Rylands Library*
ChauR	*Chaucer Review*
CS	Camden Series
EETS	Early English Text Society
ELH	*English Literary History*
ELN	*English Language Notes*
EIC	*Essays in Criticism*
E&S	*Essays and Studies*
EWS	*English Wycliffite Sermons*, vols I and III, ed. A. Hudson, vol.II. ed. P. Gradon (Oxford, 1983, 1988 and 1990).
HLQ	*Huntingdon Library Quarterly*
JEGP	*Journal of English and Germanic Philology*
LSE	*Leeds Studies in English*
MED	*Middle English Dictionary*, ed. H. Kurath (Michigan, 1956-)
MESGK	*Middle English Studies Presented to George Kane*, ed. E.D. Kennedy, R. Waldron, and J. Wittig (Cambridge, 1988).
MLR	*Modern Language Review*
MP	*Modern Philology*
NM	*Neuphilologische Mitteillungen*
N&Q	*Notes and Queries*
OED	*Oxford English Dictionary*, ed. J.A.H. Murray, H. Bradley, W.A. Craigie, C.T. Onions (Oxford, 1933).
PQ	*Philological Quarterly*
PBA	*Publications of the British Academy*
PMLA	*Publications of the Modern Language Association of America*
PRIA	*Publications of the Royal Irish Academy*
RES	*Review of English Studies*
RS	Rolls Series
SAC	*Studies in the Age of Chaucer*
SCH	*Studies in Church History*
SEWW	*Selections from English Wycliffite Writings*, ed. A. Hudson (Cambridge, 1978).

Introduction

This study is primarily concerned with four alliterative poems: *Pierce the Ploughman's Crede, Richard the Redeless, Mum and the Sothsegger,* and *The Crowned King.* Since these poems may not be generally well known, and because most of my discussion will take the form of detailed focus on passages and individual usage of words and phrases, I shall make a few general and introductory points about the poems here.[1]

The four poems were written between 1393 and 1415. All four, though in different ways, and to differing degrees, were inspired by *Piers Plowman.* Their literary indebtedness to *Piers* is shown in the recall of key words and phrases and in the reminiscence of important episodes. Like *Piers,* they are written in alliterative long lines, within a plain alliterative register.[2] It is clear that the authors of all four poems had substantial knowledge of *Piers,* though of which version, or composite versions, it is hard to tell. It is likely that the poets knew *Piers* beyond the ending of the Visio. The most extensive acquaintance with the earlier poem is seen in *Mum:* echoes of *Piers* range from the Prologue to its closing lines.

The poems in the tradition respond to *Piers* primarily as a social document. Will's urgent, spiritual quest is scarcely reflected. All the poems show stalwart support for a hierarchically maintained society directed by a strong secular power. *Richard, Mum* and *The Crowned King* show support for a limited monarchy and *Mum,* in particular, criticises civil disobedience. In all of the poems there is scrutiny of institutions and their representatives, with criticism of the legal system, the church, and the decisions of government.

Although this scrutiny never compromises civil allegiance, two of the poems, *Crede* and *Mum,* overstep the bounds of orthodoxy in their analysis of the church. *Crede* is overt in its declared support for Wyclif and Wycliffite criticism of the church. *Mum,* influenced no doubt by the

---

[1] All references are to my edition of the poems in *The Piers Plowman Tradition* (London, 1993). The introduction and notes to the texts give a much fuller coverage of the points that I shall raise here briefly.

[2] I explore this point more fully in Chapter Two.

anti-Lollard legislation which had been passed since the completion of *Crede*, is much more guarded. Nonetheless, to a reader familiar with Wycliffite ideas and terminology, the anticlericalism bears witness both to Lollard ideas and to their suppression.[3]

The four new poems display a range of ideas and literary techniques. *Crede* is the earliest and adopts the name and figure of Piers Plowman to write an urgent and vigorous polemic against the friars. The narrative scheme of *Crede* is derived from Will's meeting with the friars in Passus VIII of *Piers*, and adapts Will's quest for spiritual insight. The narrator is introduced as one who wishes to find instruction in the basic articles of Christian belief and accordingly, he consults in turn the four orders of friars, hoping to find one of them prepared to teach him his creed. All that each friar gives him, however, is boasting of his own sanctity and rule, and slander of other fraternal orders.

Exhausted and disillusioned from his search, the narrator chances to meet a poor ploughman, his wife and three children. Like his namesake in *Piers*, Peres is introduced abruptly into the poem and immediately commands a position of authority. The simple ploughman is shown to have greater spiritual understanding and insight than any member of the institutionalised church. It is Peres, not the friars whom he denounces, who is able to teach the narrator his creed. The literary strategy of the poem contrasts the hypocrisy and selfishness of the friars with the sincerity and generosity of the abjectly poor ploughman. The friars' aggression and sinful living is contrasted with the true teachings of Wyclif.

Richard the Redeless is written directly after Henry Bolingbroke's accession to the throne, following Richard II's deposition in 1399. There is no explicit mention of Piers Plowman by name, but the new poem takes up many of the concerns about government that are explored in *Piers*. *Richard* uses the example of the errors of Richard II's reign, most especially the king's choice of unwise councillors, his excesses, and his disregard for law and order, to write an 'advice to princes' poem which is of benefit for future rulers. The poem laments the absence of anyone prepared to speak out against contemporary corruption and abuse. There is particular emphasis on the way that the legal system is corrupted through maintenance and bribery so that wrongs are unredressed because people are afraid to speak out. *Richard* supplies redress through its truthtelling criticism.

The poem often refers quite specifically to recent events. The last passus of the poem is a satirical account of a parliamentary meeting, and

---

[3] These points are examined in more detail in Chapter Four.

shows knowledge of the business of the 1398 session, which met in Shrewsbury.[4] There is also focussed criticism of Richard II's unjust treatment of three noblemen: the duke of Gloucester, and the earls of Arundel and Warwick, who accused him of misrule in 1397-8. In 1397, the September parliament accused these men of treason and sentenced them to death. Gloucester had already been murdered, and Warwick's sentence was commuted to permanent exile, but Arundel was executed on Tower Hill. The poem regards these events as contrary to natural justice and describes how the people of England flocked to Henry Bolingbroke on his return from the banishment imposed by Richard, to help him to redress this injustice. Henry's destruction of Richard's hated ministers is described, and throughout the poem Henry's example of good kingship is used as a foil to Richard's criminal misrule.

In many ways *Mum* continues where *Richard* left off. It discusses events and issues current in the first decade of the reign of Henry IV (1399-1409). The focus of the poem includes the civil disturbances of Henry IV's reign, the inadequacies of the universities, the corruption of the contemporary church, and the dishonesty and inefficency of the legal system and government. There is a sweeping review of the estates of society which weighs them all in the balance and finds them wanting.

The narration of events is less direct in *Mum*, probably because the poem considers events which concerned people who currently held positions of power. The poet may have had to exercise more caution because, as a result of the persistent unrest during the early years of Henry's reign, laws were promulgated to regulate the production of political verse. The restraint may also be attributable to the writer's sympathy with Wycliffite views.

Mum's founding narrative principle is the competition between speaking the truth and keeping Mum, out of self-interest and fraudulence. The poem adopts the quest strategy with the narrator going off in search for a truthteller, and travelling to all estates of society in the hope of finding one. Instead he finds that everyone is in league with Mum. Eventually, in a dream vision, he meets a beekeeper, who turns out to be the truthteller for whom the narrator has been seeking. He assures the narrator that Mum is the cause of all civil disturbance and church corruption. He encourages the narrator to continue his practice of speaking truthfully about faults in society, and to make a book of them. The narrator turns to a bag of books that had been confiscated by Mum and his confederates, and reads out a list of their contents. The bibliography contains a mixture of criticisms directed against the

---

[4] This is discussed in more detail in Chapter Two.

nobility, the legal system, government and the church. The poem breaks off abruptly in the middle of comments about the contemporary church.

Mum is the most ambitious of the four poems in literary terms. It catches something of *Piers*'s explorations of genres. In addition to dream vision, *Mum* uses the quest motif, debate, personification allegory and extended allegorical narrative sequences. The use of the bag of books as a narrative strategy to deflect the consequences of writing topical criticism away from the poet must rank as one of the most self-reflexively bookish moments in Middle English literature. It is a self-conscious proclamation of the political significance of literacy.

The Crowned King is much the shortest of the four poems. It is written in response to the start of Henry V's military campaign against the French in 1415. What interests the writer of *Crowned King* is the *cost* of the war. This focus on the consequences of taxation is similar to the pragmatic tone of the political vision in *Richard* and *Mum*. The poem is a dream vision in which a clerk offers a petition to the king. He urges him to consider the welfare of his subjects and to cherish their allegiance, because it is much more valuable than material wealth. The advice which the clerk offers to the king is typical of the comments in 'advice to princes' literature, but in the context of commenting on a recent tax ordinance to finance a military invasion, these topoi are given a topical and political edge.

There are clear echoes of the Prologue of *Piers*. The clerk recalls the 'lunatik', who kneeling 'clergially' before the king, urges him to rule his kingdom justly to earn allegiance (123-5). The echoes of *Piers* are appropriate. Just as the lunatic's comments occur in the context of the public ritual of coronation, in *Crowned King*, the poem's narrative strategies cut through the public triumphalism surrounding the preparations for Henry V's military campaign.

All four poems question institutions and institutionalised, public issues in terms of what they mean for the community and for anonymous individuals. My present study is concerned with the linguistic implications of that interrogation. It addresses the significance of the types of literary language that are used in the poems, and how literary 'traditions' and poetic diction relate to the official discourses of church and state.

1

Locating Tradition

It is by no means a foregone conclusion that *Pierce the Ploughman's Crede, Richard the Redeless, Mum and the Sothsegger* and *The Crowned King* constitute 'the *Piers Plowman* tradition'. In two separate studies published in 1977, Thorlac Turville-Petre and Derek Pearsall categorised a mode of alliterative poetry which addressed social and political issues in a style that was plainer and more informal than poems in the 'classical' alliterative corpus. This alternative alliterative corpus included *Piers Plowman*, together with *Crede, Richard, Mum* and *Crowned King*, but neither Turville-Petre or Pearsall labelled these later poems 'the *Piers Plowman* tradition'.[1] Turville-Petre commented that *Richard* and *Mum* continued a 'tradition of political satire in alliterative verse after Langland',[2] and Pearsall referred to the poems not as a tradition but as a group.[3] A decade later, Anne Hudson included these poems in her discussion of the *Piers* legacy, but while she referred to literary traditions in general there was no mention of a *Piers Plowman* tradition in particular.[4]

By contrast, David Lawton used the label 'the *Piers Plowman* tradition' both in his discussion of the four poems as a corpus of informal alliterative poetry, and in the title of an article.[5] Even if the term 'tradition' is used, however, there are problems in determining which poems could be said to belong, or not to belong, to a *Piers* 'tradition'.

---

[1] Thorlac Turville-Petre, *The Alliterative Revival* (Cambridge, 1977), pp.31-32; Derek Pearsall, *Old and Middle English Poetry* (London, 1977), pp.150-58. The distinction between these two modes of poetry is explored more fully in Chapter Two.

[2] *Alliterative Revival*, p.32.

[3] See also his later discussion in 'The Alliterative Revival: Origins and Social Backgrounds' in David Lawton, ed., *Middle English Alliterative Poetry* (Cambridge, 1982), 34-53, p.40.

[4] Anne Hudson, 'The Legacy of *Piers Plowman*', in *A Companion to Piers Plowman*, ed. J.A. Alford (Berkeley, 1988), 251-66, 254. (1988²)

[5] David Lawton, ed., *Middle English Alliterative Poetry* (Cambridge, 1982), p.2 and pp.9-10 and 'Lollardy and the *Piers Plowman* Tradition', *MLR*, 76 (1981), 780-93.

Lawton has made the case for the influence of the A text of *Piers* on *The Parliament of the Three Ages*, *Death and Life*, *St Erkenwald* and *Winner and Waster*, and has argued elsewhere that the early sixteenth century historical poem *Scottish Feilde* and a poem by John Audelay, are clearly indebted to *Piers Plowman*.[6] Thomas Usk's *Testament of Love* has been thought to have been influenced by the C text of *Piers*,[7] and it has been suggested that Chaucer's *General Prologue* was broadly influenced by the satirical techniques of *Piers*.[8]

These diverse views make it clear that 'the *Piers Plowman* tradition' is a contested classification. Even without the attributive label of *Piers Plowman*, the word 'tradition', especially when preceded by the definite article, is not a term than can be thought of as natural.[9] In many ways, however, this is an advantage. It is unsurprising that a discourse such as literary criticism should contain sites of competition;[10] and the contest over 'tradition' foregrounds some the connotations of this loaded word that might otherwise remain opaque. David Lawton has profiled some

---

[6] David Lawton, 'The Unity of Middle English Alliterative Poetry', *Speculum*, 58 (1983), 72-94; cf. Lawton (1982), pp.10-11; '*Scottish Field*: Alliterative Verse and Stanley Encomium in the Percy Folio', *LSE*, 10 (1978), 42-57. Audelay's poem is the second in *The Poems of John Audelay*, ed. E.K. Whiting (EETS 184 1931) and is discussed in 'The Diversity of Middle English Alliterative Poetry', *LSE*, 20 (1989), 143-72, p.163.

[7] W.W. Skeat, ed., *Chaucerian and Other Pieces*, *The Complete Works of Geoffrey Chaucer* (Oxford, 1897), VII 465-66.

[8] J.A.W. Bennett, 'Chaucer's Contemporary' in *Piers Plowman: Critical Approaches*, ed. S.S. Hussey (London, 1969), 310-24, Jill Mann, *Chaucer and Medieval Estates Satire* (Cambridge, 1973), 208-12 and Helen Cooper, 'Langland's and Chaucer's Prologues', *YLS*, 1 (1987), 71-81. Hudson (1988²) reviews these cases, pp.253-54. Even outside the complications of dating, if these works were influenced by *Piers*, not one of them demonstrates all aspects of the indebtedness which characterises *Mum*, *Crowned King*, *Crede* and *Richard*, namely: the adoption of narrative strategies; the reprise of episodes and verbal echoes; the sustained use of serious wordplay and the perpetuation of a social poetic temper. These points are discussed more fully in the course of this book.

[9] This point is based on the discussion in G. Kress, *Linguistic Processes in Sociocultural Practices* (Oxford, 1985), pp.10-11 of the way that modes and terms of communication appear natural and common sense if they are discussed within a single mode of discourse that has dominated how a topic should be discussed. A colonising discourse makes what is conventional appear natural because it edits out the contradictions and objections which are apparent when a subject is the site of competing discourses.

[10] The term discourse derives from M. Foucault, *The Archaeology of Knowledge*, trans. A.M. Sheridan Smith (London, 1972), pp.50-2. My use of it follows the definition of linguists such as Kress, pp.4-32: 'Discourses are systematically-organised sets of statements which give expression to the meanings and values of an institution. . .A discourse provides a set of possible statements about a given area, and organises and gives structure to the manner in which a particular topic, object, process is to be talked about in that it provides descriptions, rules, permissions and prohibitions of social and individual actions', p.7. See also David Lee, in *Competing Discourses* (London, 1992), pp.14-16 for analysis of sites of contestation in discussion of the discourses which compete in narrating Australian history. In literary criticism, the quotation marks around 'tradition', or 'canon' are signs of an emergent critical discourse which contests these terms with those such as 'cultural studies', and 'subjectivity'.

of these implications in his discussion of the critical significance of the attempt to locate a 'unity' of alliterative poetry:

> It is as if the terminology insists on a unitary phenomenon, a 'continuum' or 'tradition', whereas all the hard evidence – the evidence we review when looking at texts and their readers – points towards a bewildering plurality and diversity. Who is to say, and with what meaning that they add up to one tradition?[11]

While the location of 'tradition' even within a smaller group of alliterative poems than those which Lawton is considering, is to some extent an act of territorialism, drawing boundaries is an inescapable fact of critical behaviour.[12] What should not escape attention however, is investigation of the agency behind those boundaries. In terms of literary history and criticism, the 'who' to whom Lawton adverts are quite simply the previous critics who have been given institutional authority by being published and then quoted, if only in disagreement, in subsequent publications. This institutional authority, as the work of Kuhn and Foucault on 'paradigms' and 'epistemes' has shown, is itself but a discourse.[13]

While I recognise the territorial implications of employing the term 'tradition' (which henceforward I shall use without quotation marks), no label I might have used to group together *Crede*, *Mum* and *Richard* and *Crowned King* could have been free of ideological positioning.[14] In my view, to examine these four poems as an affiliated group which is demonstrably dependent on *Piers Plowman*, that is, as a tradition, is appropriate to enable reading the poems individually and the kinds of response which *Piers Plowman* generated. My grouping of these poems under the term 'the *Piers Plowman* tradition' is but one choice of classification, a classification which the material offered in this book, and the conclusions I have drawn from it, is intended to explain.[15]

[11] D. Lawton, 'The Diversity of Middle English Alliterative Poetry', p.151. His terminology is akin to the 'colonisation of dominant discourses' discussed by Kress, p.7.
[12] Since literary critical practice must use language, and since individual words themselves are, at a very basic level, classificatory devices, (see further, Lee, pp.1-23) the process of selection and classification cannot be avoided.
[13] Thomas S. Kuhn, *The Structure of Scientific Revolutions* (Chicago, 1962); M. Foucault (1972).
[14] While 'tradition' annexes four alliterative poems of dubious literary reputation into the illustrious territory of *Piers Plowman*, and grants them a cohesion and status as a result, 'legacy' has connotations of personal property, and 'progeny' is not free of Bloom-derived Oedipal anxieties, (Harold Bloom, *The Anxiety of Influence* (New York, 1973)). These connotations are inappropriate to my argument. 'Group' is a more neutral term but given that it is meaningful only in the context of distinguishing types of alliterative poetry from each other, its use would still imply territorialism without making the kinds of distinctions for which the term 'tradition' is appropriate.
[15] This is not to suggest the absence of various other contexts within which *Piers* and the

From a less theoretical perspective, it is important to consider whether tradition, in the sense of literary tradition, is an appropriate critical category to apply to Middle English works. N.F. Blake has argued that there was no feeling of tradition in medieval English literature in that people knew and remembered the words of English literary works:

> No single English text was sufficiently well known for an author to assume that his readers would be so familiar to it that he could allude to its verbal expressions.[16]

He contrasts this absence of vernacular literary tradition to the function and use of literary echoes in the works of later writers such as Pope and T.S. Eliot.[17] Blake's caution about verbal correspondence between works is echoed by A.C. Spearing and R.A. Axton.[18] Axton, in considering the relationship between Chaucer and Gower, makes an important distinction between 'symbiosis of ideas' and the extent to which one poem exercises 'textual force' on another.[19]

In locating tradition, both these caveats, the awareness, or not, of vernacular tradition, and the demonstrable existence of textual force between works, are crucial. It is possible, however, as Spearing shows, to be cognisant of this caution and still to locate a sense of tradition in Middle English literature which is more precise than 'symbiosis of ideas'. Spearing notes how Chaucer was concerned with the accurate transmission of his poetry to the future: he was not content that it should simply be absorbed into a body of changing and fading verses. One way in which he took care to establish his fame as an author was by including in his writings several lists of his own works.[20] Chaucer's awareness of his writings as an oeuvre and of his place in literary

poems indebted to it can be profitably examined, English and non-English, verse and prose. The literary contexts of *Piers* are discussed in the following: T. Turville-Petre, *The Alliterative Revival*; B.S. Levy and P. Szarmach, *The Alliterative Tradition in the Fourteenth Century* (Ohio, 1981); S.S. Hussey, 'Langland's Reading of Alliterative Poetry', *MLR*, 60 (1965), 163-70; E. Salter, '*Piers Plowman* and *The Simonie*', *Archiv*, 203 (1967), 241-54; 'Alliterative Modes and Affiliations in the Fourteenth Century', *Neuph. Mitt.*, 79 (1978), 25-35; 'Langland and the Contexts of *Piers Plowman*', *E&S*, 32 (1979), 19-25, D.A. Lawton, 'Lollardy and the *Piers Plowman* Tradition'; ed., *Middle English Alliterative Poetry and its Literary Background*; 'The Unity of Middle English Alliterative Poetry'; 'Alliterative Style' in *A Companion to Piers Plowman*, ed. J. Alford (Berkeley, 1988), 223-50 and 'The Diversity of Middle English Alliterative Poetry'. Of the poems in the tradition, the contexts supplied, for example, by other political poems, chronicles and Wycliffite tracts are obviously important, and blur the distinctions between verse and prose, English and Latin.
16 N.F. Blake, *The English Language in Medieval Literature* (London, 1979), p.21.
17 ibid., p.28.
18 A.C. Spearing, *Medieval to Renaissance in English Poetry* (Cambridge, 1985), pp.59-120; R.A. Axton, 'Chaucer's Heir' in *Chaucer Traditions*, ed. Ruth Morse and B. Windeatt (Cambridge, 1990), 21-38.
19 Axton, p.23.
20 Spearing, p.59.

posterity, gave impetus for later writers, as Barry Windeatt has argued, to view him as an 'auctor'. With Chaucer's 'auctoritee' established, English poetry could, for the first time, look back on that tradition in the conscious way that was necessary for a sense of the seriousness, the dignity and the worthiness of their own literary culture.[21]

There are, of course, different kinds of Chaucerian indebtednesses, different traditions. Hoccleve names his revered literary father and leaves a space for his portrait,[22] but despite his indebtedness to the rhyme royal stanza, there are far fewer verbal echoes of Chaucer than one would expect to find in the work of an immediate follower.[23] The anonymous *Partonope of Blois*, by contrast, never names Chaucer, but the romance is steeped in echoes of a range of Chaucer's works: in precise verbal detail; in the connotations of its original context; and in the typical handling of the Chaucerian narrator.[24]

Chaucer, however, is not *Piers Plowman* and my imbalance of author and work is deliberate. There is nothing in *Piers Plowman* equivalent to Chaucer's naming and framing of himself as a vernacular author within the context of classical, continental, and even native tradition.[25] No Dantesque eagle scoops up the narrator of *Piers Plowman* from the writer's block engendered by the anxiety of influence and treats him to an aerial lecture tour on Boethian physics (*House of Fame*, 529-864). At no point in *Piers Plowman* does its author gives us a list of his works by name, even if only to poke fun at his 'lewed' versification (*CT*, II 46-76) or to retract those that 'sownen into synne' (*CT*, X 1085). Chaucer bequeathed to posterity a poem addressed to Adam the scribe, threatening grievous bodily harm if he failed to copy his work accurately (ll.3-4). At the end of *Troilus and Criseyde*, the narrator fears that his work will be mismetred because of the diversity of the English tongue precisely at the point where he has just included himself amongst the classical oeuvre of worthy writers in the 'sixth of sixth' topos (V 1786-99).[26] In *Piers*, by contrast, the absence of good versification is attributed

---

[21] Barry Windeatt, 'Chaucer Traditions' in *Chaucer Traditions*, 1-20, p.7 and cf. Helen Cooper, 'Generic Variations on the Theme of Poetic and Civil Authority' in *Poetics: Theory and Practice in Middle English Literature*, ed. P. Boitani and A. Torti (Cambridge, 1991), 83-103, p.90.

[22] Hoccleve, *Regement of Princes*, 4978-98, ed. F.J. Furnivall (EETS ES 72 1897).

[23] J.A. Burrow, 'Hoccleve and Chaucer' in *Chaucer Traditions*, 54-61, p.59.

[24] Barry Windeatt, 'Chaucer and Fifteenth Century Romance: *Partonope of Blois*' in *Chaucer Traditions*, 62-80.

[25] Chaucer's own *Tale of Sir Thopas* may be seen as a burlesque example of Chaucer's framing himself in the tradition of East Midland tail-rhyme romance.

[26] In *Inferno*, IV 102, Dante is admitted into the company of Homer, Horace, Ovid, Lucan and Virgil: 'Si ch'io fui sesto tra cotanto senno', *The Divine Comedy*, ed. and trans. C.S. Singleton (Princeton, 1970). Chaucer's treatment of the topos is discussed by P. Boitani, *Chaucer and the Imaginary World of Fame* (Cambridge, 1984), p.156.

to children who are baffled by grammar (B XV 372-75. cf. C XVII 107-10) and complaints about inaccurate scribes are restricted to the context of Scripture (A XI 225 and C XI 97).

Chaucer is named both by his followers and in his own works. The Dantesque eagle names him 'Geffrey' in the *House of Fame* (729) and in his *Prologue*, the Man of Lawe refers to the tales told by 'Chaucer', albeit a Chaucer who writes bad verse (47).These are acts of naming within self-consciously literary moments. *Piers Plowman* stands in great contrast. It has been possible to construct an author for *Piers* out of the correspondence of manuscript inscription with a cryptogram in the text, but it was many years before there was a consensus of opinion on the name 'William Langland'.[27] It is still by no means agreed how much, or which versions, of *Piers Plowman* we can attribute to this name.[28]

While the narrator of *Piers* is called 'Wille', since this term names also a faculty of the soul, it is not a 'kynde name' of the same equivalence as 'Geffrey'.[29] Further, the line in which the author is thought most clearly to have encoded his name: ' "I haue lyued in londe" quod [I], "my name is longe wille" ' (B XV 152), is found only in B version manuscripts,[30] and is located in the context of determing where 'charite' – 'a frend wiþ so fre an herte' (XV 151) may be found. In contrast to Chaucer, and indeed to Gower in *Vox Clamantis*, the riddle occurs neither in the context of declaring the contents of the poet's literary oeuvre, nor in claiming prophetic status for the author at the start of a long Latin poem.[31]

---

[27] A very early fifteenth century note in a C text manuscript, Trinity College Dublin MS 212, ascribes the poem to 'Willielm[us] de Langlond'. The arguments in G. Kane, *The Evidence for Authorship* (London, 1965) settled previous critical debates on the question. There is a recent examination of the question, together with full bibliographical details in Ralph Hanna III, *William Langland* (Aldershot, 1993), pp.1-6.

[28] The Z text of *Piers Plowman* is a classic case. The arguments for regarding the text of Bodleian Library MS Bodley 581 as a unique copy of an authorial version of the poem ante-dating the A version, are set out in *Piers Plowman: The Z Version*, ed. A.G. Rigg and Charlotte Brewer (Toronto, 1983). George Kane dismisses this argument in his review of the edition, G. Kane, 'The "Z version" of *Piers Plowman*', *Speculum*, 60 (1985), 910-30 but it is defended on metrical grounds by A.V.C. Schmidt, 'The Authenticity of the Z-text of *Piers Plowman*: Further Notes on Metrical Evidence', *Medium Aevum*, 56 (1987), 25-45. See also ref. to Ralph Hanna in preceding note.

[29] The experiential significance of Will's authorial identity is discussed by Anne Middleton, 'William Langland's "Kynde Name": Authorial Signature and Social Identity in Late Fourteenth-Century England' in ed. Lee Patterson, *Literary Practice and Social Change in Britain, 1380-1530* (Berkeley, 1990), 15-82.

[30] C reads: 'Ich haue yleued in Londone monye longe ȝeres' (XVI 286). MS U reads 'londe' for 'Londone'.

[31] In the Prologue to Book I of *Vox Clamantis*, Gower advises the reader who wishes to know the name of the author to take the first three feet from 'Godfrey' add them to 'John', plus the initial of Wales, and the sequence 'Ter' without its head (20-24). Gower concludes the prologue by asking guidance from St John, whose name he bears, who on the Isle of

To be sure, there are moments in *Piers* which are self-conscious about the making of poetry. But it is significant that at these moments, with the exception perhaps of the comment in C V 24 that Will is 'to long, lef me, lowe for to stoupe', the narrator does not draw attention to his own name. One cannot read these episodes as statements of 'auctoritee' which stake a claim to a place in literary tradition. Ymaginatif's rebuke to the narrator is well known:

> . . .Þow medlest þee wiþ makynges and my3test go seye þi sauter,
> And bidde for hem þat 3yueþ þee breed, for þer are bokes y[n]owe
> To telle men what dowel is, dobet and dobest boþe.   (B XII 16-18)

'Makynges' do not constitute a poetic oeuvre, and the other books to which Ymaginatif refers are concerned with 'doing' not 'makyng' – and they are not 'auctored'. The discussions about poetry in *Piers Plowman* centre not on the anxiety of influence, but on the anxiety of the spiritual worth of the activity of writing and the social consequences of its reception.[32] Will is more anxious as to whether his name is written in the Legend of Life (B X 380-2) than in a House of Fame, and is more anxious about the effects of his work on those who 'reden it in Retorik to arate dedly synne' (B XI 102) than about comparing his literary efforts with those of others. This is not to suggest that *Piers* is concerned solely with message and is heedless of form: *Piers* is self-conscious about language[33] but not about the literary fame of its author.

In *The Arte of English Poesie* (1589), George Puttenham surveys the work of previous poets, listing Chaucer, Gower and Lydgate, and then: 'that nameles, who wrote the Satyre called Piers Plowman'.[34] In its early reception, *Piers Plowman* was more often associated with the name of Piers Plowman than William Langland. In manuscripts, the name 'Piers Plowman' predominates in incipits and explicits. Eighteen manuscripts contain explicits which refer to the work variously as the dialogue, vision, debate or book of Piers Plowman.[35] Not only is the dreamer

Patmos, received the revelation of the apocalypse (56-8). Gower's cryptogram is more self-consciously delivered than that in *Piers*, and his named alliance to St John makes the highest claims for the prophetic voice of his poem. Gower also names himself at the close of *Confessio Amantis*, VIII 2321-2.

[32] This is discussed by James Simpson, 'The Constraints of Satire in *Piers Plowman* and *Mum and the Sothsegger*' in ed. Helen Phillipps, *Langland, the Mystics and the Medieval English Religious Tradition* (Cambridge, 1990), 11-30.

[33] The studies by A.V.C. Schmidt, *The Clerkly Maker: Langland's Poetic Art* (Cambridge, 1987) and M.C. Davlin, *The Game of Heuene* (Cambridge, 1989) fully illustrate the linguistic complexity of the poem.

[34] George Puttenham, *The Arte of English Poesie* quoted from *Elizabethan Critical Essays*, ed. G.G. Smith (Oxford, 1937), 2nd edn, vol. 2, pp.62-3.

[35] Marie-Louise Uhart, *The Early Reception of 'Piers Plowman'* (unpublished Leicester PhD thesis, 1986) p.48.

conflated with Piers[36] but Piers Plowman assumes the status of 'auctor'. In two manuscripts in the A tradition which add lines to the end of the text; one, The Library of the Society of Antiquaries MS 687 bids that God will grant us everlasting joy to dwell in his bliss with 'pers the plowman';[37] and the other, British Library MS Harley 3954, bids its readers to pray for 'pers the plowmans soule'.[38] This manuscript heads the work 'Perys Plowman' and contains an expansive explicit:

> Explicit tractatus de perys plowman quaþ herun
> Qui cum patre et spiritu sanctu viuit & regnat per omnia secula
> seculorum. Amen.

If 'qui' refers to 'perys plowman', then it grants him a status far exceeding that suggested by incipits or explicits which refer by name to Will or to Langland.[39]

Rubrication in the manuscripts of *Piers* frequently draws attention to the name Piers Plowman both in the division of the poem into sections and by marking the appearance and actions of the figure in the poem.[40] By contrast, Bodleian Library MS Rawlinson Poetry 38 is unique in supplying a 'nota' in red at XV 152, where the narrator says that his name is 'longe wille'.[41] The closest that any other manuscript rubrication comes to drawing attention to Will in the poem is Huntingdon Library MS Hm 143. This manuscript is accompanied by glosses which provide a commentary on the narrative action of the poem. In Passus V, the rubricator adds 'hyer conscience arated Wille for his lollynge' and 'hyer Wille answers to rayson' but does not pick up on Wille's activity as a

---

[36] The confusion between the dreamer and Piers is explicitly registered in the annotation in a C text manuscript. On fol. 26a in British Library MS Harley 2376, the passage V 140-66 is underlined and annotated 'William and PP', information derived from Uhart, p.130.

[37] Kane, *The A Version*, p.49.

[38] Kane, *The A Version*, p.48.

[39] Kane, *The A Version*, p.8. A late annotator to Society of Antiquaries MS 687 refers to 'Piers Plougman's vision: The author Robert Langland, a chiefe disciple of John Wickliff', Uhart, p.245. Liverpool University MS F.4.8 has 'Explicit liber Willelmi de petro le plouȝman', Uhart, p.248; Huntingdon Library MS HM 137 has 'hic incipit visio Willelmi de petro plouhman', and concludes 'explicit peeres plouhman', Uhart, p.269. The incipits and explicits of Sterling MS V.17, Uhart, p.271 and Trinity College Dublin MS 212 follow a similar pattern, Uhart, p.273.

[40] Uhart, p.48. In my use of annotation to manuscripts of *Piers*, I am aware that interpretation of such comment is necessarily subjective. While to a modern reader a 'nota' placed beside a line may seem to suggest that its author found its substance of particular value, all annotation, whether medieval or modern, is written for a variety of reasons, sometimes simply to mark a place in a text to resume reading from. A striking example of the plurality of interpretations that can be placed on a jotting is Derrida's discussion of a line of Nietzsche's found amongst his papers, 'I have forgotten my umbrella', *Spurs* (Chicago, 1978), pp.123-43. My use of the annotation to manuscripts of *Piers* is based on the premise that such commentary foregrounds certain parts of the text, whatever meaning is subsequently attached to them by a later reader.

[41] Uhart, p.261.

writer either here, or in his later rebuke by Ymaginatif.[42] In sum, with an exception to a continuation to an A manuscript which is discussed in more detail below, the early response to *Piers*, as evidenced by scribal activity and annotation, shows small enthusiasm for William Langland as named author of the poem but much interest in the figure of Piers Plowman and in the issues which the poem raises.[43]

What this evidence suggests is that in locating a tradition of poetry which looks back to *Piers Plowman* as a source of inspiration, we must regard the corpus in a different light from the self-naming and self-fashioning literary tradition authored by Chaucer. As will be discussed in the next chapter, *Mum, Crede, Crowned King* and *Richard* follow not so much an author and and his style as the socially-orientated poetic temper discernible in all versions of *Piers*. Unsurprisingly, none of the poems in the *Piers* tradition names William Langland as exemplar or guide. *Pierce the Ploughman's Crede* explicitly seeks authority in the name, speeches and actions of Piers Plowman. As will be discussed further in Chapter Five, the 'auctorising' of all four poems is accomplished not by reference to dead poets with illustrious names but with reference to standards of legal propriety and truth.

In this respect, the poems in the *Piers* tradition are of a spirit with the attitude towards tradition which Elisabeth Salter posited with respect to *Piers Plowman*: that the only declared allegiance of the poem was to a tradition more conceptual than literary, one of pursuing the truth, a tradition which accepts the help of whatever texts and authors may be available.[44] The poems are also consonant with the aims and voice of the kind of public poetry which Anne Middleton has discussed, that which sees the making of poetry as an activity in the world, where the 'I' of the poetry is simply one worker amongst others, whose talent is used for the public good.[45] This is not to suggest, however, that *Piers Plowman* did

---

[42] The annotations are recorded in full in Uhart, pp.332-9 and those from Passus XI-XV are published in G.H. Russell, 'Some Early Responses to the C-version of *Piers Plowman'*, *Viator*, 15 (1984), 276-91.

[43] Uhart notes that there are six main centres of interest amongst the rubricators: the noting of moral qualities and their personifications; general and individual personae of the poem; attention to structural elements of the poem associated with sermon literature; noting of key incidents; Piers the Plowman, and prophecy, p.83. G.H. Russell identifies two main types of rubrication: the identification of names, personae and auctores, historical exempla and biblical texts; structural devices such as legal documents, preaching and prophecy, the sins, the appearance of Piers and the various other key episodes and structural elements of the poem, (1984), p.276. Wendy Scase examines the significance of the annotations to manuscripts of *Piers* throughout her study, *Piers Plowman and the New Anti-Clericalism* (Cambridge, 1989).

[44] E. Salter (1979), p.25.

[45] Anne Middleton, 'The Idea of Public Poetry in the Reign of Richard II', *Speculum*, 53 (1978), 94-114, p.99.

not exert 'textual force' on the poems which followed it. Public poetry and poetry as social action are not incompatible with direct textual reference. The letters of John Ball provide an interesting case.

John Ball, one of the leaders of the 1381 uprising, used a variety of pseudonyms in letters sent to his confederates to rally the cause.[46] These letters weave together scraps of proverbs and vernacular verse popularised in sermons with references to *Piers Plowman*.[47] Alongside the name 'Peres Ploughman' are what appear to be quotations from the poem. John Schep's letter bids the rebels to 'dowelle and bettre and fleth synne' and to 'chastise Hobbe the robber'; Jakke Carter's promises that he and Piers Ploughman will find food and John Ball's contrasts 'trewthe' with a catalogue of the Deadly Sins. Interestingly, like the list in A versions of *Piers Plowman*, Wrath is omitted from Ball's account.[48] This would appear to be the closest instance of *Piers* exerting textual force on the later letters, though as Anne Hudson has noted, given that there is an omission mark in the manuscript of the chronicle where Wrath ought to be included, its absence may owe as much to the context of inflammatory revolt as to the direct influence of the narrative of *Piers*.[49]

From the range of references to *Piers*, it is clear that the writer of these letters was familiar with *Piers* beyond its title. But what was the nature of this familiarity? There is more than symbiosis of ideas but is it the case that these letters 'quote' the text of *Piers Plowman*? There are no lines listed verbatim and the letters themselves hover uncertainly between verse and prose.[50] Moreover, the parts of *Piers* singled out for comment coincide with the parts of the poem most densely rubricated in the manuscripts by copyists who must be counted amongst its earliest readers.[51]

[46] The letters are preserved in varying forms in the contemporary chronicles written by Thomas Walsingham, *Historia Anglicana*, ed. H.T. Riley (RS 1864), 2 vols, II.33-4 and Henry Knighton, *Chronicon*, ed. J.R.Lumby (RS 1889-95), 2 vols, II.138-40. The texts of the letters are collected in R.B. Dobson, *The Peasants' Revolt of 1381* (London, 1970), pp.379-83.
[47] This is discussed by Richard Firth Green, 'John Ball's Letters: Literary History and Historical Literature' in ed. Barbara A.Hanawalt, *Chaucer's England: Literature in Historical Context* (Minnesota, 1992), 176-200.
[48] This is noted by Green, p.182 and Helen Cooper (1987), pp.73-4.
[49] Anne Hudson '*Piers Plowman* and the Peasants' Revolt: A Problem Revisited' (paper delivered at the Cambridge Langland Conference, July 1993, forthcoming *YLS*). She notes that the omission in British Library MS Cotton Tiberius C.vii (Knighton's chronicle) may have been inadvertent; simply a copying slip.
[50] A point made in Hudson's Cambridge paper.
[51] See note 37. For discussion of scribes as readers and critics, see E.T. Donaldson, 'The Texts of *Piers Plowman*: scribes and poets', *MP*, 1 (1952), 269-73; 'MSS R and F in the B Tradition of *Piers Plowman*', *TCAAS*, 39 (1955), 177-212; B.A. Windeatt, 'The Scribes as Chaucer's Earliest Critics', *SAC*, 1 (1979), 119-42; P. Strohm, 'Chaucer's Fifteenth Century Audience and the Narrowing of the 'Chaucer tradition', *SAC*, 4 (1982), 3-32.

The activities of Piers Plowman are consistently annotated and his name predominates, as we have seen, in incipits and explicits. Next to Piers, the most consistent centre of attraction is the list of the Deadly Sins. In nearly all manuscripts, even in those which have little other annotation, these sins are underlined, or boxed and their names often written out in the margin.[52] Visually, this section of the poem commands attention. The same is true of references to Dowel and Dobet: the rubrication which divides the poem into passus frequently employs these terms and the words are often marked by underlining where they appear in the text.[53] Furthermore, the names of the actants in John Ball's letters blend fictional representation and plausible historical identity[54] and it is interesting that names of this type in *Piers*, from Letyse at the Style, Chichester the Mayor, to Robert the Robber himself, often attract the interest of rubricators.[55] So too do the prophetic passages in *Piers*. The texts of Ball's letters do not explicitly draw on the verbal details of prophetic passages in *Piers*, but menacing phrases such as 'ygrounde smal, smal, smal;/The Kynges sone of heuene schal paye for al'; 'Loke thy mylne go aright, with the foure sayles, and the post stande in stedfastnesse' and 'for now is tyme' create a tone similar to that of the

---

[52] Examples of manuscripts which rubricate the sins yet nothing, or scarcely anything, else, include: Bodleian Library MS Rawlinson Poetry 137 (Uhart, p.281); Huntingdon Library MS Hm 128 (Uhart, pp.299-300); Newnham College Cambridge, MS Yates-Thompson (Uhart, p.314) and Corpus Christi College, Cambridge MS 293 (Uhart, p.328).
[53] For instance, in Bodleian Library MS Laud.Misc.581, a rubric at the beginning of Passus VIII reads: 'passus octauus de visione & primus de dowel (et hic explicit et incipit inquiscio prima de dowel). In this manuscript, Latin quotations and principal actants are often underlined and boxed in red. At XII 268, in the line 'What were dowel and dobet and dobest atte laste' the 'dowel' triad is underlined and partitioned in red ink (fol. 49b) and XIII 152-4, which contains the line 'fast ybounde Dowel', is marked off in red (fol. 54b). Bodleian Library MS Digby 171 is given a title in 1531 which reads: 'This book is clepped: Sayewell, Doowell, Doo Better and Doo Best', (Uhart, p.267).
[54] This is a point made in Hudson's 1993 Cambridge paper.
[55] Bodleian Library MS Laud Misc. 581 places a nota at XIII 270 and boxes 'chichestre' and 'maire' in red (fol. 56a). Robert the Robber is marked by a paraph in University College MS 45 (Uhart, p.282) at V 233; by a 'nota' in British Library MS Add.35287 at V 460 (Uhart, p.354), and in Huntingdon Library MS Hm 143 there are additional subject headings, including 'Robber ryffler' at VI 316 and 'hyer was letise at stile y schent for sche tok hali bred to rathe' at VI 145 (Uhart, p.334). Letyse is also marked in Huntingdon Library MS Hm114 at VI 145-6 (Uhart, p.303) and in Bodleian Library MS Digby 102 at VI 145 (Uhart, p.333). This interest in names is also shown by the insertion into Trinity College Dublin, MS D.4.12 (A text) at II 76, which adds three people to the witnesses of Mede's charter, Kane, *The A Version*, p.49. The textual variations at this point, e.g.: 'poulynes doctour/ douȝter/ Paulyns doctrine (B II 109)/ Sent Poules chirche (Z II 80); Bette/Bernard; bukyngham shire/Bekyngham/Bannebury sokene; Randolf/Reynald/Ranald; rutelondis sokne/Roteland/rokelond; Munde/Mundy/Maclum/Maude; myllere/Mellere/mylnere/ melleward/mullere'; and 'manye mo oþere/of malwiche strete' suggest both active interest amongst the scribes and uncertainty between fictional representation and the names of actual people and places. (variants selected from Kane, p.212, Kane Donaldson, p.261 and Pearsall, II 110-13)

prophetic passages in *Piers* and indicate a centre of interest shared both by the author of these letters and by those responsible for the layout of the poem in its manuscripts.[56]

The correspondence between the nature of reference to *Piers* in these letters and the dominant centres of interest of the rubricators may be no more than coincidence. It would be extreme to suggest that Ball's familiarity with *Piers* extended no further than knowledge of its rubrics, but perhaps it is plausible to posit a reading response to *Piers* that was guided by the emphases of manuscript layout. Given that these letters are coded utterances whose communicative value depends upon a shared knowledge between sender and receiver, it would be an appropriate tactic to allude to those parts of *Piers* which, by virtue of their visual predominance on the page, Ball might have expected his readers to recall. Just as Ball's use of traditional pieces of preaching material makes them inflammatory in their new context, so too does his reference to comparatively tame parts of *Piers Plowman*.[57]

Whatever the precise nature of the textual force which *Piers* exerted on these letters, it is clear that the response viewed the poem not as a verbal icon but as a work to be used in social action, a response which corresponds to Middleton's interpretation of a public poetry which presents a common voice rather than a privileged speaker, a worker with a talent to be used for the 'common good'.[58] While the 'common good' envisioned by Ball is hardly identical to the tone of bourgeois moderation which Middleton identifies as integral to the public voice, his use of *Piers* recognises neither a text anchored to an 'auctor', nor a controlling 'I' whose fame is indistinguishable from its status as personal property. To Ball, *Piers* is, quite literally, a 'text amongst others' that is set to work.

In this respect, the response to *Piers* evinced by Ball's letters shares points of similarity with the four alliterative poems which are my main focus of study, and as such, may be seen as a part of an incipient *Piers*

---

[56] Letters quoted from Dobson, pp.381-3. The interest of the *Piers* rubricators in prophecy has been noted above, see n.37. G. Kane, 'Some Fourteenth Century "Political" Poems' in *Medieval English Religious and Ethical Literature:Essays in Honour of G.H. Russell*, ed. G. Kratzmann and James Simpson (Cambridge, 1986), 82-92 categorises these letters as 'commonplace apocalyptic' p.92 while Norman Cohen, *The Pursuit of the Millenium* (London, 1957), classifies them as 'millenarian', p.203. R.F. Green (1992) has challenged this, noting that Ball excises the potential chiliasm of phrases quoted from proverbial wisdom, p.186.

[57] Ball's use of conventional preaching material is discussed in R.F. Green (1992). The relationship of Ball's letters to *Piers Plowman* is discussed in John M. Bowers, '*Piers Plowman* and the Police: Notes Toward a History of the Wycliffite Langland', *YLS*, 6 (1992), 1-50.

[58] Middleton (1978), p.99.

tradition. One crucial difference, however, is that while the question of quotation is debatable in the letters, these later poems quote lines of *Piers* verbatim.

In advancing this argument, I am aware that the whole question of verbatim quotation in Middle English literature at this time is not clear-cut. By 1555, there is clear evidence that *Piers* was quoted in support of an anti-government, anti-Catholic, anti-Mary invective. S.L. Jansen has shown that a mixture of prophecies, protest and propaganda from *Piers* B VI 321-31 and X 322-5 are copied continuously into British Library MS Sloane 2578. The composer has carefully mined the fourteenth century text for lines which were especially meaningful in his own day. Jansen notes that what makes the Sloane prophecy so unusual is its use of the very text of the original poem.[59]

This is an unequivocal case. Is there such clarity over 150 years earlier? Richard Axton has drawn attention to the uncertainty as to whether Chaucer quoted himself verbatim[60] and N.F. Blake has argued that no medieval reader would attach importance to single words as a guide to the poet's source; he would recognise that certain words and ideas occurred together to form what linguists would call a collocational set.[61] These are important comments, and as we shall see, the notion of recall of collocational sets is certainly apposite to describe the reading response of the alliterative poems under study. But, as Blake acknowledges, there are signs of changes in the treatments of verbal recall towards the end of the medieval period. He cites John Clanvowe(?)'s quotation of two lines from Chaucer's *Knight's Tale* at the start of *The Boke of Cupid* but goes on to say that although the poem as a whole is full of Chaucerian language, there are no other direct echoes, an argument which he extends to fifteenth century Chaucerian imitators: 'who went in for a Chaucerian style rather than deliberate echoes of his poems'.[62]

These remarks are an important caveat against making assumptions about the relationship between texts in a chirographic culture that may be more appropriate to the intertextuality characteristic of a print culture.[63] The instability of texts copied by hand must make us pause

[59] S.L. Jansen, 'Politics, Protest and a New *Piers Plowman* Fragment', *RES*, 40 (1989), 93-99, p.98.
[60] *Chaucer Traditions*, p.37.
[61] Blake, p.29.
[62] ibid., pp.31-2.
[63] The instability of the works of medieval authors in a chirographic culture compared with the comparative fixity granted by print and more sophisticated editorial methods of a print culture, is discussed in relation to the 'canon' by Thomas J. Heffernan, 'Aspects of the Chaucerian apocrypha: animadversions on William Thynne's edition of *The Plowman's Tale*', in *Chaucer Traditions*, 155-67, p.155.

before assuming that authorial lines can be automatically transferred verbatim from one text to another. However, the example of *Partonope of Blois* offers empirical evidence that just such citation could occur.[64] Moreover, while texts may show minor verbal variations from manuscript to manuscript, this does not mean that a reader who possessed just one copy of the text was incapable of commiting lines from it to memory verbatim and then writing them elsewhere. That these lines may not be identical to a modern edited version of the text does not necessarily mean that they were only a loose approximation to the words of the particular manuscript which the reader was using.[65]

Examination of features of the textual traditions of *Piers Plowman* shows that its readers could quote the poem. I should say at the outset of the discussion of the texts which follows that I am not concerned with adjudicating whether lines or versions are examples of authorial revision or editorial intervention; it is an exercise which lies beyond my competence to undertake. What interests me is the question of verbal recall which the presence of textual variation in *Piers* poses in rather an interesting fashion.

Leaving aside the cases of extensive revision which have strong cases for being considered authorial reworkings,[66] there is evidence of 'contaminations' between the various versions of *Piers*. Huntingdon Library MS Hm 114 is basically a text which corresponds to a B version but which contains, in addition to its individual variants, substantial 'borrowings' (Russell and Nathan's term) from A and C texts, more or less adroitly woven into the basic B text to produce a new, edited

---

[64] The verbal correspondences between *Partonope* and *The Knight's Tale* are listed by Windeatt, *Chaucer Traditions*, p.76.

[65] This is shown by the fact that quotations from *Piers* in the poems of the tradition are a mixture of citations which are close to editorially accepted lines, of lines from versions of *Piers* other than those which the poem usually appears to be following, and of textual variants of editorially accepted lines. For an example, see *Mum*, 348, 'And laide leuel and lyne a-long by the squyre' which is closest to the C version of Study's remarks (*Piers* C XI 126-8); line 655, 'For in thre lynes hit [lith] and not oon lettre more', which preserves the reading 'lettre' not found in any extant B MSS (cf. B VIII 111 and A VIII 93 and C IX 286; and line 1373, '[Po]peryng on thaire palefrays fro oone place to an other', which recalls the reading 'Poperyng' attested only in A XI 213 (The MS reads 'properyng' which I have emended, partly on the basis that A MSS scribes also had some difficulty with the word). At 1456, 'That is the richeste royaulme that reyne ouer houeth' recalls B III 208 and A III 195 but is not in C. See also, the discussion of 'culorum', in *Richard*, Chapter 2, pp.29-33.

[66] See material cited in n.28 and the question of the second textual tradition of the C version as exemplified by the Prologues of Huntingdon Library MS Hm114 and Sterling Library MS V 88 (the Ilchester MS). Ilchester is discussed by Derek Pearsall, 'The "Ilchester" Manuscript of *Piers Plowman*', *Neuph Mitt*, 82 (1981), 181-93, Huntingdon by G.H. Russell and Venetia Nathan, 'A *Piers Plowman* Manuscript in the Huntingdon Library', *HLQ*, 26 (1963), 119-30, and the possibility of an authorial second tradition by Wendy Scase, 'Two *Piers Plowman* C Text Interpolations: Evidence for a Second Textual Tradition', *N&Q*, 232 (1987), 453-63.

version.[67] Might we re-name these 'borrowings' 'extended quotations'? They are, after all, major evidence of verbatim recall between texts of the poem.[68] Even if the scribe had two copies before him, one of a B version and one of a conflated A/C version, the moving around of material evidenced in Huntingdon HM 114 would require a substantial knowledge of the text. *Piers* is not a poem which is schematically organised, and the re-allocation of material in this manuscript could have been achieved only by a scribe who had a very strong recall of different parts of the poem. Equally, on a more reduced scale, the 'contaminations' between versions of *Piers* which are listed in the editions by Kane and Kane Donaldson necessitate the verbatim transferral of lines preserved in one version of the poem to the text of another,[69] as do those lines which belong to the same textual tradition but which have been inserted earlier or later in the poem than the place to which the weight of modern textual criticism has assigned them.[70]

For the purposes of textual criticism, the insertion in the B manuscript Corpus Christi College Oxford MS 201 of: '& summe be Clerkis of þe kyngys bench þe cuntre to shende' after Prologue 94 is a 'contamination' from A Prol.95: 'And ben clerkis of þe kinges bench þe cuntre to shende'. Equally, the insertion in the A manuscript Bodleian Library MS Ashmole 1468 after III.29: 'The lest brolle of here blod a baronys pere' is a displacement from its proper place at III 192.[71] From the viewpoint of literary criticism, however, especially if we consider scribal activity as evidence of the earliest reading response to a poem,[72] we might re-term these lines 'direct quotations'.

There are also 'contaminations' in the manuscripts of *Piers Plowman* arguably composed from scribal memory[73] which show how the poem exerted textual force on its reader, not resulting in verbatim recall of whole lines but in the redeployment of collocational sets. For instance in the A version manuscript British Library MS Harley 875, there are a number of unique lines which are extremely close to textually accepted

[67] Russell and Nathan, p.121. My comments here are concerned not with the Prologue, see previous note, but with the rest of the text.
[68] These substantial borrowings are listed by Russell and Nathan, pp.122-26. For instance, in Passus II, after line 70, there is an insertion from A II 35-53; and further insertions at 73a [A II 56], 74 [A II 58], 92 [A II 64], 100 [A II 61-2(?), 65-66], 108 [A II 73], 112 [A II 77 or C III 114], 113 [A II 78], 177 [A II 139]; there is a long passage from C following line 117 [C III 120-36, omitting 126] and insertions of single lines after lines 12 [C III 13], 161 [C III 175], 162 [C III 176], 170 [C III 185] and 177 [C III 187], quoted from Russell and Nathan, p.122, who work from Skeat's parallel text version of *Piers* (1886).
[69] Kane, *The A Version*, pp.30-1; Kane Donaldson, p.221.
[70] Kane, *The A Version*, pp.44-5; Kane Donaldson, p.221.
[71] Kane, *The A Version*, p.48. The line moved in A is quoted in *Crede*, 748.
[72] See the studies listed in n.51.
[73] Kane, *The A Version*, pp.44-50; Kane Donaldson, pp.221-24.

lines of A, or which pick up collocations frequently found in the text. Examples include the addition after I 175, which contains the line: '& þerwiþ knoweþ me kyndely of þat I ʒou sende', and after II 129: 'þoruʒ comburance of coueytyse clymben aʒeyn truþe' (cf. A I 170: '3e ben acumbrid wiþ coueitise, ʒe [conne] not out crepe').[74] We might regard these 'contaminations' as an incipient tradition of reader response.

The case for regarding these interpolations as something more than textual refugees from the authorised version may be strengthened by examining some slightly longer additions. After V 55, British Library MS Harley 6041 adds the following four lines to an A text:

> And chastite to seke as a chyld clene
> The lust of his likam to leten for euere
> And fle fro felyschipe there foly may a rise
> For that makith many man mysdo ful ofte.[75]

This interpolation weaves together echoes from different parts of *Piers* to extend the confession by Lechery. It is interesting that C texts also interpolate at this point with material from the later Haukyn episode in B, one line of which, in contrast to B, uses the word 'likame'.[76]

The first line in the Harley addition recalls the collocation in Holy Church's speech: 'as chast as a child' (I 154), and the second, with the collocation 'lust of his likam', recalls the stress on the word earlier in Holy Church's sermon: 'Ne liflode to þe lykam þat lef is to þe soule./ Leue not þi lycam for a li[ʒ]er hym techiþ' (I 35-6). This is the moral which Holy Church draws from the exemplum of Lot, who committed the sin of lechery with his daughters because of the influence of drink. Significantly, the lines in Harley are inserted before Lechery resolves to abstain from drink (V 56-7). The remaining two lines recall vocabulary from the Mede episode. The last seems a direct echo of a comment about Mede at A III 112: 'She makiþ men mysdo manye score tymes,'[77] while the fellowship from which one is advised to flee before folly arises is reminiscent of the references to Mede's 'Felasshipe' four lines earlier (III 98) and her established reputation in Passus II and III for encouraging criminal 'felaweship'.[78]

---

[74] Kane, *The A Version*, p.45.

[75] Kane, *The A Version*, p.48.

[76] 'As in likynge of lecherye my lycames gultes' (C VI 176, cf. B XIII 343).

[77] The echo may reflect a typical alliterative collocation; there is a parallel in *Richard*, III 188: 'This makyth men mysdo more than oughte ellis' though this could itself be a recall of a collocation used of Mede, given that *Richard* shows familiarity with the episodes in *Piers* where Mede appears, see Chapter Two, pp.41-2.

[78] The legal connotations of 'felaweship' are noted by J.A. Alford, *Piers Plowman: A Glossary of Legal Diction* (Cambridge, 1988), p.57.

This interpolation into the confession of Lechery shows direct verbal recall and an understanding of the textual networks of both Passus I and III. Its author responds to *Piers* by composing a new, if tiny, alliterative text which blurs the distinction between symbiosis of ideas and textual force. It illustrates in miniature, the techniques of writerly response to *Piers* which developed more fully in the separate poems of the *Piers* tradition.

Some other aspects of an incipient tradition of response to *Piers* can be glimpsed in the additions which were supplied to the end of the poem. Amongst a number of things which *Piers* inspired seems to have been confusion as to where it stopped.[79] There are additions to the end of the poem in six manuscripts of the A version. These select significant aspects of *Piers* and use them to sum it up with a more resounding conclusion than that offered by A XI 313.

Two of these continuations show no direct verbatim recall of *Piers* but are interesting for their selection of aspects of the poem felt worthy of summary and restatement. Library of the Society of Antiquaries of London, MS 687 adds these six lines:

> For þey I rede alle men þat on crist be leuyn
> Asken mercy of god for here misdedes
> And coueiten non clergie ne catel on þis erþe
> But alwey to seruen god & hendyn in hise werkys
> And þat he graunte vs þe Ioie þat euere schal lastyn
> With pers þe plowman to wonyn in his blysse Amen Amen.[80]

At first sight this seems a badly executed commonplace, yet the one regularly alliterating line produces a telling collocation of 'coueiten . . .clergie. . .catel', and moreover, the sequence contrasts this greed for learning and property with the true Christian life exemplified by Piers Plowman. Since this is the life that will earn heavenly reward, conventional though the ending may seem, it encodes a dynamic which juxtaposes a saved Piers Plowman against the corruption of the church.

A similar reading response can be observed in the lines added to MS Harley 3954:

> For þei leuyn as þei be leryd & oþer wyse nouth

---

[79] In CUL MS Ll i 14, *Richard the Redeless* follows straight on from the preceding copy of *Piers Plowman*. It is written in the same hand; there is no rubrication to suggest the start of a new poem, and at the end of the text, the scribe writes out a list of words whose sense might cause difficulty, and provides glosses. The list includes words from both *Piers* and *Richard*. The rubrication which concludes the C version in Bodleian Library MS Laud Misc. 656 reads: 'Explicit passus secundus de dobest incipit passus tercius' (quoted from Uhart, p.45)

[80] Kane, *The A Version*, p.49.

Musyn in no materes but holdyn þe ryth beleue
He þat redyth þis book & ryth haue it in mende
Preyit for pers þe plowmans soule.[81]

This is inserted two lines earlier than the conventional ending of the A version. The 'þei' are the 'pore peple' of the previous lines: the ploughmen, cattleherds and shepherds, cobblers and seamstresses. According to this continuator, these 'lewide iottis' believe as if they were learned and hold the *right* belief, a faith which contrasts to musing over scholastic debates. The patron of this anti-clerical true living is Piers Plowman. Once again, a writer considers that a 'ryth' reading of *Piers* produces a statement where Piers Plowman exemplifies the true Christian life in contrast to the skewed priorities of the contemporary church. In both of these continuations, there is a reading response analogous to that of *Pierce the Ploughman's Crede*; a much lengthier alliterative composition which is grounded on the narrative principle of contrast between the over-learned, greedy friars who 'folwen nought fully the feyth' and Peres Ploughman – the 'lewed' exemplar of 'sanctite'.[82]

The two remaining conclusions to A (one of them found in varying degrees of advancement in three manuscripts)[83] are much closer to the verbal detail of *Piers*. Seven closing lines are added by a marginal commentator to the Westminster version:

And when I was wytterly awakyd I wrote all thys dreame
And theys marvellys þat I met on mawlverne hyllys
In a seyson of sommer as I softe nappyd
For þe people after ther power wold persen after dowell
That þe tresure moost tryed and tryacle at neede
now god gravnt hys grace to make a good ende
And bryng vs all to þe blysse as he bowghte vs on þe Roode   Amen
R H.[84]

This is primarily concerned to round off the poem by waking up the dreamer, have him acknowledge his responsibility for writing the poem and provide a conventionally pious ending. There is a reprise of the

[81] ibid., p.48.
[82] See David Lampe, 'The Satiric Strategy of *Pierce the Ploughman's Crede*' in *The Alliterative Tradition in the Fourteenth Century*, ed. B.S. Levy and P.S. Szarmach (Ohio, 1981), 69-80.
[83] University College Oxford MS 45 has lines 1-19 of Passus XII after which the manuscript breaks off damaged; Pierpoint Morgan Library MS M818 has lines 1-88, ending with two lines at the top of the leaf, implying that this is where its exemplar stopped; and Bodleian Library MS Rawlinson Poetry 137 has lines 1-117.
[84] Kane, 'The Text', in *A Companion to Piers Plowman*, ed. J.A. Alford (Berkeley, 1988), 175-200, p.182.

collocational sets of the opening of the poem: 'seyson. . .sommer. . . softe; (cf. Prol. 1); a conflation of 'met' and 'marvellys' (cf. Prol. 11) with the 'mawlverne hyllys (cf. Prol. 5) and an alliterative linking of 'tresure. . . tryed. . .tryacle' which recalls the 'tresours arn triȝed' of I 83, 124 and 126. Interestingly, 'tryacle' is not in A at this point, but is present in both B I 148 and C I 146 where it collocates with 'Treuthe' in a description of love. The continuator lifts the collocation from its original context and associates it with 'dowell'. In its awareness of narrative voice, its collation of collocational sets and the sentiment of the closing line, this addition recalls the techniques of the interpolation in Passus V in MS Harley 6041 and anticipates aspects of the reading response discernible in the more ambitious *Crowned King*.

Westminster's reference to 'make a good ende' matches a phrase found in the much more subversive reading of *Piers*, attested by the letters of John Ball.[85] It also matches a phrase used in the longest continuation to the A text, that preserved in Bodleian Library MS Rawlinson Poetry 137.[86] John But states that he 'made þis ende' at XII 109 but it is by no means clear how much of the 'ende' he made. It is possible that it extends to the whole of Passus XII.[87]

Anne Middleton, in her illuminating study of this passus has argued that But's 'ende' focusses attention on the spiritual worthiness of writing poetry, and on the pious practices he saw as the pervading intention of the author of *Piers the Plowman*. She argues that But's work is not: 'a scribal explicit, but a tribute in kind, a "makyng" about making; an act both of literary criticism and literary imitation'.[88]

Alone amongst continuators, But names the author of the poem and refers to his oeuvre:

> Wille þurgh inwit [wiste] wel þe soþe
> þat þis speche was spedelich, and sped him wel faste,
> And wrouȝthe þat here is wryten and oþer werkes boþe
> Of peres þe plowman and mechel puple also.   (99-102)

By Chaucerian standards this is modest. The collocation 'wille. . .inwit' is capable of allegorical interpretation and recalls IX 118: 'Here is wil wolde wyte ȝif wit couþe hym teche'. No family name is given, in contrast to the literal 'Iohan but' of XII 106. Equally, the 'oþer werkes'

---

[85] In Knighton's Chronicle, Jakke Carter's letter bids the rebels to 'make a gode ende of that ye haue begunnen'; John Balle's 'to make a gode ende', Dobson, p.382.
[86] Quotations are from Kane's edition of the A version.
[87] The evidence is assessed in Anne Middleton, 'Making a Good End: John But as a Reader of *Piers Plowman*', in *MESGK*, 243-266, p.245.
[88] ibid., p.246.

are vague. But's tribute is not so much to a named author but to a type of writing. Indeed, one might view But's comment:

> And whan þis werk was wrouȝt, ere wille myȝte aspie,
> Deþ delt him a dent and drof him to þe erþe   (104-5)

as a strikingly early example of the 'death of the author' brand of literary criticism.[89] 'Wille' may be 'closed vnder clom' but his 'werke' lives on, a work which But interprets as 'dowel' despite the fact that the phrase taken from *Piers* to describe his own activity – 'medleþ of makyng' (XII 109), shows that he read Ymaginatif's rebuke to Will for writing poetry, which Middleton has described as: 'perhaps the most devastating systematic indictments of "making" anywhere in Middle English literature'.[90]

Passus XII weaves together reminiscences of episodes of *Piers* with quotation of vocabulary. The first fifty lines recall the action of the previous Passus, with the debate between Will and Study recast as an argument between Will and Scripture. In Scripture's earlier appearance, her first words are: 'I nile not scorne' (XI 225), but Passus XII introduces her thus: 'Skornfully þo scripture shet vp here browes' (12) and later terms her 'scripture þe skolde (34). This characterisation is more in keeping with the dismissive Scripture introduced in B XI 1 and C XI 163, and/or of Study's criticism of Wit in A XI 1-16 for teaching Will.

Just as Wit, at his wife's words, falls silent and confused and draws to one side (XI 93-5), so Clergie in Passus XII is embarrassed into silent retreat: 'Clergie into a caban crepte anon after' (35); a line which recalls Mede's accusation of cowardice against Conscience: 'Crope into a caban for cold of þi nailes' (III 178). Will's submission to Scripture in Passus XII, that he will 'be hure man ȝif I most for euermore after' (39) recalls his humble obeisance to Study in XI 101-2: 'your man shal I worþe/For to werche your wil while my lif duriþ'. In Passus XI, in recompense for Will's humility, Study sends him off to her cousin Clergy, while in Passus XII, Scripture promises to send him to her 'cosyn' Kynde Wit (43). Study in Passus XI gives Will both an allegorical route to Clergy and a 'signe' to take with him to ensure that he is accepted. In Passus XII, Scripture calls a 'clerion' to go with Will (49) on a short allegorical journey composed entirely of quotation from earlier parts of the poem (56-7).

Unfortunately, Will never makes his destination. He goes through 'ȝouþe' (60) and then meets Hunger and Fever, the messenger of Death.

[89] Roland Barthes, 'The Death of the Author', in *Image, Music, Text*, ed. and trans. Stephen Heath (London, 1977), 142-48.
[90] Middleton (1988), p.247.

Hunger's feeding of Will until his guts groan recalls Hunger's speech in Passus VII 241-51 and also the confession of Gluttony in B Passus V 340. The sequence as a whole, culminating in Will's desire to seek death is reminiscent partly of the diversion into the 'Lond of Longyng' (B XI 8-60) and also of the final Passus of B and C, where Will is assailed by 'Elde', and emerging from the encounter toothless, bald and impotent, pleads despairingly to Kynde that he be 'taken out of care'. Kynde refuses and bids Will enter Unitee and learn the craft of love (B XX 183 208). In Passus XII, Fever refuses Will's plea to die and instead, commands Will to 'dowel whil þi dayes duren' (94). Will's response is to write *Piers Plowman*. That accomplished, Death finishes him off, and John But the Passus.

To judge the coherence of the scheme as a whole is made complicated by the problem of knowing just how much of this 'ende' is John But's. But whether it is the work of one hand or more, in MS Rawlinson Poetry 137 we have 117 lines of continuous text which produces a new alliterative poem out of selective readings of *Piers Plowman*. There is direct quotation of whole lines: 'Many ferlys me byfel in a fewe ȝeris' (58; cf. A Prol 62) and recall of significant lexical collocations from more than one version. In addition to those already noted are: XII 47: 'And þanne I kneled on my knes and kyste her fete sone'(cf.Will's response to Holy Church: 'þanne I knelide on my knes and criȝede hire of grace' (I 77), and verbal recalls which show familiarity with B or C texts, for instance, 'medleþ of makyng' (109) as already discussed. In XII 50-2 and 56-7, the biblical texts 'omnia probate' and 'quod bonum est tenete' recall Conscience's denunciation of Mede's reading practice in B III 338-53. In Passus XII, 'omnia probate' is the 'clerioun' who attempts to direct Will to the court 'quod bonum est tenete'(50-2). Line 50: 'Hyȝt omnia probate, a pore þing withalle' recalls the 'lunatik' of B Prol. 123 who is 'a leene þyng wiþalle' and also continues the alliterative practice of *Piers* of incorporating some Latin quotations into the metrical structure of the line.

Passus XII knits up diverse threads from diverse texts of *Piers* and in so doing, produces a new poem with its own distinct emphases. In its addition of 117 lines, Passus XII exemplifies techniques of construction used in the four new, and separate, alliterative poems of *Mum*, *Richard*, *Crede* and *Crowned King*. Similarities of vocabulary and narrative episodes are put to new ends, and unsurprisingly, with some different results. For example, while in Passus XII, the debate about learning, and who is entitled to clerical knowledge, is reflected at other parts of *Piers Plowman* (e.g. Trajan's speech in B XI 140-319), the appearance of 'kynde wit' (43) is incompatible with the portrayal of this actant anywhere else in *Piers*.[91] Moreover, the closing lines of Passus XII grant a directness of political context unparallelled at any other point in *Piers*:[92]

> Furst to rekne Richard, kyng of þis rewme,
> And alle lordes þat louyn him lely in herte
> God saue hem sound by se and by land.   (113-5)

These lines are more than a conventional bidding to a sovereign; they encode a partisan response to a political situation. A king is not 'rekned', he is 'crouned'[93] and lurking silently behind the restrictive clause of all the lords that 'louyn him lely in herte' are those who in the 1380s and 90s were not so loyal, to the extent that in 1399, some of them took King Richard's crown from him. These lines parallel exactly the response to *Piers* witnessed by the poems in the *Piers* tradition. Like Passus XII, they weave together reminiscences of parts of *Piers* to form a response to actual political issues.[94]

The readings of *Piers Plowman* witnessed by the letters of John Ball and the annotations, interpolations and continuations by its earliest copyists show signs of an early community of response. There is consensus of interest in *Piers* not as an 'auctored' act of literary play but as a communal work for society. There is also clear evidence of verbal affiliations which show a mixture of symbiosis of ideas, direct citation and creative misprision. With the exception of Passus XII of the A text, these works are miniaturist and pragmatic. The response of *Crowned King*, *Mum*, *Richard* and *Crede* is much extended and transformed in scope, but, as we shall see, it perpetuates both the interests and the techniques of these early fragmented witnesses. It is in this incipient *Piers Plowman* tradition that we can locate seeds of its fruition.

[91] Middleton (1988) notes that Scripture's recommendation of Will to Kynde Wit in A XII is : 'radically at odds with both Langland's definition of this faculty's powers early in A and in the B continuation, and with the allegorical logic of the immediately preceding episode', p.259.

[92] While there is extensive discussion of political matters in *Piers* (for a review and discussion of the scholarship on this, see Anna Baldwin, 'The Historical Context' in *A Companion to Piers Plowman*, ed. Alford, pp.67-86), the only unequivocal references to fourteenth century named people are to John Chichester, mayor of London during the great dearth of 1370 (XIII 270) and the Folville brothers, who were a notorious criminal gang in Lincolnshire in the 1330s, XIX 247; see Alford, *Glossary*, p.60.

[93] Turville-Petre (1977), notes that 'crouned' and 'king' is a common alliterative collocation, p.85.

[94] *Crowned King* is an exception amongst the poems of the tradition in containing no reference to named contemporaries, but it does focus on a specific political event, namely the grant of two tenths and two fifteenths which Henry V extracted from parliament on 19 November 1414 to finance his military campaign against France, see note to line 36 in Barr (1993). *Richard* names Richard II and March and Mowbray (see note to *Richard*, IV 6-7) and refers to other contemporaries by well-known nicknames (see notes to lines II 152-92; and III 19-30. *Mum*, names Henry IV at 206 and *Crede* names John Wyclif at 528 and Walter Brut at 657.

2

Reading Tradition

At the end of Passus III of *Piers Plowman* Conscience gives Mede a lesson in 'right' reading (B.337-53). It is a lesson which John But must have read since he re-uses the texts with which Conscience illustrates the dangers of selective reading.[1] There is no such direct reference in the continuation of MS Harley 3954, yet it replicates Conscience's teaching in the concern that whoever reads *Piers Plowman*, should 'ryth haue it in mende'.[2] This concern for 'right' reading is evidenced in all the poems of the *Piers* tradition. In this chapter I explore this 'right reading' by showing how the poems' interest in the social importance of reading correctly is put into practice in their attentive reading of individual words and phrases from *Piers*, and also in their broader reading response to the alliterative temper of *Piers Plowman*.

On one level, the importance of reading 'right', is inseparable from the moral and social consequences of failing, or being unable, to read properly. Reading is not assumed to be a private, recreational activity divorced from one's responsibilities to the larger community, but an act of labour integral to the fulfilment of one's social position.[3]

In *Crede*, the Carmelite accuses the Dominicans, the fraternal order most famed for their learning,[4] of being unable to read well:

---

[1] Like Conscience, A XII 50-2 and 56-7 separates the texts 'omnia probate' and 'quod bonum est tenete', this time over consecutive lines rather than pages, and transforms them into an actant and an allegorical journey. While the new context is not concerned with reading, the separation of the texts recalls the techniques of Passus III, and the fact that Will never reaches 'quod bonum est tenete' might be considered a reflection of the dangers of travelling with 'omnia probate' alone.

[2] Kane, *The A Version*, p.48.

[3] This is an emphasis seen also in *Piers*, most sharply in Trajan's denunciation of ignorant priests, and bishops who ordain those who do not know how to: 'Synge ne psalmes rede ne seye a masse of þe day' (314). The analogy drawn between framing a legal charter, and the presence of legal diction in the accusation (see below, pp.142-3) emphasises that the priests and bishops betray the responsibilities with which society has entrusted them (B XI 303-17).

[4] The Constitutions of the Dominicans laid down that they were to be intent on study and

Loke a ribaut of hem that can nought wel reden
His rewle ne his respondes but be pure rote,
Als as he were a connynge clerke he [c]asteth the lawes,
Nought lowli but lordly and leesinges lyeth.   (375-79)

The only way that the Dominicans are able to 'read', in the sense of 'learn',[5] is by rote; by repeating their rule and responses in the same kind of empty repetition of mere sounds as Chaucer's Summoner in his drunken, jay-like rehearsal of his few scraps of Latin, (*CT*, A 638-43).[6] The accusation suggests that the Dominicans are illiterate and that their behaviour is centred on the outward sounds of the words, not their sense. As a result, their religious offices are empty of spiritual content – ornament without substance.[7] Moreover, because they can reproduce only the sounds of their founding rule, they are unable to behave according to its strictures. Far from practising humility, as the rule demands, the friars are 'lordly'; that is, not only are they proud, but they defraud their spiritual role in society by behaving like secular lords.[8]

For some Franciscan friars in *Mum*, their failure to read riddles 'a-right' (416) results in hanging. They, like the Dominicans in *Crede*, have betrayed their proper place in society, but with the capital offence of fuelling civil dissent.[9] This is a theme to which the poet returns towards the end of the poem in considering the way that people interpret old prophecies:

teaching, R. Southern, *The Making of the Middle Ages* (London, 1967), p.182. Thomas Aquinas and Albert Magnus were both Dominicans. Famous English Dominican scholars included Nicholas Trivet, Robert Holcot and John of Bromyard.

[5] MED 'reden' v(1); 3a).

[6] cf. *Friar Daw's Reply* in *Jack Upland, Friar Daw's Reply and Upland's Rejoinder*, ed. P.L. Heyworth (London, 1968), which says of Jack that he 'jangelist as a jay and woost not what þou menest' (808). The image is also used in *The Simonie*, ed. Dan Embree and Elizabeth Urquhart (Heidelberg, 1991) of an uneducated parish priest who does not know what he says or what he reads: 'þanne is a lewed prest no betre þan a iay' (A 103-8).

[7] This accusation against the friars reflects Lollard denunciations of the recitation of elaborate ceremonies such as mass or matins, which are spiritually void because the ritual is unintelligible, e.g. *Lanterne of Light*, ed. M.L. Swinburne (EETS OS 151 1917), p.50/29ff: 'But preiars in þe fendis chirche maken miche noise mumling wiþ her lippis, þei reche neuir what so þat men preise fast her feyned occupacioun as Crist seiþ in his gospel'. Mat. XV 'Populus hic labijs me honorat cor autem eorum longe est a me'. þis peple worschipiþ me wiþ her lippis but her herte is feer fro me' and cf. 'Lorde! wheþer þis chauntyng of Kyries, Sanctus, and Agnus wiþ Gloria in excelsis and Patrem maken þat men heren nout þo wordis but onely a sowne' (Arnold, III 481/13).

[8] One of the criticisms against the friars in Wycliffite texts is that they defy secular authority. The Lollard *Tractatus de Regibus* states that the friars fail in their clerical allegiance to the king because they do not fulfil their spiritual duties, *Selections from English Wycliffite Writings*, ed. Anne Hudson (Cambridge, 1978), pp.129-30; cf. *The Plowman's Tale*, in *Six Ecclesiastical Satires*, ed. James Dean (TEAMS, 1991), which accuses the friars of compromising secular obedience by behaving like lords, ll.181-207.

[9] This passage is discussed on pp.113-14.

Yit is there a poynt of prophecie how the peuple construeth
And museth on the meruailles that Merlyn dide deuyse,
And redith as right as the Ram is hornyd,
As helpe me the high God, I holde thaym halfe a-masid.
For there nys wight in this world that wote bifore eue
How the winde and the wedre wol wirche on the morowe,
Ne noon so cunnyng a clerc that construe wel couthe
Ere sunneday a seuenyght what shal falle.
Thus thay muse on the mase on mone and on sterres
Til heedes been hewe of and hoppe on the grene,
And al the wide world wondre on thaire workes.   (1723-33)

In 1402 and 1406, laws were passed to prevent the dissemination of old prophecies.[10] Because of their coded writing, such prophecies were regarded as a highly effective means of fostering dissent because a forecast of the future could reflect dissatisfaction with the present.[11] A poem known as *The Six Kings to Follow John*, which was often attributed to the Merlin of Geoffrey of Monmouth's *Historia Regum Brittaniae*[12] was circulated by the supporters of Glendower and the Percies in their revolt against Henry IV.[13] The reference to 'mone and sterres' in *Mum*, 1731-2, may be a coded reference to the Percies, and to the deaths of two of them in the Battle of Shrewsbury of 1403.[14]

[10] The 1402 statute links such divinations with the Welsh rebels (*Rot.Parl*, III 508). The 1406 law accuses the Lollards of publishing false prophecies which predicted the overthrow of the princes and lords temporal and spiritual (*Rot.Parl*, III 583ff).

[11] This is a point made by R.E. Lerner, 'Medieval Prophecy and Religious Dissent', *Past and Present*, 72 (1976), 3-24, p.7.

[12] Geoffrey of Monmouth's 'Book of Merlin' (Bk VII of his *Historia Regum Britanniae*) was the source for most of the prophecies composed in England for the next four centuries. Some are direct translations, some use its conventions, some simply use the name of Merlin for authority. They are discussed in R.W. Southern, 'Aspects of the European Tradition of Historical Writing: History as Prophecy', *Transactions of the Royal Historical Society*, 22 (1972), 159-60 and R. Taylor, *The Political Prophecy in England* (New York, 1911), pp.1-47.

[13] This is discussed by V.J. Scattergood, *Politics and Poetry in the Fifteenth Century* (London, 1971), p.32.

[14] Caroline Eckhardt, 'Another Historical Allusion in *Mum and the Sothsegger*, *Notes and Queries*, 225 (1980), 495-7, has argued that these lines contain a reference to the executions of the Percies since their heraldic sign was a cresent moon. 'sterres' could refer to a marvellous comet which appeared at around 1402. *The Dieulacres Chronicle*, ed. M.V. Clark and V.H. Galbraith, *BJRL*, 14 (1930), 164-81, says that the 'stella comata' was a prognostication of the Battle of Shrewsbury, p.175 and the *Eulogium* narrates that after the beheadings of the Percies, an eclipsed moon appeared covered in blood, and over the head of Henry Percy appeared the starry comet, 'signifying the evil event', *Eulogium Historiarium*, ed. F.S. Haydon (RS 1863), III p.397. But the moon and the stars might allude more simply to the characteristic language of prophecies. The closing passage of Monmouth's *Book of Merlin* refers to the moon and the stars in an extended astrological periphrasis. In *Dives and Pauper* there is a discussion of the evils of astronomy in which the collocation 'moon and sterrys' is frequent, e.g. 'þow þey wacchyn and staryn after þe sterrys tyl þey lesyn here hedys moun nought lettyn hym ne sauyn oo mannys lyf þat the kyng wele han ded', ed. P.H. Barnum (EETS OS 275 1976 and 280 1980), I 118/31-3.

The point of this passage is that reading badly – attempting to use old prophecies as a prognostication of the future – not only offends against common sense, but is actually treasonable and results in unnecessary bloodshed. The proverb in 1725: 'redith as right as the Ram is hornyd' is paralleled in a poem by Lydgate and *The Tale of Beryn*.

In *Ryght as a Rammes Horne* Lydgate reverses the world-upside-down topos of complaint poetry[15] by writing the fantasy scenario of a world-right-side-up in which law has outlawed bribery, the priesthood has refused all riches and the labourers work themselves to the bone all day. All is as 'right as a rammes horne', a refrain which shows how the society that is depicted in the poem is exactly opposite to the state of affairs in the actual world.[16] In *The Tale of Beryn*, the Pardoner, the Miller and 'other lewde sotes', a group who are described as 'counterfeting gentilmen' (150), take it upon themselves to interpret the coats of arms in a church window. The Pardoner interprets a spear as a stout stick like a rake handle. His mistake shows his fraudulent attempt to usurp a higher social station than the one to which he naturally belongs. His reading is as: 'right as rammes horned!'(152).[17] In all of these poems, but most gravely in *Mum*, reading like a ram's horn, rather than reading 'right', is inseparable from the proper functioning of society, with each fulfilling the obligations of the roles for which they have been ordained.

In all four poems of the tradition, proper learning enables proper behaviour. In *Crowned King* the king is advised to learn literature in his youth, 'as a lord befalleth' (113) so that when he appears in parliament he will be wise enough to speak for himself and not have to go as a beggar to broker for 'pore mennes wittes' (118), a situation which is described as the worst 'myscheef' that can happen to a king (119). According to *Richard the Redeless*, the 'moste myscheff' in the world is an action performed against the ordinances of nature (III 9-10). The narrator instructs Richard to learn a 'lesson other tweyne' of 'alegeance' (I 96), and one of the lessons meted out is to appoint counsellors appropriate to the hierarchical and natural divisions of society:

> Thanne wolde [right dome] reule if reson where amongis us,
> That ich leode lokide what longid to his age,
> And neuere for to passe more oo poynt forther,

---

[15] The topos is conventional in 'evils of the age' complaint poetry, and is discussed by Scattergood, pp.302-3 and Thomas J. Elliott, 'Middle English Complaints Against the Times: To Contemn the World or to Reform it?, *Annuale Mediaevale*, 14 (1973), 22-35, p.23.
[16] *Minor Poems of John Lydgate*, ed. H.N. McCracken (EETS OS 109 1934), pp.461-4. There is a poem which operates on an identical principle in *Historical Poems of the XIVth and XV Centuries*, ed. R.H. Robbins (New York, 1959), no. 63, pp.150-2.
[17] *The Tale of Beryn*, ed. John M. Bowers (TEAMS 1992), 147-156.

> To vsurpe the seruice that to sages bilongith
> To be-come conselleris er they kunne rede,
> In schenshepe of souereynes and shame at the last.
> For it fallith as well to fodis of xxiiij yeris,
> Or yonge men of yistirday to yeue good redis,
> As becometh a kow to hoppe in a cage!   (III 254-62)

These comments are made directly after the narrator has set out the need for each in society to behave according to their proper function.[18] Those who assume the place of counsellors to the king before they can read are usurpers, they disrupt natural hierarchy and violate the principles of natural law.[19] Reading is a political activity of the highest importance in *Richard*: a good reader is one who can both read the right books and give the right advice. Throughout the poem, there is play on the twin senses of 'reden' as an active verb meaning both to read a book and to counsel.[20] Instead of 'myghthffull men of the mydill age' (III 252) to advise him, Richard II adhered to:

> The tale of a trifflour in turmentours wede,
> That neuere reed good rewle ne resons bookis!   (III 118-19)

His youthful counsellors preferred entertainment to reading serious books,[21] as a result of which, Richard himself ends up 'redeles' (I 88). He is not just devoid of counsel, he is without a book to 'wissen him better' (I 31). *Richard the Redeless* is itself the book to supply his lack, a book that is of benefit, not just to Richard (who was certainly no longer king at the time of writing, and was probably dead)[22] but to 'euery Cristen kyng that ony croune bereth' (I 43). There is an important proviso, however:

> So he were lerned on the langage my lyff durst I wedde
> Yif he waite well the wordis and so werche ther-after.   (I 44-5)

---

[18] *Richard*, III 250-3 divides society into 'thre degres' (249). The traditional three-fold division into those who fight, those who pray and those who work receives altered emphasis. The clergy are omitted and the narrator stresses the proper rule of mature magnates, the fighting strength of men in their prime and the work of the labourers. This classification may be deliberately anti-clerical or may simply stress the role of sound government, internal and external cf. Dan Embree, 'The King's Ignorance: A Topos for Evil Times', *Medium Aevum*, 54 (1985), p.125.

[19] This is discussed in Helen Barr, 'The Treatment of Natural Law in *Richard the Redeless* and *Mum and the Sothsegger*, *LSE*, 23 (1992), 49-80, p.56.

[20] MED 'reden' v (1) senses 3a) 'to learn by reading' and 8a) 'to counsel; give advice'.

[21] The 'turmentours wede' refers to costumes used in drama. *The Simonie* satirises the costumes of the courtiers and says that: 'Hii ben desgised as turmentours that comen from clerkes plei', (A 285). The line compares the courtiers to the Roman soldiers in the Mystery Cycle play of the scourging and crucifixion of Christ.

[22] The reference to the Cirencester uprising at II 17 shows that *Richard* must have been composed after January 1400. See Helen Barr, 'The Dates of *Richard the Redeless* and *Mum and the Sothsegger*', *Notes and Queries*, 235 (1990), 270-5, pp.271-2.

For good 'rede' to result in good work, there has to be right reading, one which requires proficiency in the language of the text and serious consideration of the meaning of its words.

These lines set out a model of reading practice that is apposite to describe the way in which the poems of the tradition read *Piers Plowman*. Their own 'work' sees right reading as inseparable from right doing. This is apparent in the explicit comments in their poems about the significance of reading, and also from the way in which they considered very seriously the significance of the words and phrases they read in *Piers Plowman*. It is to this aspect of their concern for right reading that I shall now turn.

At the start of *Crowned King*, the narrator is part of a company which beguiles its time in melody and mirth: 'With redyng of romaunces, and reuelyng among' (22). He is implicated in the kinds of pleasurable reading which in *Richard* are associated with empty-headedness. As such, it is only proper that it is not the narrator of the opening of *Crowned King* who advises the king, but a cleric, who in the dream vision, offers him some 'sawes of Salomon'.

The passage in which the cleric asks for permission to advise is indebted to the Prologue of *Piers Plowman*, and shows, despite the absence of explicit verbal recall, close attention to the precise meaning of its words:

> With that a clerk kneled adoun and carped these wordes:
> 'Liege lord, yif it you like to listen a while
> Sum sawes of Salomon y shall you shew sone,
> Besechyng you of your souerainte that y myght be suffred
> To shewe you my sentence in singuler noumbre
> To peynte it with pluralites my prose would faile. (42-7)

One of the speakers who addresses the king in the B version of *Piers* is the 'lunatik':

> And knelynge to þe kyng clergially he seide,
> 'Crist kepe þee, sire kyng and þi kyngryche'. (Prol. 124-5)

This is not in A, and in C, the passage is altered. The speaker becomes Kynde Witt:

> Thenne Kynde Witt to þe kynge and to þe comune saide,
> 'Crist kepe þe, kynge, and thy kyneriche'. (Prol. 147-8)

Omitted here are the reference to kneeling and the word 'clergially'. As David Burnley has shown, the term 'clergially' in B indicates a particular type of speech appropriate to clerics, a speech in which it is appropriate to address the king using the singular form of the second person pronoun. The pronoun carries 'all the implications of learned authority borne by a recognizably clerkly idiom'.[23] Despite his description as a 'lunatik', the speaker in B addresses the king with the authority of a cleric, and with the form of the second pronoun to which he is entitled.

The use of 'clergially' in *Piers* clearly exerted textual force on *Crowned King*, even though the word itself is not quoted. The speaker is a cleric, who kneels down in a gesture reminiscent of the lunatic and asks permission from the king to address him in 'singuler noumbre', that is, with the clergial 'þou' pronoun which befits his status. When the king gives his assent the clerk switches from the 'pluralites' of the 'ʒe' form of the pronoun, and addresses the king with two 'þou' pronouns and the clerkly 'sawe' of 'nosce te ipsum': 'Sir, crowned kyng, thow knowest well thyself' (51).[24]

This is a 'right' reading of *Piers* of which Conscience would approve, for he is himself a reader who is acutely aware of verbal subtlety. His reading lesson to Mede is preceded by a demonstration of the right reading of her name, which in C, is extended by deft analysis of the grammatical relationship between antecedents and pronouns, to include an explication of the distinction between 'mede' and 'mercede' (C III 332-405).[25] Present in the A, B and C versions just before this, is a comment made by Conscience which draws attention to his process of argument: 'The culorum of þis cas kepe I noʒt to shewe (B III 280).[26] 'Culorum' is used again in X 415: 'The culorum of þis clause curatours is to mene.' It is a distinctive word, an abbreviated form of 'seculorum' from the phrase 'secula seculorum' – for ever and ever, commonly used at the end of prayers and graces. It

[23] David Burnley, 'Langland's Lunatik Clergial' in *Langland, The Mystics and the Medieval English Religious Tradition*, ed. Helen Phillips (Cambridge, 1990), 31-38, p.38.
[24] J.A.W. Bennett has noted the the use of this concept in *Richard*, III 200 and *Mum*, 130, in *Middle English Literature* ed. and completed by Douglas Gray, (Oxford, 1986), p.56. Bennett traces the influence of St Bernard's dissemination of this idea in ' "Nosce te ipsum": Some Medieval Interpretations', in *J.R.R. Tolkein: Scholar and Storyteller*, ed. Mary Salu and Robert T. Farrell, (Ithaca, New York, 1979), 138-58.
[25] For discussions of this see M. Amassian and J. Sadowsky, 'Mede and Mercede: A Study of the Grammatical Metaphor in *Piers Plowman* C IV 335-409', *NM*, 72 (1971), 457-76; R. Adams, 'Mede and Mercede': The Evolution of the Economics of Grace in the *Piers Plowman* B and C Versions' in *MESGK*, 217-32 and S. Overstreet, ' "Grammaticus Ludens": Theological Aspects of Langland's Grammatical Allegory', *Traditio*, 40 (1984), 251-96.
[26] In Z Passus III concludes with lines unique to that version, 147-176.

means both 'end' and also, as the usage in X 415 indicates, 'meaning', or 'sense'.[27] It occurs twice in *Richard the Redeless*:

> And constrewe ich clause with the culorum   (I 72)
>
> Ho-so toke good kepe to the culorum   (IV 61)

Outside of *Piers* and *Richard*, the word is not recorded,[28] a coincidence which is best explained as the result of the textual force of *Piers* on *Richard the Redeless*. *Piers*, X 415 occurs in the context of an exemplum which likens those who made Noah's ark to the contemporary clergy. The line describes a reading process in which the speaker[29] translates the literal sense of his preceding clause 'men þat maden it amydde þe flood adreynten' (X 414) into the spiritual sense of 'curatours' of Holy Church (415). In Passus III, Conscience relates the story of how Saul disobeyed God's instructions to destroy Amalec and kill Agag, its king. Conscience's comments at III 269-72, which record God's instructions to Saul not to touch any property, either for 'Mede ne for monee' (271) are an addition to the biblical story. While the moral of 1 Samuel 15 is Saul's punishment for disobeying God,[30] the moral of Conscience's story is that Saul is destroyed by cupidity and avarice which led him to spare the city and its king:

> Swich a meschief Mede made þe kyng to haue
> That god hated hym for euere and alle hise heires after.   (III 278-9)

It is the 'culorum' of this 'cas' that Conscience elects not to declare, and his reasons are significant:

> On auenture it noyed m[e] noon ende wol I make,
> For so is þis world went wiþ hem þat han power
> That whoso sei hem soþe[s] is sonnest yblamed.   (281-3)

These are lines which exhibit textual disturbance[31] and attract the

---

27 Some of the B MSS have difficulty with 'culorum', substituting 'culor', 'colour' and 'conclusioun', Kane Donaldson, p.432. The line is not in A but is present in C XI 249.
28 Under 'culorum' MED gives only these examples from *Piers* and *Richard*.
29 In B, the speaker is supposed to be Will, but he speaks with such conviction and authority that the poet appears to taken over the voice of the poem. In C, the speech is given to Rechelesness.
30 This passage is discussed by James Simpson, 'The Constraints of Satire in *Piers Plowman* and *Mum and the Sothsegger*', in *Langland, the Mystics and the Medieval English Religious Tradition*, ed. H. Phillipps (Cambridge, 1990), 11-30, pp.13-14.
31 Lines 282-3 are not in A. And in B, MS Harley 3954 omits lines 281-2. In A, MS Harley 875 omits 259 (B.281). There are also substantial variants in individual words, see Kane, *The A Version*, p.251 and Kane Donaldson, p.287. Notably, the majority of the B MSS read 'men' rather than 'me' in line 281.

attention of the annotators.[32] Given the sense, this is hardly surprising. Conscience explains that he will not explain the 'culorum' of the exemplum because he fears retribution from those who wield secular power. It is not simply the 'ende' which Conscience is loth to declare in omitting the 'culorum', but, as suggested by the legal punning on 'cas', 'shewe' and 'ende', it is also the 'sentence' or 'meaning'.[33] What Conscience (or the poet) is too scared to spell out explicitly is the resemblance of the avaricious, greedy Saul to his own king.[34]

It is striking that 'culorum' is used in Passus IV of *Richard* in the context of describing a parliamentary meeting, an assembly preceded by an explicit account of Richard II's extravagance and his dubious economic policy (IV 1-15). The parliament is one in which those who attempt to speak out with the truth fall under grave suspicion:

> And somme were tituleris and to the kyng wente,
> And formed him of foos that good frendis weren,
> That bablid for the best and no blame serued
> Of kynge ne conceyll ne of the comunes nother,
> Ho-so toke good kepe to the culorum.   (IV 57-61)

If one pays good heed to the 'meaning', one sees that, like those who 'sei hem soþe' in Passus III of *Piers*, those who in Richard's reign speak without blame 'for the best' are 'sonnest blamed'. While the verbal recall is not exact, the use of 'culorum' in *Richard*, Passus IV suggests a close understanding of the textual – and social – connotations of vocabulary used in *Piers*, Passus III.

It is also possible that Passus III of *Piers* exerted a closer textual force on *Richard* than may be immediately apparent from using only the texts provided by modern editions. Two A manuscripts have the reading

---

[32] In British Library MS Additional 10574, there is a hand pointing at III 283, Uhart, p.291; in Huntingdon Library MS Hm 143, 'he sayþ trewþ shal be shent' is written in the margin at III 435, Uhart, p.333. There is also a 'nota' at III 436 in CUL MS Dd.3.13, Uhart, p.317. In BL MS Additional 35287 'the culore' is written beside III 280, Uhart, p.353.

[33] The legal senses of 'cas', 'shewe' and 'ende' are discussed on pp.153, 135, 137.

[34] The versions of *Piers* have traditionally been dated as follows: A, some time after 1362; B between 1377 and 1379 and C some time in the 1380s. There is a review of the literature on dating the versions, together with a full bibliography in Hanna, pp.11-24. Dating the poem is still a contentious issue and papers read at the 1993 Langland conference questioned the traditional chronology of the versions and their dates: see Hudson's paper on *Piers Plowman* and the Uprising of 1381 and Jill Mann, 'The Tyranny of the Alphabet: The Relationship of the A and B Versions of *Piers Plowman*' (both forthcoming *YLS* 8 1994). Mann's paper proposed that the A version was written after B. The king in question at *Piers* B III 281-3 would have been either Edward III, or Richard II. Although the nature of the criticism would be applicable to both kings, if the traditional dating of *Piers* stands, then Richard would have been too young to have been the precise target of the remarks at the time of writing the poem.

'culorum of þis clause' at A III 258.[35] This is no closer to *Richard*, IV 61, a line which in any case may be corrupt[36] S, but it is a reading closer to the first use of 'culorum' in *Richard*, at I.72. While it is possible that the writer of *Richard* remembered the collocation 'culorum. . .clause' from Passus X, it is equally the case that he could have derived it from a version of Passus III which preserved the readings of MSS T and H².[37] In its use in Passus I of his own poem, the collocation suggests a thorough understanding of the textual issues of Conscience's hesitation.

Richard explicitly associates the collocation 'culorum. . .clause' with reading poetry that is designed to correct faults and redress corruption. His own book will be a corrective to young readers, even if they dawdle through it only half way, and if elderly readers:

> . . .opyn it other-while amonge,
> And poure on it preuuly and preue it well after,
> And constrewe ich clause with the culorum,
> It shulde not apeire hem a peere a prynce though he were
> Ne harme nother hurte the hyghest of the rewme,
> But to holde him in hele and helpe all his frendis.   (I 70-5)

Unlike Conscience, who must hide the culorum for fear of reprisal, the reader of *Richard* can construe each clause with its sense without harm. Such judicious reading is healthy both to the king and his nobles. It is a secret reading, however, and for the writer who is prepared to offer up both 'clause' and 'culorum', there is still a sense of danger. The passage continues:

> And if ony word write be that wrothe make myghte
> My souereyne, that suget I shulde to be,
> I put me in his power and preie him, of grace,
> To take the entent of my trouthe that thoughte non ylle.   (I 76-79)

Here, the writer as subject of his own verse, sues his sovereign for protection and grace. The legal flavouring of line 78[38] shows the poet

---

[35] Trinity College Cambridge MS R.3.14 and MS Harley 6041, see Kane, *The A Version*, p.251.

[36] By normative standards of alliteration both I 72 and IV 61 lack a stave in the b-verse. IV 61 also lacks an alliterative stave in the a-verse, and while this may be characteristic of a looser style of alliteration; (there are 72 a-verses which scan xa) it is possible that the a-verse originally read 'kepte' and 'toke' was substituted because the scribe read the device of polyptoton as dittography. Polyptoton is used elsewhere in *Richard*, e.g. at I 31; 92; 120; II 147 and IV 56.

[37] There appears to be a further echo of *Piers* Passus X in the use of 'so ballid and bare was the reson' (IV 70), see below, p.44. The annotator to British Library MS Cotton Vespasian BXVI marks the C equivalent of the exemplum on Noah's Ark with the word 'experimentum', Uhart, p.322.

[38] 'grace' has the sense of 'the power to show mercy or pardon', Alford, *Glossary*, p.66.

anxious to write within the bounds of accepted hierarchy at the same time as urging a reading process in which a subject 'rede's his sovereign. The passage shows an attentive reading of Conscience's own reading lesson, and a keen awareness of the transference of its topical 'culorum' to the political climate of his own poem.

Conscience's is not the only reading lesson of *Piers* which attracted the attention of a poet in the tradition: the interchange between Piers and the priest in Passus VII is echoed in *Crede*. The pardon is written in Latin and the priest says that he 'moste' read the pardon for Piers and 'construe ech clause and kenne it þee on english' (VII 107-8).[39] Literally, the priest can find no pardon in the words of the document; an explanation which is deeply dissatisfying to the ploughman, who proceeds to tear it up and abandon the active for the contemplative life.[40] He cites scriptural texts in support of his action, prompting the lines:

> '. . .Peter! as me þynkeþ
> Thow art lettred a litel; who lerned þee on boke?'
> 'Abstynence þe Abbesse myn a b c me tauȝte,
> And Conscience cam afte[r] and kenned me [bettre]'
> 'Were þow a preest [Piers]', quod he, 'þow myȝtest preche [whan þee
>   liked]
> As diuinour in diuinite, wiþ *Dixit insipiens* to þi teme'.
> 'Lewed lorel!' quod Piers, 'litel lokestow on þe bible;
> On Salomons sawes selden þow biholdest:
> E[ji]ce derisores & cum eis ne crescant &c.'   (VII 136-43a)

The priest's response to Piers is that he is unlicensed to preach texts because he is not a priest. But Piers does not claim priestly learning for himself, merely a knowledge of the a b c. and instruction by some rather interesting teachers. Abstinence is a nun, not a male cleric, and she is

---

[39] There are a number of occasions in *Piers* when attention is drawn to the difference between writing in Latin and English. In C III 342, the king asks Conscience to explain his grammatical terms: 'for Englisch was it neuere'. In B XIII 70 Will quotes St Paul's 'Periculum est in falsis fratribus' in Latin, and says that he will not write it in English in case it is repeated too often. He writes the context in full in Latin so that grammarians can read it and then comments that he has never known a friar take that text as his theme when he preached in English. The passage shows awareness of the propriety of reserving certain topics for discussion in Latin but this stance is also heavily ironic in that the failure to translate is also because the joke on 'brothers/friars' in the Latin 'fratribus' is lost in English translation. At XV 117 when Anima quotes a long section from John Chrysostom, he does not translate it and warns of the 'wonder' that would happen if uneducated people knew what the Latin meant.

[40] The tearing is omitted in C and the change from active to contemplative life signalled much more clearly by the citation of the marriage feast from Luke 14 (C VII 292-306). The revision is discussed in Malcolm Godden, *The Making of Piers Plowman* (London, 1990), pp.185-90; E.T. Donaldson, *Piers Plowman: The C Text and its Poet* (New Haven, 1949), pp.161-68. See also R.W. Frank, 'The Pardon Scene in *Piers Plowman*' *Speculum* 26 (1951), 317-31 and R. Woolf, 'The Tearing of the Pardon' in Hussey (1969), pp.50-75.

the embodiment of sober living, not clerical display. Conscience is his next teacher, not a doctor of divinity.[41] Further, the aural pun on 'abbesse' and 'a b c' invokes the world of orality precisely at the point where alphabetisation, the symbol per se of the literate mind,[42] is mentioned.[43] These resonances destabilize the hierarchies of institution-alised learning, an instability which is continued in Piers' retort to the priest that he is a 'lewed lorel. . .litel lokestow on þe bible'. An issue raised by this many-layered episode is the proper use of biblical texts and the right relationship of written language to spiritual conduct. While the narrator refuses to adjudicate the quarrel, the interchange foregrounds the way that the church limits the users of its written language to those within its institutionalised hierarchy.[44]

A similar dynamic is at work in the opening of *Crede*. The narrator's framing remarks concern the state of his literacy:

> A. and all myn A.b.c after haue y lerned,
> And [patred] in my pater-noster iche poynt after other,
> And after all, myn Aue-marie almost to the ende;
> But all my kare is to comen for y can nohght my Crede.
> Whan y schal schewen myn schrift schent mote y worthen,
> The prest wil me punyche and penaunce enioyne. (5-10)

He lives in fear of institutional penance for failing to know all the texts which canonical decree considered elementary for Christian learn-ing.[45] What is interesting is that the narrator prefaces his proficiency in the Paternoster and the Ave Maria with his knowledge of the 'a b c'. Given that this new poem adopts the figure of Piers Plowman as its

---

[41] Significantly in Passus XIII when Conscience takes his leave from the banquet where the Doctor of Divinity has paraded his fraudulent learning, he whispers in Clergy's ear as he leaves that he would rather have perfect patience than half his pack of books (201).

[42] W.J. Ong, *Orality and Literacy*, (London, 1982), p.91.

[43] The pun is discussed by B.F. Huppé, 'Petrus id est Christus': Wordplay in *Piers Plowman* the B Text', *ELH*, 17 (1950), 163-70, p.167. See also J.K. Tavers, 'The Abbess's ABC', *YLS*, 2 (1988), 137-42.

[44] There is an interesting comment peculiar to the Z version on this question where Hunger cuts short his exposition of the parable of the talents: 'Of thys matere Y myght make a longe tale/Ac hit fallet nat for me, for Y am no dekne/To preche the peple wat that poynt menes' (VII 230-2). See further J.B. Allen, 'Langland's Reading and Writing: Detractor and the Pardon Passus', *Speculum*, 59 (1984), 342-59 and M. Aston, 'Lollardy and Literacy' in *Lollards and Reformers: Images and Literacy in Late Medieval Religion* (London, 1984), pp.193-218. The issue of who has the right to the institutionalised language of the church is crucial also in *The Wife of Bath's Prologue*, see J.A. Alford, 'The Wife of Bath versus the Clerk of Oxenford: What Their Rivalry Means', *ChauR*, 21 (1986), 108-32; A. Blamires, 'The Wife of Bath and Lollardy', *Medium Aevum*, 58 (1989), 224-42 and S. Schibanoff, 'Taking the Gold out of Egypt: The Art of Reading as a Woman' in *Gender and Reading*, eds. E.Flynn and P.Schweickart (Baltimore, 1986), 83-106.

[45] The Council at Beziers in 1246 ordered that children attaining the age of seven should be taught the Salutation of the Blessed Virgin Mary, the Paternoster and the Creed.

presiding authority, it is not fanciful, I think, to suggest influence of the episode in *Piers* where Piers disputes the nature of institutional reading with one of its inadequate representatives, and to see in the narrator's own statement of his proficiency in the a b c, an echo of that of Piers.[46]

Unlike *Piers*, however, the narrator's command of Latin is unsure. In contrast to Piers's fluency with biblical texts he can plod only awkwardly through the Latin texts which the ecclesiastical hierarchy requires him to recite. But his own 'litel' learning stands in great contrast to the pedagogy of the friars, who are so caught up in their mutual calumny that they are unable to teach the narrator his creed. The instruction of institutionalised figures of authority fails. It is Peres the Ploughman who eventually teaches the narrator his creed, a labourer who, in contrast to the friars, lives a holy and godly life and practices what he preaches.[47] Peres is the embodiment of the view expressed by an anonymous Wycliffite writer:

> 'A symple pater noster of a plouȝman þat his in charite is betre þan a þousand massis of coueitouse prelatis & veyn religious ful of coueitise and pride & fals flaterynge and norischynge of synne.'[48]

At the beginning of the poem, the echo of *Piers* sets the stage for the interrogation of the actions of those who are entitled to preach ecclesiastical texts.[49]

On the surface, this interrogation of the right uses of literacy, with a ploughman ultimately proving a better teacher than a member of the institutionalised clergy, sits rather uneasily with Peres' own castigation of making literacy available to the sons of cobblers and beggars:

---

[46] The use of 'abc' in the short poem *Defend us from all Lollardry* is discussed below, pp.110-12.

[47] The figure of Peres is discussed more fully in Chapter Four.

[48] Matthew, pp.274/7. cf. the penultimate line of the A version of *Piers* (also preserved in B and C). Clerics with knowledge of many books are no sooner saved than the unlettered, (including 'plouȝmen' who 'percen wiþ a paternoster þe paleis of heuene' (XI 312) and 'Ye, men knowe clerkes þat han corsed þe tyme/That euere þei kouþe [konne on book] moore þan Credo in deum patrem,/And principally hir paternoster; many a persone haþ wisshed' (B X 472-4). This is a passage which attracts the attention of annotators in: CUL MS Dd.1.17, with a 'nota' (Uhart, p.295); CUL Ll 4.14, and Oriel College MS 79 with the words 'exemplum bonum' (Uhart, p.295 and p.309). See also the end of B Passus X and the distinctive emphasis that is given in the C version of the lines: 'So lewede laborers of litel vnderstondyng/Selde falleth so foule and so depe in synne/ As clerkes of holy chirche þat kepe sholde and saue/Lewede men in good bileue and lene hem at here nede' (C XI 302-5). In *Crede*, Peres's first words to the narrator are that if he lacks sustenance: 'lene the ich will' (445).

[49] cf. *The Friar's Answer*, Robbins, 69, where the narrator, who is a friar, is alarmed that 'lewed men' know the Scriptures because it enables them to expose the hypocrisy of the friars.

Now mot ich soutere his sone setten to schole,
And ich a beggers brol on the booke lerne,
And worth to a writere and with a lorde dwell,
Other falsly to a frere the fend for to seruen.
So of that beggers brol a bychop schal worthen,
Among the peres of the lond prese to sitten,
And lordes sones lowly to tho losells aloute,
Knyghtes crouketh hem to and crucheth full lowe,
And his syre a soutere y-suled in grees,
His teeth with toylinge of lether tatered as a sawe.
Alaas that lordes of the londe leueth swiche wrechen,
And leneth swiche lorels for her lowe wordes! (*Crede*, 744-55)

The substance of the passage recalls Will's criticism in *Piers*, C V 61-81, of the chaos caused to social hierarchy when bondsmen's children are made into bishops and the sons of cobblers can buy themselves knighthoods. But in contrast to *Piers Plowman*, Peres's chief concern in *Crede* is not with simony and barratory: the fault lies not with the labourers themselves, but with those who make such education available, namely the friars.

In their own empty reading practices, the friars are accused of abusing their learning, as we have already seen. Here, through their teaching, and recruitment of young children, they are accused of overturning secular hierarchy more widely. Line 745 echoes a collocation used in the interchange between Mede and Conscience: 'The leeste brol of his blood a Barones peire' (III 205).[50] It invests Peres' attack with resonances of the harmful effects on a king who listens to the advice of one who reads to her own advantage rather than for the common good. As a result of the friars' programme of education,[51] the brats of beggars are elevated into a position where they are able to sit amongst the peers of the realm and offer advice.[52]

Unlike the cobbler's son, however, Peres has no pretensions to a bishopric, or a place as a king's counsellor. Although he is a ploughman, he is no advocate of secular upheaval, as his remarks on literacy prove. His own command of learning is used not to further his own position but to remedy the spiritual impasse of another. In his matching of words

[50] The A manuscript Bodleian Library MS Ashmole 1468 displaces this line from III 192 to after III 29. See above, p.15.

[51] The friars often undertook teaching in the local community but the lines in *Crede* may also allude to the fraternal propensity for forcible recruitment, often of young children. This is a staple of anti-fraternal satire, e.g. Richard Fitzralph, *Defensio Curatorum*, in *Trevisa's Dialogues*, ed. A.J. Perry (EETS OS 167 1925), pp.55-6 and *Vox*, IV 981ff.

[52] *Crede*, 362-5 criticises the friars for becoming king's counsellors, with particular reference to Richard II's maintenance of an ecclesiastical clique which included the friar bishops Burghill and Rushook, see A. Steel, *Richard II* (Cambridge, 1962), p.220.

and deeds, Peres proves a better 'brother' to the narrator than the friars. Their lessons promote civil confusion and corruption; his own lesson to the narrator provides understanding and an exemplar of holy living.

The response of *Crede* to reading lessons in *Piers Plowman* shows an awareness of the social and institutional implications of the words and phrases that are recalled. This is an awareness that can be parallelled across the four poems in the tradition. They are 'lerned on the langage' of *Piers* not just in the sense of being able to reproduce some of its verbal collocations, but also in their perpetuation of the social poetic temper in which the whole poem is written. At the beginning of Chapter One, I alluded to the fact that *Piers* was written in a 'plainer' alliterative style than poems of the classical corpus, and it is a feature of the tradition's 'right reading' of *Piers* that they reproduce this alliterative temper in their own new works. The rest of this present chapter will examine this aspect of the tradition's reading response to *Piers Plowman*.

A number of critics have suggested that amongst poetry which employs alliteration as a sustained structural device, the alliterative temper of *Piers* is distinctive.[53] While the range of alliterative writing is such that it cannot be considered a homogenous group,[54] within its ambit it is possible to discern a verbal texture that is more characteristic of *Piers* and the poems of the tradition, than of any other poem or group of poems. *Piers* does not employ the formal, elaborate mode of archaic, decorative diction and regular alliterative style that is prevalent in poems such as *The Wars of Alexander* and *Morte D'Arthure*. The diction of *Piers* is less sumptuous and less locally-defined, its narrative sequences less stately and its metrical patterns more informal.[55] As James Simpson has observed, *Piers* is detached in 'matters both of genre and style from the courtly mode of alliterative writing'.[56]

While there exists across the range of alliterative writing, a concern with serious moral issues, and often indeed, doctrinal quandaries,[57] the social imperative of *Piers* and its tradition informs the verbal texture of these poems in a way that sets them apart. At the opening of *Piers*, the

[53] See references in Chapter One, n.1 and E.Salter, '*Piers Plowman* and *The Simonie*', *Archiv*, 203 (1967), 241-54; 'Langland and the Contexts of *Piers Plowman*', *E&S*, 32 (1979), 19-25, D.A. Lawton, 'Alliterative Style' in *A Companion to Piers Plowman*, ed. J. Alford (Berkeley, 1988), 223-49; J. Simpson, *Piers Plowman: An Introduction to the B Text* (London, 1990), p.9; Hoyt Duggan, 'Langland's Meter', *YLS*, 1 (1987), 41-71.
[54] See references cited in Chapter 1, note 15.
[55] On the absence of decorative diction, see also G. Kane, 'Music Neither Unpleasant nor Monotonous' in *Medieval Studies for J.A.W. Bennett*, ed. P.L. Heyworth (Oxford, 1981), pp.43-63.
[56] Simpson (1990), p.12.
[57] This is discussed in Lawton (1983) and also in G. Shepherd, 'The Nature of Alliterative Poetry in Late Medieval England', *PBA*, 56 (1970), 57-76.

narrator goes in search of 'wondres' (B Prol. 4) and, while out walking on the Malvern Hills, experiences a 'ferly, of Fairye me þoȝte' (Prol. 6). The diction suggests the marvels of courtly alliterative writing: heroic deeds; fantastic Arthurian adventure; or supernatural mystery,[58] but the Prologue to *Piers* redefines its affiliations. When the collocation reappears in the Prologue: 'Manye ferlies han fallen in a fewe yeres' (65), it refers to marvels of the institutionalised kind – those provoked by disorders within the discourses of government or the established church.[59]

While the collocation 'ferly. . .befalle' is not uncommon in alliterative poetry, its use in *Piers* to refer to social disorder is shared only by new poems in the later tradition.[60] In *Mum*'s redeployment of the 'ferlies' of Prol. 65 at line 222: 'Lest feerelees falle withynne fewe yeres', the marvels feared by the narrator are the disorders resulting from inefficient kingship. The line is recalled towards the end of the poem where the narrator picks up a roll:

> Y-write ful of wordes of woundres that han falle,
> And fele-folde ferlees wythynne thees fewe yeris,
> By cause that the clergie and knighthoode to-gedre
> Been not knytte in conscience as Crist dide thaym stable.
>
> (*Mum*, 1736-39)

In considering the written correction of social disharmony, *Mum* is concerned not with the 'ferlies' of serpents coming out of eggs, impossibly green knights and wondrous battles (however morally informative these marvels may be), but with the disruptive consequences of institutional failure.[61] In its handling of 'ferly' and 'wondre', *Mum* is both attuned to the social connotations of the verbal texture of

---

[58] When the collocation is used in *Gawain and the Greeen Knight*, 23 it refers to the marvellous happenings of Arthurian history; in *The Destruction of Troy*, Prol.95, it refers to heroic deeds and at 421 to Medea's witchcraft. In *The Wars of Alexander*, 501, the 'ferly' is the sudden entrance of a bird into the king's court, who lays an egg in the king's lap, from which a tiny serpent hatches; and in *Cleanness*, 1529, 1563 and 1629, 'ferly' refers to the mysterious writing on the wall.

[59] The argument here is indebted to Simpson (1990), pp.13-14.

[60] When the phrase is used in A Passus XII 58 its resonances are closer to the marvellous incident that Prol. 6 promises. Will's adventures on his abortive journey to 'quod bonum est tenete' are without the emphasis on institutional difficulties that characterise the use of the phrase at Prol. 62. A similar phrase is used in *Dives and Pauper* in the context of discussing the signs and miracles which have happened recently in the land: 'Y may well assentyn to þyn speche for so many wondris han fallyn in þis londe withynne a fewe ȝeris' (I 213/42-45).

[61] Lawton (1983) has drawn attention to the morally instructive nature of alliterative romance.

Piers and consonant with the social emphases of other poems in the tradition.[62]

Integral to the social temper of *Piers*, is the absence of alliterative decoration and courtliness. Where any such embellishment appears, it is foregrounded by its difference from the verbal texture of its context. For instance in the adoption of traditional alliterative poetic diction, together with the strict aa/ax pattern in the description of Mede's arrival at court,[63] verbal elaboration becomes associated with corruption.

This is a technique used fleetingly in *Wynnere and Wastoure*. The poem is written predominantly in the classical mode of alliterative writing,[64] but there are, within this temper, changes of register. Occasionally, the texture moves closer to the plainer style of *Piers* and its tradition[65] and at other points, courtly or decorative language is foregrounded in a fashion similar to that in the Mede episode. For instance, the banner of the Augustinian friars is: 'Whitte als the whalles bone whoso the sothe tellys' (181). The collocation in the a-verse is more usually found in descriptions of courtly women.[66] Its use here suggests the pampered luxury of the friars. While much of the description in the poem is sumptuous (the account of the opposing armies (50-100) or of the king's clothes (90-8)), the most ostentatiously formal verse describes Wastour's elaborate feasting.[67] Stephanie Trigg has illuminatingly demonstrated how the poem as a whole contests the rival discourses of winning and

---

[62] cf. *Richard* where the 'selcouthe thingis,/A grett wondir to wyse men'(I 5-6) and 'wondirffull werkis' (I 18) are the events surrounding the deposition of England's anointed king. In *Crowned King* 'the most merveylous' dream (12) prefaces a vision which questions the economic and political wisdom of levying heavy taxation for the purposes of war. The only 'wonders' in *Crede* are the narrator's astonishment at the extravagance of the building at Blackfriars (172).

[63] J.A. Burrow, *Ricardian Poetry* (London, 1971), p.34; Simpson (1990), pp.10-11.

[64] The dialect of *Wynnere and Wastoure* is almost identical to that of *The Parlement of the Thre Ages* and suggests a provenance of the extreme North West Midlands, possibly South Lancashire. There are, however, many East Midland forms, which may reflect the spread of the London dialect. On the basis of this 'mixed dialect', Trigg suggests that the poem may have been written by a clerk in the service of one of the lords who had both estates in the North-West Midlands and connections with the court in London, *Wynnere and Wastoure*, ed. Stephanie Trigg (EETS OS 297 1990), pp.xviii-xxii.

[65] e.g. the speech of the herald forbidding the two opposing armies to breach the king's peace, 124-135. The syntax is hypotactic; there are only three adjectives – and these are functional; there is an even distribution of nouns and verbs and the only distinctive vocabulary is 'beryn' (126; 131). This may be a result of the poet's echo of legislation passed to prevent the practice of leading armed bands of men; see Trigg (1990), pp.25-6. The speech at lines 191-201 is also free of ornament and embellishment, and the king's concluding judgement, 456ff, contrasts with the more ornate style of the rest of the poem.

[66] e.g. *The Harley Lyrics*, ed. G.L. Brook (Manchester, 1956), no. 7/40; no. 9/1.

[67] 332-65. Trigg notes that the lavishness of the feast is emphasized by the similar shape of the a-verses between 349-54, p.xxxiii.

wasting,[68] and while this contest does not extend to the verbal texture of the whole poem, there is, within what is predominantly a formal mode, some evidence both of the plainer mode of alliterative writing and the foregrounding of its most elaborate embellishments.

This principle of contrast is taken much further in *Crede*. Fundamentally, the poem is written in the plain alliterative style. On the relatively few occasions where the texture is embellished, decoration equals a betrayal of spiritual truths. One such occasion is the description of the elaborate convent of the Dominicans.[69] Given that the account of Blackfriars is severely critical of the practice whereby the friars rewarded their benefactors by recording their names in stained glass windows, it is possible it shows awareness of the alliterative register of the description of Mede.[70] The narrator gapes (156 and 191) at the elaborate costliness of Blackfriars, London, 'a woon wonderlie well y-beld' (172):[71]

> With arches on eueriche half and belliche y-corven,
> With crochetes on corners with knottes of golde,
> Wyde wyndowes y-wrought y-written full thikke,
> Schynen with schapen scheldes to schewen aboute,
> With merkes of marchauntes y-medled bytwene,
> Mo than twenty and two twyes y-noumbred.
> Ther is none heraud that hath half swich a rolle,
> Right as a rageman hath rekned hem newe.
> Tombes opon tabernacles tyld opon lofte,
> Housed in hirnes harde set abouten,
> Of armede alabaustre [alfor] for the nones,
> [Made vpon marbel in many maner wyse,
> Knyghtes in her conisantes clad for the nones,
> All it semed seyntes y-sacred opon erthe;
> And louely ladies y-wrought leyen by her sydes.   (173-87)

---

68 Trigg (1990), pp.xlvi-xlviii and 'Israel Gollancz's *Wynnere and Wastoure*: Political Satire or Editorial Politics', in *Medieval English Religious and Ethical Literature: Essays in Honour of G.H. Russell*, ed. G. Kratzmann and James Simpson (Cambridge, 1986), pp.115-27.

69 In *Piers*, B XV 77-8, Anima criticises the friars who spend foolishly on housing, clothing and proud displays of learning. *Vox* criticises the lavish buildings of the friars at IV 1141-58. *The Lanterne of Light* criticises the fraternal orders for building extravagant houses to dwell in like lords of the world, p.41/7-10 and states that curious church building was forbidden by the Fathers; walls, pillars, glittering gold beams and other ornaments, are anti-apostolic, p.37. *Wynnere and Wastoure* notes that stored up wealth will be used by the friars to paint their pillars or plaster their walls, 300-1.

70 In *Piers* a friar offers to absolve Mede if she agrees to glaze the window in his friary. Mede's acquiescence to this arrangement calls forth from the narrator a denunciation of the practice of writing the names of benefactors in windows, (III 47-72 and cf. similar criticism of the practice at XIV 199-200).

71 In keeping with the social temper of *Piers*, this, the only use of 'wonder' in the *Crede*, associates it with ecclesiastical disorder. Mede is described as 'wonderlich ycloþed' (B II 8). Many B MSS read 'worþiliche' at this point but A II 8 and C II 9 both read 'wonderly'.

With its use of catalogue and emphasis on surface decoration and ornaments, the account of the friary is reminiscent of the elaborately rich descriptions of buildings in poems of the classical alliterative corpus.[72] As a whole, however, *Crede* refuses the validity of sumptuous expression both in its statements and in its alliterative practice. Peres teaches the narrator the 'graith' in contrast to the friars' 'gladding tales/ That turneth vp two-folde vnteyned opon trewthe' (516).[73]

In *Richard*, there is a strong case for the poet's cognisance of the alliterative techniques of the Mede episode in *Piers*: there is a verbal echo of the description of Mede in the list of the allegorical properties of the stones in the king's crown:

> Crouned with a croune that kyng vnder heuene
> Mighte not a better haue boughte, as I trowe;
> So full was it filled with vertuous stones,
> With perlis of pris to punnysshe the wrongis,
> With rubies rede the righth for to deme,
> With gemmes and juellis joyned to-gedir,
> And pees amonge the peple for peyne of thi lawis.
> It was full goodeliche ygraue with gold al aboughte;
> The braunchis aboue boren grett charge;
> With diamauntis derue y-douutid of all
> That wroute ony wrake within or withoute;
> With lewte and loue yloke to thi peeris,
> And sapheris swete that soughte all wrongis,
> Ypouudride wyth pete ther it [pounced] be oughte,
> And traylid with trouthe and treste al aboute;
> For ony cristen kynge a croune well ymakyd.
> But where this croune bicome a clerk were that wuste.
>
> (*Richard* I 120-36)

Lines 120-1 recall: 'Ycorouned [in] a coroune, þe kyng hath noon bettre' (*Piers*, II 10),[74] and the use of 'boughte' in I 121 recalls the financial nexus of the debate surrounding Mede.[75] The list in *Richard* is conspicuous for its formal organisation and its strict adherence to an aa/ ax alliterative pattern which is much less rigidly observed elsewhere.[76]

---

[72] e.g. the descriptions of the siege tower in *Siege of Jerusalem*, 645-80, of Troy in *Destruction of Troy*, 1537-1618, and St Erkenwald's tomb, *St Erkenwald*, 38-55.

[73] R.D. Kendall, *The Drama of Dissent: The Radical Poetics of Non-Conformity 1380-1590* (N. Carolina 1986), observes the Wycliffite predilection for the 'monophonic' (p.29) and observes that there is no polyphony in the plowman's field – only the plainsong of hunger, p.78. But cf. the discussion of wordplay in *Crede* in the following chapter.

[74] Substantial numbers of A and B MSS read 'with' for 'in', Kane, *The A Version*, p.206; Kane Donaldson, p.255. The C version II 11, reads 'with'.

[75] The collocation 'crouned. . .croune' is not listed amongst those collected by Oakden, see J.P. Oakden, *Alliterative Poetry in Middle English: The Dialectal and Metrical Survey* (Manchester, 1968), pp.263-363.

[76] 72.34% of lines in *Richard* alliterate on aa/ax. If we exclude I 130 (aa/aa) and I 133

The formality is foregrounded, and, as such, becomes the subject of the narrative. In one sense ritualised verse is entirely appropriate to a king's coronation but the recall of the Mede episode alerts us to a deeper significance. By using the formal discourse of regular alliterative composition, in metre, in the use of catalogue[77] and in the enumeration of sensuous detail characteristic of the description of clothes and finery,[78] the narrator points up the gap between the institutional discourse of regal investiture and the economic and political realities over which Richard II effectively (or ineffectually) presided.

In order to display the ideal virtues of a king, the narrative employs the traditional associations of lapidaries[79] but the authority of the lapidary tradition is exhausted by the immediate political context of its poetic application. The poet gives us a textbook display of kingly virtue which is unmatched by the political realities of the time: 'But where this croune bicome a clerk were that wuste'. We have already learned that covetousness has crashed Richard's crown for ever (I 95). Formal symmetry, alliterative neatness and static lapidary associations are effective means of portraying the ceremonial clothes of kingship but in this poem, as we soon learn, fine clothes and political mismanagement go hand in glove.[80]

In *Piers*, this interrogation of established discourses is a very characteristic poetic technique.[81] Its perpetuation in the poems in the tradition suggests it was one of the chief stylistic lessons learnt from reading *Piers Plowman*. Often, institutionalised discourses provide the narrative schemes of the poetry but with the result that the inadequacies or contradictions of these discourses are exposed. The poems can be seen to supplement institutionalised discourse in the Derridaen sense of 'supplement': that which is simultaneously both an enrichment of

---

(corrupt), then in this passage there is 88.23% aa/ax alliteration. There are four other places where significant stretches of the narrative alliterate predominantly on aa/ax: I 37-60, (exceptions: aaa/ax (45); aa/aa (53); III 14-31, exceptions: aaa/ax (15); aa/aa (22)); III 181-206, exceptions: aa/aa (181); aaa/ax (188); III 291-306, exception: aa/aa (293). None of these passages has the formal syntactical organisation of the crown sequence.

[77] G.Shepherd discusses the ubiquity of the catalogue in alliterative poetry in 'The Nature of Alliterative Poetry in Late Medieval England', *PBA*, 56 (1970), 57-76, p.60.

[78] e.g. *Parlement of the Thre Ages*, 118-132; *St Erkenwald*, 77-91; *The Wars of Alexander*, 1652-75; *Gawain*, 151-220, *Wynnere and Wastoure*, 90-98; 108-22.

[79] The catalogue begins with a pearl, which Isidore of Seville calls the: 'prima candidarum gemmarum' (*Etymologiarum*, XVI. x.1, *PL*, 82, p.575); the ruby is traditionally associated with lordship, *English Medieval Lapidaries*, ed. J. Evans and M.J. Serjeantson (EETS OS 190 1933), p.21; the diamond is traditionally the hardest of stones, ibid., p.83 and a sapphire is a most suitable stone for a ring to be set on a king's finger. It is associated with 'gentillesse', ibid., p.22.

[80] A substantial section of *Richard* inveighs against over-dressed courtiers, III 116-242.

[81] Simpson, p.14.

something already full, and a replacement of something which is deficient.[82]

For example, as in *Piers*, sections of poems in the *Piers* tradition are generated out of the discourses of legislative topoi.[83] The stimulus for the political comment of *The Crowned King* is the ordinance recently passed by parliament designed to raise taxation for Henry V's military campaign against France.[84] The extent of the award was unprecedented: 'A soleyn subsidie to susteyne his werres' (36). The poem supplements the institutional discourse of an 'ordenaunce. . .made in ease of his peple' (41) by giving a voice, outside the official discourses of parliamentary procedures, to a representative of the people who have to bear the cost. As we have already seen, this is accomplished within a narrative scheme drawn from the Prologue to *Piers*.

A similar poetic operates in *Richard*. Passus IV opens with a list of the revenues which Richard customarily received. The narrative is lexically marked by technical fiscal vocabulary, e.g. 'fee-fermes', (IV 4) 'for-feyturis', (5) 'nownagis', (6) and 'issues of court' (8). Lines 14-16 incorporate the wording of a statute passed at the 1398 Shrewsbury session, which in an unprecedented move, granted to Richard the subsidies on wools, leathers and woolfells for the rest of his life in addition to a levy of a fifteenth and a tenth:[85]

> Withoute preiere at a parlement a poundage biside,
> And a fifteneth and a dyme eke,
> And with all the custum of the clothe that cometh to fayres. (14-16)[86]

The narrative proceeds to question the wisdom and propriety of such a grant by moving into the discourse of parliamentary debate. The Chancellor's traditional opening formula: 'monstra & pronunca la cause del sommonce du parlement'[87] is reproduced in alliterative idiom:

---

[82] J. Derrida, *Of Grammatology*, trans. Gayatri Chakravorty Spivak (Baltimore, 1976), p.144-5.
[83] Simpson (1990), pp.2-3.
[84] On 19 Nov. 1414, Henry exacted from Parliament two tenths and two fifteenths, *Rot.Parl.*, IV.35. In the previous Parliament, eight months earlier, Henry had stated that the usual grants of a tenth and a fifteenth would not be imposed, *Rot.Parl.*, IV.16.
[85] *Statutes of the Realm*, II 106: 'they [the people of the realm] have made at this Time of their good Will *more than they have done to any of his progenitors before this Time*, that is to say, the Subsidy of the Wools, Leathers and Woolfells for Term of his Life and a Disme and Quinzime and an half, to be paid in Manner comprised in their said Grant' (emphasis mine).
[86] Line 15 completely lacks alliteration in its direct reference to the terms of the grant. There is a comparable line in *Piers*, XIII 270 where Haukyn refers to John Chichester, Mayor of London. None of the variants supplies the lack of alliteration. The line is omitted in C.
[87] *Rot.Parl.*, III 347.

43

Than, as her forme is frist they begynne to declare
The cause of her comynge and than the kyngis will.
Comliche a clerk than comsid the wordis,
And prononcid the poyntis aperte to hem alle.   (IV 33-6)

The debate which follows is chaotic and corrupt. The narrative subverts the authority of parliamentary discourse from within its stated terms. Far from debating the truth, the representatives are either too stupid to contribute or have been bribed to speak fraudulently. At the collapse of the meeting, the narrative deploys the traditional analogy between the State and a ship[88] and demonstrates the incompetence of the parliament by describing the inability of a ship's crew to control their vessel in stormy weather (71-82). This recalls the storm topos of formal alliterative poems[89] but the gesture towards this formal mode of composition within the depleted terms of parliamentary discourse serves to highlight the social truth-telling function of a different style of alliterative poetry. There are a number of verbal echoes of *Piers* in this sequence in *Richard* the 'culorum' (IV 61), 'so ballid and bare was the reson' (IV 70); and in the last line of the poem (IV 93), where the fraudulent representatives forsake 'Do-well'[90] Almost as if in mimesis of the breakdown of institutional resources to redress grievance and corruption (and inspired perhaps by narrative schemes in *Piers*) the supplementary narrative of *Richard the Redeless* breaks off.[91]

Mum and the Sothsegger also dramatises this lack in institutionalised discourses, again from within their very terms, and in a fashion reminiscent of the poetic temper of *Piers*. In his search for a truthteller, the narrator interrogates the Seven Liberal Arts at the universities. As in Passus IX to XII of *Piers*, the narrative is generated out of the discourses of academic learning[92] There are verbal echoes of Study's disquisition on academic pursuits in Passus X.[93] The Doctor of Philosophy's words to

---

[88] cf. Gower, *Vox Clamantis*, I 1593-2078 and the macaronic sermon preached on the government of Henry V, ed. R.M. Haines, 'Our Master Mariner, Our Sovereign Lord: A Contemporary Preacher's View of Henry V', *Medieval Studies*, 38 (1976), 85-96.

[89] Shepherd, p.61 and N. Jacobs, 'Alliterative Storms: A Topos in Middle English', *Speculum*, 47 (1972), 695-719.

[90] cf. *Piers*, III 280; and X 55: 'And bryngen forþ a balled reson, taken Bernard to witnesse'. In C the phrase becomes 'ballede resones' XI 38. The only other example of 'balled reson' cited by MED apart from *Piers* and *Richard* is *Castle of Perseverance*, 1278.

[91] For instance the scheme to plough the half-acre, see discussion in Simpson, (1990), pp.67-71. See also Steven Justice, 'The Genres of *Piers Plowman*', *Viator*, 19 (1988), 291-306, who notes that the poem seeks its provisionality; it enables narrative progress and approaches religious authority by discontinuous choices of genre that progressively abandon claims to poetic authority, p.305.

[92] Simpson (1990), pp.132-6.

[93] The echo is closest to the C reading: XI 126-7: 'Of carpentrie, of keruers, and contreuede þe compas,/And caste mette by squire, bothe lyne and leuele'. B X 184 lacks the reference to 'square'.

the narrator: 'And seide, soon, seest thou this semble of clercz/How thay bisien thaym on thaire bokes and beten thaire wittz' (366-7) echo Holy Church's words to Will: 'sone, slepestow, sestow þis peple/How bisie þay ben aboute þe maze' (I.5-6). The reprise in *Mum* serves to belittle the activities of the academics.

In *Piers*, the use of academic debate questions the premises of such a mode of enquiry. Ultimately, the narrative moves on to search for a more sapiential, affective knowledge of Truth.[94] *Mum's* interrogation of the effectiveness of academic discourses exposes more radically the redundancy of university institutions, prompted by the fact that 'sum of the semble' (383) are friars.[95] The narrative is marked lexically by the terms of academic debate: 'moeued my matiere' (326); 'bothe sides' (334); 'reherce' (340); 'caas' (341); 'question' (381). But whereas in *Piers* the disputants are able to argue the pro and the contra, in this episode in *Mum* the arts are incapable of working within their own discursive rules because they are each so enmeshed in the jargon of their particular discipline:

> Sire Grumbald the grammier tho glowed for anger
> That he couthe not congruly knytte thaym to-gedre.
> Music and Mvm mighte not accorde,
> For thay been contrary of kynde, who-so canne spie.
> Phisic diffied al [the] bothe sides,
> Bothe Mvm and me and the soeth-siggre;
> He was accumbrid of oure cumpaignye, by Crist that me bought,
> And as fayn of oure voiding as foul [of his make].
> Astronomy-ys argumentz were alle of the skyes,
> He-is touche no twynte of terrene thinges.
> Rethoric-is reasons me luste not reherce,
> For he conceyued not the caas, I knewe by his wordes;
> But a subtile shophister with many sharpe wordes
> Sette [the] soeth-sigger as shorte as he couthe.
> But he wolde melle with Mvm ner more ner lasse,
> So chiding and chatering [as choghe was he euer].
> Ieometrie the ioynour iablid faste,

---

[94] Simpson (1990), pp.150-6.

[95] In *Piers*, Anima's criticism of inadequate academics in B XV 377-84 is in C, given to Liberium Arbitrium, where an explicit reference to the seven arts is added. The passage suggests the corrupt influence of the friars in the reference to 'Flaterer': 'Go we now to eny degre and bote Gyle be holde a maister/And Flaterere for his vscher, ferly me thynketh./ Doctours of decre and of diuinite maistres,/That sholde þe seuene ars conne and assoile a quodlibet,/Bote they fayle in philosophie – and philosoferes lyuede/And wolde wel examene hem – wonder me thynketh!' (C XVII 111-16). While the friars are not explicitly mentioned, in B Passus XX, it is 'Frere Flaterere' (315; 323) who destroys the Barn of Unity by selling contrition for money. In the same Passus, Envy commands the friars to go to 'scole' to learn logic and law (274) and philosophy (295).

> And caste many cumpas, as the crafte askith,
> And laide leuel and lyne a-long by the squyre.
> But I was not the wiser by a Walsh note
> Of the matiere of Mvm that marrid me ofte,
> And stoode al a-stonyed and starid for angre
> That clergie couthe not my cares amende. (330-52)

The section recalls the terse, intellectual punning characteristic of *Piers* by playing on 'termes' from technical language to obfuscate the points of debate.[96] 'Congruly' (331) has the sense of grammatical congruence which Grammar is unable to perform; 'accorde' (332) chimes on the senses of 'come to an agreement' and 'being harmonious, in tune'; and while line 334 is corrupt, in addition to its sense 'denounce/scorn', 'diffied' may pun on 'digest/assimilate'.[97] 'Skyes' (338) has the technical astronomical meaning of 'a sphere of the celestial realm' together with the figurative suggestion of 'being foggy or misty'. 'Reasons' (340) puns on the senses of 'a proposition in logic' and 'a riddle or joke'; 'conceuyed' (341) has the senses of 'to comprehend' and a grammatical term meaning 'to join the elements in a sentence or phrase', and 'caas' (341) has the senses of 'matter' and 'grammatical case'.[98] 'Ioynour' (346) has the geometrical sense of 'to connect two points by a straight line' and the grammatical sense of 'connecting words or clauses', both of which pun ironically with 'iablid'; 'cumpas' (347) puns on the sense of 'a geometrical drawing instrument' and 'a crafty plan'; and 'crafte' (347) has the senses of 'liberal art' and 'trick or deceit'.[99] 'Lyne' (348) puns on a 'builder's or mason's line' and 'a line in geometry'; and 'squyre' (348) is both an 'implement or tool for determining right angles' and a geometrical term meaning 'a plane figure having the form of a carpenter's square'.[100]

The narrator's matter is left unresolved – indeed, unaddressed. Logic sets the sothsegger as short as he knows how (343), an ironic echo of *Piers* XII 121-2 in which Ymaginatif counsels against despising 'clergie' and setting short 'by hir science'. The obfuscatory mode of narration demonstrates how far the universities are from a truthtelling discourse: earlier, a 'sothsegger' is defined as one who:

---

[96] A.V.C. Schmidt, *The Clerkly Maker* (Cambridge 1987), M.C. Davlin, *A Game of Heuene* (Cambridge 1990) examine the wordplay of *Piers* in depth. The following chapter examines its use in the tradition.

[97] MED 'congru' (adj) b); MED 'accorden' 1a) and 5a; MED 'defien' (v)1 and 'defien' (v)2.

[98] MED 'skie' 1b) and 2a); MED 'resoun' 9b)a) and 8d); MED 'conceiven' 6a) and 'concepcioun' 4): 'concepcion of case is whenne a nominatyf case is joynyd wyth an ablatyf case and a preposicion j sette by twene'. MED 'cas' 6a) and 10).

[99] OED 'join' 1d); MED 'joinen' 2d); MED 'compas' 5) and 1b) and MED 'craft' 5) and 2b).

[100] MED 'line' 2a) and 6) and OED 'square' 1) and 3).

> . . .can not speke in termes ne in tyme nother,
> But bablith fourth bustusely as barn vn-y-lerid;
> But euer he hitteth on the heed of the nayle-is ende
> That the pure poynt pricketh on the sothe. (*Mum*, 49-52)

By contrast, the academics can speak only in 'termes',[101] and it is precisely within those terms that the narcissistic inadequacies of their institutionalised discourse are exposed.[102]

Crede in its entirety is grounded on a very similar poetic agenda. The narrator goes in search of a text: the creed which he is required to know by institutional authority. The friars whom he meets offer him only mutual backbiting, in one case authorised by scriptural quotation.[103] This misuse of institutionalised texts[104] is matched by the friars' vaunted abuse of ecclesiastical practices, documents and writing: annuals (414);[105] testaments (70; 410);[106] letters of fraternisation (417) and books

---

[101] Following the discussion in Jill Mann, *Chaucer and Medieval Estates Satire* (Cambridge, 1973), p.194, Lee Patterson, in *Chaucer and the Subject of History* (London, 1991) has noted how *The General Prologue* is packed with the 'termes' of the vocational objects of the pilgrims, such that they appear to speak in their own voices, pp.27-29.

[102] In Chapter Four, the Wycliffite allegiances of *Mum* are explored. It is likely that the criticism of the universities is indebted to Wycliffite polemic against the useless techniques of university learning. Wycliffite texts often argue that university learning is fatuous, see Hudson, *The Premature Reformation*, pp.225-6, At *Mum*, 320, the narrator goes to 'clergy' to 'deme his doute'. 'Doute' is a word often used in Wycliffite texts to ridicule the techniques of university learning. Its use in *Mum* suggests that the premise of the narrator's quest is useless, cf. 'doctour of doutz' (360) and. *EWS*, II no. 96/38: 'Bysyde lettre of þis gospel may men moue doutus of scole; but me þinkuþ now it is betture to touche lore of vertewys'. Similarly 'in scole' (line 324) echoes the denigratory use of 'scole' in Wycliffite texts, Hudson (1988), p.226. The description of Logic as a 'subtile shophister' (342) is suggestive of the Lollard use of 'sophister' as a derogatory term, see Hudson (1988¹), p.226 and Matthew, 6/8; *EWS*, I no. 30/77 and II no. 96/38.

[103] The Franciscan quotes Philippians 3:18-19 against the Carmelites (89-92). The narrator explicitly criticises this backbiting, quoting Matthew 7:3-5, on removing the beam first from one's own eye before attempting to pluck the mote from another's, as support (138-45). The same text is quoted in *Piers* B X 268-70 in Clergy's warning against those who undertake correction of others without addressing faults in themselves.

[104] The failure of the friars in *Crede* to instruct the narrator recalls Will's meeting with the two friars in Passus VIII, in which they are unable to offer satisfactory instruction but merely laud their own merits. In *Crede*, the friars' further and consistent ignoring of the narrator's needs, and the concentration solely on attempting to absolve him in return for payment, is similar to the actions of Friar Flatterer in Passus XX, who sells contrition for money (363-79).

[105] An 'anuell' was money given for saying a yearly mass for a departed soul. *The Orders of Cain* states that the friars have become so wealthy from annuals that the monks are not able to maintain their dress; see Robbins, no. 65/141-44 and at 155, that friars have become 'annuel prestes'. i.e. in their procuring of annuals, they have usurped the position of the parish priest.

[106] Friars are often presented trying to persuade people to leave them donations in their wills or to be buried at their houses rather than the parish church, e.g. *On the Council of London* which states that if a rich man falls sick, a friar rushes immediately to him and asks him to bequeathe his corpse to the friars; see Wright, I 257. Fitzralph criticizes this practice in *Defensio Curatorum*, p.42. cf. 181-8.

confirming fraternity (326-7),[107] and windows written thick with the names of benefactors (175-80).[108] The narrator is invited to read his name in the glazing of the visible church as a substitute for being taught the text he needs to know (128). The treatment in *Crede* of the institutional-ised texts held so dear by the friars is reminiscent of Will's meditation on the validity of 'pardons', 'provincials lettres' the 'fraternite of alle the foure ordres', 'indulgences' 'patentes' and 'pardon' in *Piers*, VII 192-200. It is tempting to speculate that statements such as: 'I sette your patentes and youre pardon at one pies hele!' (200) were read by the author of *Crede* with enthusiastic assent.[109]

Although both the narrator of *Crede*, and Peres himself, authorise their criticism of such corruption with scriptural citation,[110] the alliterative poem ultimately supplements the institutional discourses of the established church. The conclusion of *Crede* rehearses the Apostles Creed. However, the illocutionary force of this recitation is not the ritualised rote learning exemplified by the narrator's knowledge of the Paternoster and the Ave Maria, nor the friars' parroted renditions of their rule and antiphonal responses. Instead, its significance is profound.

The recitation of the creed is more radical than in *Piers* where Anima quotes the opening and closing clauses of the Apostles' Creed in Latin in the context of urging Church prelates to convert non-Christians (B XV 598-613).[111] In *Crede* the creed is strikingly de-institutionalised. It is placed neither in the comparatively innocent context of preaching conversion, nor in the examination of a parishioner's understanding of basic Christian texts, nor in a liturgical setting. Instead it forms the conclusion of an alliterative poem whose basic premise questions the

---

[107] In *The Summoner's Tale*, a similarly corrupt attitude towards letters of fraternity is revealed: 2126-28: Letters of fraternity are criticised in the Wycliffite text, *The Church and her Members* as a deceitful ruse for the friars to rob the people of their money, Arnold, 377-8.

[108] cf. *Piers*, XI 54-69 where Coveitise of Eyes tells the Dreamer that he should go and confess himself to a friar. He will court him while he is prosperous, secure him in his fraternity and sue to his Prior for a pardon for him. When the Dreamer falls on ill-luck, however, the friar spurns him.

[109] In BL MS Additional 35287, there is written 'dowell superest Indulgens' beside B VII 175, (Uhart, p.354). In CUL MS Dd.3.13 there is a 'nota' beside C XI 334 (Uhart, p.318) and in Huntingdon Library Hm 143 beside XI 335 is written 'note de indulgences & pardones & trionales' (Uhart, p.335). In MS Oriel College 79, beside B VII 197 (pokeful of pardon etc.) there is a mark and the words 'Of pardoun', fol. 32a.

[110] e.g. 149-151; 260-3; 456-9; 489-95; 567-8.

[111] The Latin is absorbed into the structure of the alliterative line at XV 608; 610; 611 and 612. This is appropriate in the context of matching up words and deeds and is consonant with the alliterative absorption of a high proportion of Latin quotations into the narrative of Passus XVIII, see further, Helen Barr, 'The Use of Latin Quotations in *Piers Plowman* with special reference to Passus XVIII', *Notes and Queries*, 231 (1986), 441-8.

adequacy of discourses sanctioned by the church. The speaker who recites the creed in English is a simple ploughman, standing not in a church, but ankle-deep in a muddy field,[112] and calling not for the conversion of unbelievers but the correction of those to whom the church has entrusted its teaching.[113] Opposed to the empty formalism of the friars, and their embellishments – sartorial, architectural and verbal – is the 'graith' of a 'lewed' man.[114] In the last lines of the poem, the voices of author, narrator, and Peres all merge:

> '. . .all that euer I haue seyd soth it me semeth
> And all that euer I haue writen is soth, as I trowe,
> And for amending of thise men is most that I write.'   (836-8)

These lines stress the contrast between the 'feyned' and slanderous speech of the friars, and the true, corrective words of Peres, narrator and author. A poem speaks the truth while the friars parrot fraudulent tales. Authority is wrested from the representatives of the institutionalised church and vested in the words of a member of the laity. Alliterative poetry and the speech of a ploughman exceed the discursive practices of the established church.[115]

In my examination of these passages from the *Piers* tradition I hope to have shown how they absorbed very thoroughly the reading lessons offered by *Piers Plowman*. These four poems constitute a tradition of verse on which *Piers* has exerted demonstrable textual force, and with which it shares key ideas and techniques. Most fundamental in their indebtedness to *Piers* is the poems' perpetuation of a poetic temper primarily social in orientation. Their explicit discussion of reading practices focusses primarily on the consequences for society of either

---

[112] One Wycliffite text comments that the church is useful when it rains, a comment which implies that it has no intrinsic value by virtue of its consecration, *EWS*, II no.73/22; cf. III 486/26 and *Lanterne of Light*, p.36/13ff.

[113] At the start of his written defence of the charges against him, Walter Brut rehearses the Apostles' Creed to show that his arguments are in accordance with true Christian belief, *Registrum Johannis Trefnant*, ed. W.W. Capes (Canterbury and York Society, 1916), pp.258-7. Brut describes himself as a sinner, a layman, a Christian, and significantly, an 'agricola'. See further discussion of Brut in *Crede*, Chapter Four, pp.109-110.

[114] In contrast to the formality of the lines on the Dominican house of Blackfriars, the alliterative style of the lines which recite the creed are plain. They eschew catalogue and ornament and in their stress on 'beleue', do not attempt to fit doctrine slavishly into a normative aa/ax alliterative pattern. (This emphasis on 'beleue' is discussed more fully below, p.101). Between lines 795-818 only 6 alliterate on aa/ax (798; 801; 803; 807; 810; 817), and 2 alliterate aaa/ax (796; 808). The other patterns are aax/ax (799; 802; 815); aax/bb (795); ax/ax (797); aax/xax (800); aa/xx (804); xaa/ax (805); xaa/xa (806); xab/xba (809); xax/ax (811; 816); xx/xx (812); abb/ax (813); axa/xa (814); aax/xx (818). cf. the description of the plain style of alliterative poetry in Turville-Petre, *Alliterative Revival*, pp.113-4.

[115] This reversal is discussed much more fully in Chapter Four.

reading well or reading badly, and their own readings of *Piers* are put to work in poems which address issues and offer reform for matters relevant to the whole community.

As a response to *Piers*, they demonstrate the careful attention to language and sense which they enjoin on all members of the community in order to fulfil the roles to which they have been assigned. The tradition continues the sturdy alliterative temper of *Piers* in which the ideological and aesthetic expectations of poems in the classical alliterative corpus are re-defined. In keeping with *Piers*, and often directly echoing it, their narrative is often generated out of the discourses of institutions which their alliterative poetry supplements.

This is entirely appropriate for poetry concerned to speak the political truth. Institutions and the discourses they generate, entitle certain speakers only, who must speak from legitimate sites, according to certain programmes of information.[116] These poems were written in a climate of institutionalised censorship,[117] and all of them draw attention to the dangers of offering corrective advice outside the frameworks of institutions which are established for this purpose.[118] Nevertheless, that these poems, like *Piers Plowman* before them, speak out against abuse and corruption, means that their very existence supplements the institutions they attempt to correct. It is this supplement which the poems in the *Piers* tradition appear to have recognised in *Piers*, and to have felt the need to update in the new social contexts of their own writing.

[116] M. Foucault, *The Archaeology of Knowledge* (London, 1972) pp.50-2. The relevance of this to ecclesiastical legislation is discussed below, pp.96-98.

[117] The anxiety about truth-telling expressed by all the poems in the *Piers* tradition is not just a literary topos but a reflection of contemporary legislation passed to censor free speech both secular and ecclesiastical, see J. Barnie, *War in Medieval Society* (London 1974), pp.142-5, Anne Hudson, *The Premature Reformation* (Oxford 1988), pp.10-25 and Simpson, 'The Constraints of Satire'.

[118] Despite the fact that *Mum* notes that the proper place to speak for the realm is parliament, 1132.

3

Signes and Sothe

'My prowor and my Plowman Piers shal ben on erþe,
And for to tilie truþe a teeme shal he haue.

(Piers Plowman, B XIX 260-1)*

Thus concludes Grace's provision for the ideal community in the
penultimate Passus of *Piers Plowman.* Throughout Passus XIX, there
is play on the literal and allegorical significances of ploughing.[1] Here,
there are puns on 'tilie' and 'teeme' which equate the last of the
agricultural duties which Grace enjoins on Piers with telling the truth.
Piers requires both a team of oxen for his tilling, and a theme for his
truth telling.[2]

The importance of this injunction may be inferred from its position as
the last of Grace's provisions. Earlier in the poem, there have been
debates about the propriety of telling truth in verse, but here,
truthtelling is seen unequivocally as one of the vital components of an
ideal society. In presentation, however, as a result of the wordplay, the
injunction is multivocal. At the very point of enjoining the importance of
truthtelling, the text is polysemous.[3] This is characteristic of the
wordplay that is such a dominant feature of the poetic texture of *Piers
Plowman.*

[1] In *Piers Plowman and Christian Allegory* (London, 1975), pp.109-31, David Aers explores
the development in the allegorical use of agricultural imagery. He finds that it embodies
the theologian's view of allegory because of its historical justification and fulfilment
through Christ's acts in history. He argues that, read in total context, the diagrammatic
allegory of Passus XIX and XX, compared with that in Passus VI, supersedes its
limitations.
[2] B.F. Huppé notes this pun in 'Petrus id est Christus: Word Play in *Piers Plowman* the B
Text' *ELH,* 17 (1950), 163-90, p.168. He comments that 'the pun is simple enough but its
meaning is profoundly important for the poem'. One B witness, Robert Crowley's 1550
edition, records 'tell' for 'tilie'. There is a similar pun on 'teeme' in Passus VI 22, when the
knight replies to Piers: 'Ac on þe teme trewely tauȝt was I neuere'.
[3] The interchange between Leaute and Will on the propriety of truthtelling is discussed in
Chapter Five, p.165.

51

There has been a steadily growing attention to the polysemy of *Piers*, both as a work composed of competing discourses and voices, and as a text riddled with wordplay. It is not possible to do justice to the range and depth of scholarship on this question here,[4] but it is worth noting that while there is a broad consensus of agreement that the language of *Piers* is, in varying ways, unstable, or polysemous, the conclusions drawn from this are not unanimous. Some critics have argued that the instability of language in *Piers* is antithetical to, or subversive of, the beliefs expressed in the poem, and in particular, of its espousal of Christian doctrine.[5] Others have regarded the language of the poem as an essential part of the truth of Christian experience:

> 'Treuþe' in the poem is always beyond our full comprehension, and reveals itself only partially, in unexpected forms, people, places and words. That is why the reader must play or shift in order to be 'trewe' to the text and read it successfully.[6]

Within this sapiential, celebratory approach, it is also possible to show that linguistic instability in *Piers* often delineates corruption, moral fraudulence, or simply inadequacy. Shoaf, in analysing the pun 'speche þat spire is of grace' (B IX 104) has argued that because the text concedes that speech is capable of multiple meanings, such meanings can be perverted into frivolity, or worse. Because language is always potentially metaphoric, it is always potentially impure.[7] Schmidt has argued that there is in *Piers* a concern with the 'lele' use of words. Wordplay can be used to define and form spiritual experience and Christian teaching, or it can be abused in a fraudulent misapplication of language.[8] Simpson has shown how the use of worldly terms in *Piers Plowman* spiritualizes their meaning by enlargement and contraction of their senses: words are redefined not to reject, but to transform the world.[9]

[4] B.F. Huppé, (1950); Janette Dillon, '*Piers Plowman*: A Particular Example of Wordplay and its Structural Significance', *Medium Aevum*, 50 (1981), 40-8; A.V.C. Schmidt, ' "Lele Wordes" and "Bele Paroles": Some Aspects of Langland's Wordplay', *RES*, 34 (1983), 137-50; and *The Clerkly Maker: Langland's Poetic Art* (Cambridge, 1987) and M.C. Davlin, *A Game of Heuene: Wordplay and the Meaning of Piers Plowman B* (Cambridge, 1989). David Lawton, 'The Subject of *Piers Plowman*', *YLS*, 1 (1987), 1-30.
[5] Priscilla Martin, *Piers Plowman: The Field and the Tower* (London, 1979), p.32 and 34, Charles Muscatine, 'The Locus of Action in Medieval Narrative', *Romance Philology*, 17 (1963), 115-22, p.122.
[6] Davlin, p.114 and cf. Huppé, p.164.
[7] R.A. Shoaf, ' "Speche þat Spire is of Grace": A Note on *Piers Plowman* B IX 104', *YLS*, 1 (1987), 128-33.
[8] Schmidt (1983).
[9] James Simpson, 'The Transformation of Meaning: A Figure of Thought in *Piers Plowman*', *RES*, 37 (1986), 161-83.

At first sight, the poems in the *Piers* tradition appear to be very far removed from a poetic in which wordplay is the vehicle of truth and social correction. In all of the poems overt statements about telling the truth call for a transparent, monosemic use of language, which appears much closer to the standpoint of *Confessio Amantis* than *Piers Plowman*. [10] The narrator of *The Crowned King* promises: 'Sekerly and shortly the soth y shall you shewe' (15) and the cleric: 'y shall you shewe that soth is knowe' (129). Doubt and misconstrual are confidently refused. A similar attitude prevails in *Richard*. At several points, the narrator comments on his own activity: 'Now for to telle trouthe thus than me thynketh' (II 77); 'And also in serteyne the sothe for to telle' (II 116) and 'Now if I sothe shall saie and shonne side tales, (III 170). 'Sothe' is 'serteyne'; there is no apparent difficulty or gap between the conception and the expression of truth. 'Sothe' is singularly ready for speech, and is opposed to the misleading plurality of fraudulent 'tales'.

As already remarked in the previous chapter, this opposition between 'tales' and 'trouthe' forms the key narrative staple of contrast in *Crede*. Friars are associated with 'tales'; 'fables'; 'glose'; 'queynt wordes'; 'lesynges' and 'gestes'. Their 'gladding tales/Turneth vp two-folde vnteyned opon trewthe' (515). This dissembling plurality contrasts with the singular 'trewth' 'graithly' preached by Wyclif, the 'sothe' of Walter Brut, and the 'trewe' speech of Peres the Ploughman. The conclusion of the poem strives for univocality as the voices of Peres, narrator and poet all merge to assert that all they have ever said or written is 'soth'. [11] Finally, in *Mum*, the truthteller, as we have seen, cannot speak in 'termes' (49), is one who tells out the text and touches not the gloss (141), and who 'pleynely telleth' (1174). As in *Richard*, the narrator comments on his own speech: 'And forto saye sothe and shone long tale' (832), and 'Now forto telle trouthe, I trowe hit be no lesing' (1444). [12]

---

[10] In Gower's *Confessio Amantis* flattery and truthtelling are established as polar opposites. Flattery is equated with linguistic instability and manipulation: 'Of feigned wordes make him wene/That blak is whyt and blew is grene' (VII 2187-8); 'And thus of fals thei maken soth' (VII 2197); 'And trouthe is torned to lesinge/It is, as who seith, ayein kinde'. (VII 2214-5). Flattery produces an anarchic system of language that offends against the naturally ordained stability of created order.
By contrast, the truthteller's language is substantial, transparent and monosemic: Bot wher the pleine trouthe is noted/Ther may a Prince wel conceive/That he schal noght himself deceive/Of that he hiereth wordes pleine. . . (VII 2340-43); Whan Rome was the worldes chief/The Sothseiere tho was lief/Which wolde not the trouthe spare/Bot with his wordes pleine and bare/ To Themperour his sothes tolde (VII 2347-51); Whan suche softe wyndes blewen/Of flaterie into her Ere/Thei setten noght here hertes there/Bot whan thei herden wordes feigned/The pleine trouthe it hath desdeigned/Of hem that weren so discrete (VII 2438-43).
[11] See earlier discussion, p.49.
[12] Andrew Wawn has discussed *Mum* in relation to the tradition of truthtelling in 'Truth-

From the quotations extracted here, the poems in the *Piers* tradition would seem well to exemplify G.T. Shepherd's comment that the alliterative poet is above all a truthteller[13] But while the poems explicitly claim monosemy in a fashion that seems far removed from the wordplay of *Piers*, these are claims which are not borne out in practice. It is a mark of the textual force which *Piers* exerted on these later poems that their language perpetuates plurality and serious play. In contrast to *Piers*, however, the presence of claims to univocality sets up a potential tension between what the poems claim to be doing and what they deliver. I shall illustrate with an example from each poem.

The clerk of *Crowned King* requests permission to speak in clergial idiom: 'To peynte it with pluralites my prose would faile' (47). Unlike the friars in *Crede* the cleric eschews 'painting' but given that he speaks in verse, his claim to prose in the b-verse is a fiction. In his attempt to distance himself from the painted fictions of verse[14] the cleric's assertion is literally a lie. Of course, one might seek excuse on the basis that a word alliterating on 'p' is required to complete the metrical scheme of the line. Far from redeeming the clerk, however, appeals to metrical expediency condemn him with use of exactly the wrought adornments of poetry which he is anxious to reject.[15]

Like the cleric, the narrator in *Richard* shuns 'side tales' in favour of telling out the truth. But so far is his narrative from being transparent, that on a number of occasions he has to go back over it to explain its occlusions. At one point he interrupts himself with an imagined interjection from his reader:

> 'What is this to mene, man?' maiste thou axe,
> 'For it is derklich endited for a dull panne;
> Wherffore I wilne yif it thi will were,
> The partriche propurtes by whom that thou menest?'
> A! Hicke Heuyheed! hard is thi nolle
> To cacche ony kunynge but cautell bigynne!   (III 62-7)

Telling and the Tradition of *Mum and the Sothsegger*', *YES*, 13 (1983), 270-87 and Alcuin Blamires has examined the style of *Richard* and *Mum* in relation to *Piers* in '*Mum and the Sothsegger* and Langlandian Idiom', *NM*, 76 (1975), 583-604.

[13] G.T. Shepherd, 'The Nature of Alliterative Poetry', *PBA*, 56 (1970), 57-76, p.65.

[14] 'Prose' is often understood in a more figurative sense as the antonym of poetry. Hoccleve, in *Ars Sciendi Morendi*, 930: writes 'Translate wole y nat in rym, but prose' and cf. *Mandeville's Travels*, 419: 'And thus in proce I shall bigynne this werke, because that often in romaunce and ryme is defawt, and nouʒt accordement founden to the matir'; quotation from MED 'prose' 1a).

[15] There are, in any case, words available which would fulfil alliterative requirements without contradicting the sense of the line, e.g. 'pleynte'; 'poynte'; 'profe'; 'purpose'; 'ple' or 'appel'.

The narrator uses details of the partridge's nesting habits as an analogy to show that Henry is king by right and Richard a usurper, but as the partridge was traditionally a symbol of fraudulence, the analogy endangers the very truth he is attempting to establish.[16] These lines register the narrator's awareness that he may have entangled some unwelcome figurative associations which threaten to destabilise his sense. Abuse of the reader, however, does not conceal the fact that words may not, by their very nature, tell out the truth unequivocally. More or less may be said than intended and a hearer may, or may not, understand what has been uttered.

In *Mum* we learn that a truthteller who shuns 'termes' and appropriate times to speak, always 'hitteth on the heed of the nayle-is ende,/That the pure poynt pricketh on the sothe' (51-2). The collocation of 'pure poynt' and 'sothe' suggests that this proverbial transparency is completely efficacious. Elsewhere, however, the text shows that pithy, brass tacks speech is not necessarily pure, but performative. Towards the end of the poem, the narrator reports the direct speech of executors of wills who defend their appropriation of legacies for themselves with: 'thees [wordes]: /'Hit is no wisedame forto wake Warrok while he sl[epeth]' (1702-3). Now, this might be true if one is standing two feet from a violently-tempered hound (as the Pardoner discovers to his cost in *The Tale of Beryn*).[17] But, given that for the executors there is no dog present, the proverb functions only in its figurative sense. It licences expediency – not to tell out the truth, but to gloss over it with lies.[18] While, in one sense, the example shows simply that language can be corrupted by corrupt speakers, the very stability and transparency of the kind of truthtelling discourse which is predicated of the 'sothsegger' is threatened by the acknowledgment that proverbial directness may serve falsehood as well as truth. The recognition that language can be used performatively questions the uncomplicated existence of a 'pure poynt'.

There is a rather different kind of problematic in *Crede*. Despite the claims for monologic transparency at the end of the poem, its opening is rife with plurality. The very first word is a pun with at least four senses: 'Cros, and Curteis Crist this begynnynge spede' (1). One sense of 'cros'

---

[16] See Bartholomaeus Anglicus, *De Proprietatibus Rerum*, transl. John Trevisa as *On the Properties of Things*, ed. M.C. Seymour, et al. (Oxford, 1975), 2 vols., I 637 and Gower, *Vox Clamantis*, VI 143-4. The narrator comes close to scuppering his intended political point by associating a king who deposed his predecessor with a bird known for its deceitful conduct.

[17] *Tale of Beryn*, 640-1 where warrok is a savage dog which bites the Pardoner in the thigh. *Mum*, 1703 gives an alliterative rendering of a common proverb.

[18] We might compare Pandarus's expedient use of the saying. *Troilus*, III 764: 'It is nought good a slepyng hound to wake'.

is simply the cross of Christ, and the line a simple invocation to the instrument of Christ's passion.[19] There is also a pun on 'two lines intersecting at right angles', a mark which was sometimes used at the beginning of a book. With this sense, the very first word of the poem becomes simply a mark on the page.[20] This linguistically unsteady start to the poem is shaken further by additional senses which were presumably not intended. MED glosses this example of 'cros' from *Crede* under 1d), 'a figurative sense of the word used in oaths and exclamations'. Given that the abjuration of oaths was frequently enjoined in Lollard texts, and was also a matter on which Wycliffites were examined by the authorities,[21] it is somewhat surprising that the first word of a Wycliffite poem is capable of a signification antithetical to declared Wycliffite views. The spillage of sense is an index, perhaps, of the inherent instability and untrustworthiness of the linguistic sign. Similarly, it is possible to interpret the opening word as a reference to the sign of the cross which is made by the right hand, or the fingers (MED 5a) at the beginning of a prayer or statement of belief. In *The Lay Folks Mass Book* the instructions at the *Devotions to the Gospel* are very similar to the first line of *Crede*:

> At þe begyunnyng gud tente þou take
> A large + on þe þou make.   (175-6)[22]

Even if the sense of signing oneself with a cross be incompatible with the typical Wycliffite hostility towards outward signs of holiness, it is a sense which the opening line of *Crede* admits.[23] The polysemy of 'cros', especially in its collocation of senses to which a dyed-in-the-russet Lollard might reasonably be expected to object, stands in direct contrast

---

[19] MED 'cros' 1b). cf. *Dives and Pauper*: 'Crist in holy wryȝt oftentymys is clepyd a cros, for þe cros is his special tokene. And so sumtyme we spekyn to þe cros as to Crist hymself' (I 88/29-30).

[20] MED 'cros' 3a). There is a cross marked at the start of *Sir Launfal* in BL Cotton Caligula A ii, fol. 35. cf. *The Kingis Quair*, ed. J. Norton-Smith (Leiden, 1981), 90-1: 'And furthwithall my pen in hand I tuke/And made a [cros], and thus begouth my buke'. Norton-Smith emends MS + to 'cros'. Wyclif's opposition to 'signs' can be seen from his labelling of Ockham's disciples as 'doctors of signs', A. Kenny, *Wyclif* (Oxford, 1985), p.8. The first sentence in *Jack Upland* accuses Antichrist and his disciples of destroying and deceiving Christ's church 'bi many fals signes', p.54/1-3. The Wycliffite text *On the Sufficiency of Holy Scripture* states that: 'kynrede of hordom sekiþ signes' (Arnold, III, p.186).

[21] See *Lanterne of Light*, p.89/20. Knighton lists the injunction against swearing oaths as one of the characteristic traits of Lollardy, II 252. It is objected to by Walter Brut, Trefnant, p.374 and by William Thorpe, 'The Testimony of William Thorpe', in *Two Wycliffite Texts*, ed. Anne Hudson (EETS 301 1993), pp.76-80.

[22] *The Lay Folks Mass Book*, ed. T.F. Simmons (EETS 71 1879).

[23] e.g. *Twelve Conclusions of the Lollards* in *Selections from English Wycliffite Writings*, ed. Anne Hudson (Cambridge 1978), 25/51-61.

to the 'graith' which is sought throughout the poem, and the attempt at monologic transparency at its conclusion. One might read the closing appeals to a univocal 'soth' as an attempt to lock the stable door after the horses have bolted.

With these passages in view, we might seem to have moved to to a position beyond even that seen in *Piers*, and one which is closer to that outlined by Edmund Reiss, who has argued that in the late Middle Ages, writers were less interested in restating moral and religious commonplaces than investigating the possibilities and limitations of language:

> 'storytellers joined schoolmen in focusing not on truth itself but on such epistemological matters as the essential ambiguity of signs and the inherent complexity of language. Along with speculative grammarians, poets explored processes of signification and modifications of meaning. And along with semioticians, fiction writers investigated ways in which language altered concepts of reality. For those involved with the word, the emphasis was on inference, equivocation, and various kinds of conundrums or aenigmata.[24]

Chaucer is an obvious example. In both longer and shorter works he investigates the diversity and enigma of linguistic expression. In *The Reeve's Tale*, the anti-intellectual miller mocks the clerks who request lodging with him, that while his house is small, they can employ 'lerned art' and 'arguments' to make a place of twenty feet wide into a mile (I 4122-26).[25] Incidental comments on linguistic diversity and instability are frequent in *Troilus*[26] and the short poem *Lak of Stedfastness* takes as its subject the relationship between manipulation of language and political disarray.[27] In the *Canterbury Tales* the immoral Pardoner is superbly equipped with the linguistic skills to preach repentance,[28] and in the repeated claim that in narration the 'word mote be cosyn to the dede' the transparent relationship between language and reality is shattered by the pun on 'cozening'.[29] The 'pleyn' text that is promised by the

---

[24] Edmund Reiss, 'Ambiguous Signs and Authorial Deceptions in Fourteenth Century Fictions', in *Sign, Sentence and Discourse*, edd. Julian Wasserman and Lois Roney (New York, 1989), 113-137, pp.114-15.

[25] Reiss, p.115. See also A.S.G. Edwards, 'Chaucer and the Poetics of Utterance' in Boitani and Torti (1991), 57-67, p.59.

[26] e.g. II 22-28; III 1324-37; 1793-79.

[27] This is discussed by Liam O.Purdon, 'Chaucer's *Lak of Stedfastnesse*: A Revalorisation of the Word', in *Sign, Sentence and Discourse*, pp.144-52.

[28] See for example, Stephan A.Khinoy, 'Inside Chaucer's Pardoner', *ChauR*, 6 (1972), 255-67, and P.B. Taylor, ' "Peynteyd Confessiouns": Boccaccio and Chaucer', *Comp Lit*, 34 (1982), 116-29.

[29] This is discussed by R.A. Shoaf, 'The Play of Puns in Late Middle English Poetry: Concerning Juxtology', in *On Puns: The Foundation of Letters*, ed. Jonathan Culler (Oxford,

Prologue of the *Legend of Good Women* is delivered dressed in some finery,[30] and most striking of all, perhaps, is the discussion throughout *The House of Fame*, one which resists authoritative meanings, and nowhere more graphically than when a 'lesinge' and a 'sad soth sawe' emerge simultaneously through the same hole in the swirling house of twigs. A more deconstructive interrogation of linguistic stability is hard to imagine.[31]

Despite the fact that the tensions in the four examples from the *Piers* tradition, which I quoted above, could be read along Chaucerian lines of linguistic instability, I would argue that these poems are closer to the linguistic sensibilities of *Piers Plowman*, than those of Chaucer.[32] Just as it is possible to reconcile in *Piers* an awareness of the potential impurity of language with a 'belief in words as vehicles of truth'[33] so in the *Piers* tradition it is possible to harmonise the declared appeals to monologism with the polysemy and performativeness of language which their texts exhibit.

The reconciliation in the *Piers* tradition takes a rather different form from that in *Piers*. It rests on a distinction between the physical form of language, whether written or spoken, and the incorporeal, or intramental intention that underlies its use. This is a distinction which is voiced in many diverse works of the later Middle Ages, and with different emphases, depending on context. The widespread reference to this distinction suggests that in its broadest application, it was available to writers who did not necessarily receive a university education.[34]

A Wycliffite sermon appeals to this distinction. Its writer is anxious to uphold the view that the text from John 1:19: 'telleþ aftur þe lettre a playn storie'[35] in face of the fact that when asked if Christ was Elijah or a

---

1988), 44-61. p.56 and cf. David H. Abraham, ' "Cosyn and Cosynage": Pun and Structure in the *Shipman's Tale*', *ChauR*, 11 (1977), 319-27.
[30] See discussion in Jesse M. Gellrich, *The Idea of the Book in the Middle Ages* (Cornell, 1985), p.214.
[31] The relationship of truth and lies in *House of Fame* is discussed by Gellrich, pp.167-201. See also Sheila Delaney, *Chaucer's House of Fame: The Poetics of Skeptical Fideism* (Chicago, 1972), R.J. Allen, 'A Recurring Motif in Chaucer's *House of Fame*, *JEGP*, 55 (1956), 393-405, P. Boitani, 'Chaucer's Labyrinth: Fourteenth Century Literature and Language', *ChauR*, 17 (1983), 197-220 and R.M. Jordan, 'Lost in the Funhouse of Fame: Chaucer and Postmodernism', *ChauR*, 18 (1983), 100-15; reprinted and modified in his *Chaucer's Poetics and the Modern Reader*, (Berkeley, 1987).
[32] I explain the reasons for this more fully in my conclusion to this chapter.
[33] Davlin, p.114.
[34] There is a patristic source for this distinction in the works of Augustine. In one of his clearest expositions, he states in *De Dialectica*, ed. J. Pinborg, trans. B. Darrell Jackson (Dordrecht, 1975), that: a word, or 'verbum' is an acoustic form in contrast to an intention, a 'dicible', which is an immaterial entity percieved by the mind and not by the ear, pp.88-9. This is discussed by Marcia L. Colish, *The Mirror of Language* (Nebraska, 1983), pp.39-46.
[35] *Lollard Sermons*, ed. Gloria Cigman (EETS 294 1989), 45/2.

prophet, John's words appear to contradict those of Christ. The writer is anxious to defend John against the charges both of making a 'gabbyng' and also of using the kinds of 'sutel wordes' employed by merchants to defraud their customers. His defence is as follows:

> For Seint Austyn seiþ, and þe Maister of Stories reherceþ it, þat 'a lesinge is a false significacion' of voice 'wiþ intencioun of deceyuynge' and þis hadde not John in þe answerynge to þe messingeris, for he was not þe gret prophet bihiȝt in þe lawe, and þerfor he seide he was not a prophet (for þei menede soo), and so he deceyeued hem not, for boþe hadde oon intencioun.[36]

The writer goes on to say, quoting Augustine's *Enchiridion*, that a liar is one who misuses the signs of God, signs which God has ordained to show the truth (p.48/146-48).

Although later than the poems in the *Piers* tradition, Reginald Pecock's *Donet* makes a very similar distinction between the physical manifestation of language and the intention that supports it. Pecock is anxious to dissociate himself from any slander or heresy that might be attributed to him:

> fferþirmore, siþen an errour or heresye is not þe ynke writen, neiþer þe voice spokun, but it is þe meenyng or þe vndirstondyng of þe writer or speker signified bi þilk ynke writen or bi þilk voice spokun, and also neuere into þis daie was enye man holde iugid or condempnid for an errer or an heretyk, but if it were founde þat his meenyng and vndistondyng whiche he had in his writyng or in his speking were errour or heresie.[37]

Pecock explicitly claims the authority of Augustine as support for this defence.[38] In *Dives and Pauper*, Pauper states that:

---

[36] ibid., p.47/102-108. Cigman attributes the reference to Augustine to *Contra Mendacium*, Liber I caput XII (*PL* 40 col.537). The Master of Stories is Peter Comestor, p.249. This distinction between voice and content is analogous to Trevisa's comment on the story of Diogenes's reaction to an apparent slander, which is told in Higden's chronicle: 'Hit is wonder þat Diogenes used so lewed sophestrie for here he makeþ no difference betwene þe lyere and hym þat accuseþ þe lyere and warneþ men of his lesynges, and reherseþ þe lesynges; it is nouȝt oon to speke evel by a man and warne hym þat me spekeþ evel by hym and reherse what me seiþ' *Polychronicon Ranulphi Higden*, ed. J.R. Lumby (Rolls Series 41 1871), III 319. A dispute over the literal truth of Scripture was conducted along similar lines between Wyclif and the Carmelite John Kenningham, particularly in the discussion of what was meant by Scriptural phrases such as Amos's 'non sum propheta', see *Fasciculi Zizaniorum*, ed. W.W. Shirley (RS 1858), pp.21ff. Wyclif's answer to the debate provides a different resolution from the appeal to intention in that he concludes that each word is literally true because present in God, see J.A. Robson, *Wyclif and the Oxford Schools* (Cambridge, 1961), p.168. This factor of eternal time provides a different slant on the question from the relationship of physical and intramental language.

[37] Reginald Pecock, *Donet*, ed E.V. Hitchcock (EETS 156 1921), p.4.

[38] Hitchcock traces the source of this to *Liber de diversis quaestionibus octoginta tribus* (*PL* 40, p.34) and compares the statement in Pecock's *Repressor*, ed. C. Babington, RS 19 (1860):

speche is tokene of þouȝtis in þe herte, for it is ordeynyd þat man be his speche schulde schewyn þing to ben or nout to ben as he felyt & þynkith in his herte. . .[there follows a citation of Matt 5:37]. . .þat ȝa of þe mouth be ȝa of þe herte & nay of þe mouþ be nay of þe herte, so þat þe mouth & þe herte must alwey acordyn, for, as seint Austyn in libro Contra mendacium þe mouth beryth witnesse to þe herte'.

(II 217/7-14)

Elsewhere, there are comments in works nearly contemporary with the poems in the *Piers* tradition which do not cite Augustine as support, but which make exactly this direct contrast between the physical aspect of language and the 'meenyng' or intention which is behind it, and which may contrast to its surface corporeal appearance. One such is Criseyde's defence of her letter to Troilus, excusing its brevity by an appeal to the good intention which underwrites it: 'Th'entente is al, and nat the lettres space' (*Troilus*, V 1630).

The distinction is also made in the Prologue to *Vox Clamantis* where Gower sets out very clearly the aims and objectives of his work. The writer is asked to forgive the writer's faults; to embrace the matter, not the man; to think of the intention (mens) and not the bodily form (corpus) in which it is expressed:

Rem non personam, mentem non corpus in ista
Suscipe materia, sum miser ipse quia.
Res preciosa tamen in vili sepe Minera
Restat, et extracta commoditate placet. . .

[In this matter, take the product, not the person; the intention, not the bodily form: because I, myself, am a worthless man. But a precious thing often resides in a vile mineral, and the commodity, on being extracted, is valued. . .][39]

Alastair Minnis has argued that this defence is indebted to the analysis of the contents and purpose of books found in intrinsic prologues to scholastic texts, both in Scriptural commentary and in the tradition of medieval commentary on pagan writers such as Ovid.[40] Gower's *Prologue* to *Vox* takes the form of a complex examination of 'intentio',

'an oold Doctour Hillary seith (and sooth it is) that the wordis of a speker ben to be referrid into the entent whereto he hem spekith' (I 72). Minnis has referred to these passages in ' "Authorial Intention" and "Literal Sense" in the Exegetical Theories of Richard Fitzralph and John Wyclif', *PRIA*, 75 (1975), 1-31, p.23-24. He queries whether Pecock confuses Hilary with Augustine, and notes that intentionalism and literalism were 'two sides of a very important fourteenth century coin', p.24. cf. *The Testimony of William Thorpe*, ed. Anne Hudson (EETS 301 1993): 'þe lettre þat is touchid wiþ mannes hande is not þe gospel, but þe sentence þat is verily bileued in mannes herte þat is þe gospel' (1773-34).
[39] This is discussed by A. Minnis, *The Medieval Theory of Authorship*, 2nd edn (Aldershot, 1988), p.172.
[40] ibid., pp.170-3.

this being one of the intrinsic headings of an academic prologue. Other headings included *'nomen'*, *'materia'* and *'utilitas'*. Minnis has argued that this scheme underlies *Confessio Amantis* as the Latin commentary to Book One makes clear:

> intendit auctor ad presens suum libellum, cuius nomen Confessio Amantis nuncupatur.[41]

While the *'intentio auctoris'* is not identical with the Augustinian concept of the distinction between physical language and intention, the basic premise of the two theories is identical: namely that in its physical manifestation, words, and language more generally, are not identical to the incorporeal intention that precedes it. This in no way diminishes the status of words as vehicles of truth. Although, as we shall see in the poems of the *Piers* tradition, words may signify other words, the correspondence between words and the reality they denote may be so thoroughgoing that a person may speak the truth without knowing it. It is also possible with this distinction, as the scholastic commentators overtly discuss, for an apparently lascivious or fabulous story to have been written with the intention of moral or spiritual instruction.[42]

In *Confessio Amantis*, as Gotz Schmitz has argued, Gower appears concerned that the physical appearance of language should correspond with the sincerity of its intended use. He asserts that speech is a gift from God, which distinguishes humanity from the beasts and demands that a person's speech disclose their innermost motives:

> The word to man hath yove alone
> So that the speche of his persone,
> Or forto lese or forto winne,
> The hertes thoght which is with inne
> Mai schewe, what it wolde mene (VII 1509-13)[43]

As his denunciation of Ulysses' treacherous eloquence demonstrates, Gower is concerned with the danger inherent in the fact that language can be used to both good and evil ends. The power of words is such that they 'maken frend of fo/And fo of frend, and pes of werre/And werre of pes' (VII 1574-6).

His concern for sincerity in language use extends to consideration of his own style. Time and again, Gower refuses to 'peint' and 'pike' and

---

[41] See A.J. Minnis, 'John Gower: "Sapiens" in Ethics and Politics', in *Gower's Confessio Amantis: A Critical Anthology*, ed. P. Nicholson (Cambridge, 1991), 158-80, p.174. Latin quoted from *Confessio* I, p.35.
[42] This is discussed by Minnis (1991), pp.162-3.
[43] Gotz Schmitz, 'Rhetoric and Fiction: Gower's Comments on Eloquence and Courtly Fiction', in Nicholson, 117-142, p.126.

instead 'y have do my trewe peyne/With rude wordis and with pleyne' (VII 3106-24). As Schmitz argues, the word 'plain' and related terms are particularly common in *Confessio* and are almost invariably linked to matters of speech and the moral attitudes of speakers:

> the word should always be the expression of a person's and in particular, a prince's innermost conviction, 'The word is tokne of that withinne' (VII 1737). The wording sounds commonplace, almost proverbial, but it expresses one of Gower's central concerns, and in his view the high road to personal and public peace in a troubled world.[44]

The integrity of Gower's claims for a plain and honest discourse is clear, but in practice, his style is often very far from being rude and simple in the sense of being shallow or straightforward. In a fashion very similar to the poets in the *Piers* tradition, Gower uses wordplay and rhetoric as a means for urging exactly that integrity and social decorum that defines his honest use of language. One example must suffice as illustration. In describing the transformation of Nebuchadnezzar from beast back to man, Gower writes:

> His mannes forme ayein he tok
> And was reformed to the regne
> In which that he was wont to regne.   (I 3034-6)

Here, the polyptoton of 'forme' and 'reformed' and the 'rime riche' of 'regne' weave a web of verbal resonances which embody a number of Gower's most dearly cherished ethical concerns. The play on 'forme' and 'reformed' links the senses of changing shape with being restored to a proper model of conduct. As a result of Nebuchadnezzar's humility, he is not only restored to his man's shape, he is transformed in a moral sense; his earlier fault of pride is corrected.[45] As a result of this moral and physical reformation, he is now fit to reign.

The use of 'rime riche' here, is a further example of how an apparent chasteness of style[46] yields a fecundity of meaning. As a verb, 'regnen' has the senses of exercising royal power, and to live, to be present and to follow a certain way of life. Under the senses of 'regne' as a noun, MED includes 'sovereignty' and the 'territory over which a king's power extends'.[47] While there is no sense listed for a figurative

---

[44] Schmitz, p.131.

[45] MED 'refourmen' 1) 'to restore'; 2a) to correct; improve, remedy; 2c) transform oneself and 3b) to re-set; re-shape. MED 'form(e)' n) 1a) 'the physical shape of something'; 8a) 'the correct or appropriate way of doing something' and 11a) 'a model of life or conduct or example to imitate'.

[46] The term is Donald Davie's from *The Purity of Diction in English Verse* (London, 1967), p.32.

[47] MED 'regnen' (v) 1a) and 4a) and b); 'regne' (n) 1a) and 3a).

understanding of the noun, in the sense of 'self rule', this is surely one of the connotations which these lines suggest. Resulting from his moral and physical metamorphosis, with inner and outer 'forme' as one and the same, Nebuchadnezzar is now able to rule himself according to appropriate conduct, and as a result, is fit to resume political sovereignty. The rime riche fuses the microcosm with the macrocosm and the verbal pattern sets up a 'forme' of model conduct for a king.[48] Good political government proceeds only from ethical self-rule. The verb 'to reign', in the sense of ruling others, signifies correctly only if it is preceded and accompanied by the appropriate state of self-government. It is exactly this relationship which Gower maps out by the order of noun and verb and the identical rhyme. These lines are linguistically self-conscious but ethically sound.[49]

The poems of the *Piers* tradition demonstrate a concern for the integrity of language of just the same intensity and political conviction as that of *Confessio Amantis*. Similarly, as in Gower, this is compatible with the polysemy and performativeness of their physical language. These poems make the same distinction between physical language and intramental intention. Their appeals to sincerity of intention, and how this may be manifested in physical language which, on the surface, seems incompatible with such a stance, provides a way of resolving the declared statements about truthtelling language in these poems, with their actual practice as poetic texts. By analysing each poem in turn, I shall hope to demonstrate how it is possible to accommodate the 'sondry signes' of the poems within their declarations of 'sothe'.[50]

As we have already seen, both the narrator of *The Crowned King* and the cleric, declare that their words are true. The cleric makes a clear distinction between the physicality of the word and the incorporeal intentions that underwrite it when he warns the king of fraudulent, or incomplete, speakers:

> And kepe the fro glosyng of gylers mowthes,
> That speken to the spiritually with spiritual tonges,

---

[48] Christopher Ricks analyses the subtle effects wrought in Gower's poetry through a plain style, including the use of 'rime riche' in 'Metamorphosis in Other Words' in Minnis (1983), pp.25-49. He discusses rime riche on p.37 and the 'simplicity of genius' in the narration of the transformation of Nebuchadnezzar on pp.31-2 (the lines just before the passage I have quoted). The importance of the macrocosm and microcosm in Gower is discussed by Elizabeth Porter, 'Gower's Ethical Microcosm and Political Macrocosm' in Minnis (1983), pp.135-62. Nebuchadnezzar is discussed on pp.142-4.

[49] It is possible that that 'regne' carries a pun on its near homophone 'rein(e) n) 2 in the sense of 'guidance', 'control' cf. 'reinen' vb) 2. The image of bridling as a metaphor for self-controlled kingship is used in *Richard*, I 201 and Hoccleve, *Regement*, 4929-30.

[50] The terms are taken from *Crowned King*: 'That suche sondry signes shewest vnto man' (5).

[Momelyng] with here mouthes moche and malys in hert,
And of a mys menyng maketh a faire tale.
Vnder flateryng and fair speche falsehede foloweth);
And yif they myght with her moustres to marre the for euere,
With disceit of here derknesse – the deuell hem a-drenche! (86-92)

And though her speche be but small, the more be here thoughtes.
(116)

The corporeality of the 'verbum' is stressed by the reference to 'mowthes'; 'tonges'; 'moustre' and 'speche' in contrast to the intramental 'hert'; 'menyng' and 'thoughtes'. The lines make a clear distinction between what is perceived physically and the speakers' intentions. Simultaneously, however, the lines are also rich in word-play. At the very point of stressing that the potential plurality of the linguistic sign may be abused by corrupt speakers, the cleric employs polysemy to assert the 'sothe'. In line 89, 'menyng' can be understood in two senses: 'purpose, intention' and 'the expression of a meaning, language, words'.[51] The fracture of 'mening' into the senses of overt expression and intention is indicative of the split in the speech of corrupt speakers between the physical substance and inward thought.[52]

A similar double resonance characterises the expression 'maketh a faire tale'. One sense of 'maken' is to 'talk about' while a 'made tale' is a fabrication, or fiction.[53] Unlike the citation from Trevisa: 'Hit is no made tale but hit is sooþ as þe lettre is i-write',[54] the 'tale' that is made by a flatterer appears to be true, but is, in fact, a deception. In the last line of the first quotation 'derkenesse' also has a plural sense: both 'metaphorical or figurative meaning' and 'intentionally obscure, deceptive or malicious'.[55] The context of 'malys' and 'momelyng' in *Crowned King* suggests that 'derkenesse' has both of these senses, and the reference to 'deuell' in the b-verse picks up the ironic use of 'spiritual' five lines earlier, to suggest the sense of sinfulness.[56]

---

[51] MED 'meninge' 1) and 3c).

[52] In my examination of the use of wordplay I have drawn on the sense distinctions recorded in MED. These sense divisions pose some problems as it is not always clear whether they mark distinct separate senses of a word, or a range of collocability. This is a difficulty of semantics not confined to MED. Additionally, sometimes separate senses are listed under the same headword which, arguably, could be grouped as a separate word. An example of the latter is 'rede', see pp.27-28 above. While the senses of 'counsel' and 'read a book' have emerged from the OE 'rede', one might argue that their senses have diverged such that they are two different verbs. The example of 'meninge' is relatively straightforward; it is less a pun (cf. discussion of 'more' below), than a play on the range of collocability of a word. In my use of these sense divisions in future examples I shall note any particular points of difficulty.

[53] MED 'maken' 12a) and 5d).

[54] *Higden*, II 195.

[55] MED 'derkenes' 5); 'derk' 5).

[56] MED 'derkenes' 4).

The structure of line 116 is a chiasmus[57] but the reflection of the a-verse in the second half line gives a contradictory equivalent to 'speche' and 'smal' in 'more' and 'thoughtes'. Furthermore, 'more' is a rather interesting pun. The common sense of the word is 'a larger amount, or quantity' but there is also a homophone, which means 'the root of the tongue'.[58] It seems to me plausible to admit this sense, as a consquence of which the line may be read in two ways: first, that brief speech conceals rather more expansive thought; and second, that although their speech is outwardly and physically insubstantial, the root of it, that is, its tongue, is to be found in their thoughts.

These lines in *Crowned King*, I would argue, are of a more weighty significance than their commonplace advice topoi might suggest.[59] In their warnings against duplicity, they invoke the polysemy of the linguistic sign in the legitimate function of declared truthtelling. At the very point of illustrating the fraudulent use of double meaning, its honest, truthtelling potential is demonstrated in deed.

Within this short text there are many further examples of wordplay which are used with the intention of showing the truth. A section which is concerned with the proper treatment of the contribution of the poorer members of society to the commonwealth capitalises on the financial and spiritual connotations of words in a fashion which recalls similar instances of wordplay in *Piers Plowman*:

> And yit the most preciouse plente that apparaill passeth,
> Thi pouere peple with here ploughe pike oute of the erthe,
> And they yeve her goodes to gouerne hem euen.
> And yit the peple ben well apaid to plese the allone. (71-4)

Throughout these lines, the financial and moral connotations of words are held in tension as a means of adverting the king's attention to the true loyalty that comes from respecting the worth of his subjects rather than thinking of them as merely suppliers of goods. 'Preciouse' has the sense both of 'costly' and of 'spiritual worth, value'.[60] The pun recalls that in *Piers*, B I 152: 'And ek þe plante of pees, moost precious of

---

[57] The repetition of ideas, not necessarily the same words, in inverted order, see B.Vickers, *In Defence of Rhetoric* (Oxford, 1988), p.493. My use of classical terms of rhetoric is for economy of reference. While *Mum* refers to arguing the 'pro and the contra as clergie askith' (300), there is otherwise no hard evidence that any of these poets received university training, though it is not impossible that they did. My use of these terms is not intended to imply that they were necessarily known by the writers.

[58] MED 'more' (n)3 2a) and 'more' (n)1 2).

[59] Warnings against flatterers are prolific in works concerned with rulers, e.g: Gower, *Mirour*, 26545-7; *Vox*, VI 545-80; *Confessio*, VII 2165-2694; *On the Times*, Wright, I 270-81; Robbins, 49/29-32 and Kail, II and IV 93-6 and Chaucer, *The Merchant's Tale*, 1478-1518.

[60] MED 'precious' 1a) and 2a).

vertues'. Indeed, line 71 in *Crowned King* may recall the collocation 'precious/plant'. 'Plente' in *Crowned King* may be a spelling of 'plant' – in the sense of something planted in the earth , a sense which is brought out by line 72,[61] but there is also a pun on 'plente' which can mean both an abundance of grain and an abundance of worldly goods. The pun here is an example of what Shoaf calls 'juxtology'.[62] The most precious worldly goods are identical to the food that the labourers glean from the earth. These precious goods are distinguished from the list of finery and material possessions in the lines prior to the extract quoted. Indeed, this quotation is linked rhetorically to the worldly goods dismissed in lines 69-71 by the ploce[63] of 'preciouse stones' (69) and 'preciouse plente' (71). A similar dynamic, but without a rhetorical figure, motivates the play on 'goodes' both as material wealth and communal 'good'. Once again, this is a play used in *Piers*.[64]

Another pun which is used in *Piers* forms the pivotal pun of line 74. Hunger's treatment of the wastrels in Passus VI of *Piers* results in: 'ech a pouere man wel apaied to haue pesen for his hyre': (VI 195). 'Apaide' puns on 'well pleased' and 'well paid'.[65] Exactly the same pun is used in *Crowned King*. The labourers are either well satisfied to please the king rather than themselves, or – more subversively – the labourers are financially well paid (which they clearly are not) to satisfy the king rather than themselves. 'Allone' has the senses both of 'sole ruler' and also 'exclusive of all others'.[66] This latter sense is close to suggesting the king's private pleasure rather than communal interest. The double meaning of the line serves to remind the king of the political inequality which might underlie what is presented as an equitable tax system.

Underlying this use of wordplay is a sense of linguistic decorum. Signs, if they are to be used properly, must proceed both from honourable intention, and also be in accordance with true action. The cleric is aware that signs may be conventionally used in ways that are inappropriate. Given that a word is not identical to the reality it denotes,

---

[61] MED 'plaunt' 1a). Some manuscripts of *Piers* read 'plente' for 'plante', see Kane, *The A Version*, p.199 and Kane Donaldson, p.250. Two B MSS read 'plentee'. It is a word which appears to have caused difficulty; A MS V reads 'playnt' and B MS Y reads 'planetes'.

[62] MED 'plente' d). Shoaf (1988) defines 'juxtologists' as those who: 'recognized that words yoke themselves together, and together with things, in the most unpredictable ways', p.45.

[63] The repetition of the same word or words, Vickers, p.497.

[64] Schmidt (1987), pp.134-38. Simpson (1986), notes how Haukyn's opposition between 'good' and 'God' in XIII 397 shows the use of worldly, earthly terms to point towards a reformed, spiritualized world (pp.161-2).

[65] MED 'apaien' (v) 2); MED 'apaiement' (n).

[66] MED 'alone' 2 and 4a).

it is possible for a word to misrepresent reality if it is applied sloppily or if it is deliberately manipulated.

At line 121, the cleric says: 'Sir they it come to the of kynde a kyng to be called' it is necessary for him to adopt the behaviour that enables him to live up to his name. The line draws attention to the act of using the word 'king'. It is applied to the king by reason of his birth and also according to his proper occupation or profession.[67] The duality opens up a potential gap between the king's birthright to the name 'king' and the kind of behaviour which justifies his use of the title. Lurking behind the concern that the word 'king' is accompanied by the reality of kingly behaviour, is the suggestion that if this is not the case, then 'king' is a word without a true object – an empty signifier. The line goes almost so far as to suggest that a king is not born – he is named – and indeed, in the coronation ceremony, this is what literally, and ritually happens.[68] Hovering over this section of *Crowned King* are echoes of the coronation sequence in the B Prologue of *Piers*, especially the Latin quotation: 'Dum rex a regere dicitur nomen habere/Nomen habet sine re nisi studet iura tenere' (Prol. 141-2). Earlier in the poem the cleric has expressed his concern that the king's person may not match up to his name. If a king misuse his personal prowess it is: 'vnsemely for a souerain (so saue me oure Lord)/And hevy for his name that hyndren will ever' (83-4). The stress on 'name'[69] draws attention to the proper use of the linguistic sign to which he has been entrusted.

Wordplay in the form of rhetorical schemes emphasises this concern for proper naming. At line 79, the device of ploce draws attention to the reality which ought to correspond to the word of 'lord':

> For as a lord is a lord and ledeth the peple,
> So shuld prowesse in thi persone passe other mennes wittes
> The wittyest and wylyest and worthiest in armes.   (79-81)

The superlative qualitites that are necessary for the verbum 'lord' to correspond to proper 'lordship' are emphasised by the homoioteleuton of line 81.[70] Verbal repetition is used elsewhere in the poem to suggest

---

[67] MED 'kinde' 12a) and 6a).

[68] Susan Crane has analysed the coronation scenes in *Piers* with reference to the contemporary account of Richard II's coronation in *The Anonimalle Chronicle*. She notes that the archbishop asks the commons if they give their assent to Richard as king, and they answer with a great cry and noise, 'yes, we want it', 'The Writing Lesson of 1381' in *Chaucer's England*, ed. B. Hanawalt (Minnesota 1992), 201-221, p.213, quoting from *The Anonimalle Chronicle*, pp.109-10.

[69] The line does not alliterate regularly, and it is possible that 'name' is a scribal error for a word beginning with 'h' or a vowel. However, the line is not deficient in sense, and contains three alliterative staves.

[70] The repetition of the same derivational or inflectional ending on different words, Geoffrey Leech, *A Linguistic Guide to English Poetry* (London, 1969), p.82.

the proper correspondence of sign and reality. Full correspondence, however, is reserved for God's use of language. At line 100, the cleric reminds the king of Christ's new commandment of love:

> For God in his gospell asketh no thyng elles,
> But oonly loue for love; and let hym be levest.   (99-100)

In contrast to the conditionality of the ploce in line 79, in line 100 the ploce is declarative and affirmative. The repetition of 'love' suggests complete correspondence between the sign and what it represents. Fully spiritual behaviour closes the earthly, partial relationship between what is named and what is. In *The Crowned King*, such closure is reserved solely for God. A tiny variation in grammatical detail demonstrates this more fully.

When the dreamer falls asleep, he comments: 'Me thought y herd a crowned kyng of his comunes axe' (35). The uncertainty of reference extends further than the verb: the article used of the king is indefinite. This contrasts to the use of 'crowned king' elsewhere in the poem. The opening line: 'Crist, crowned Kyng, that on Cros didest' (1) contains two subjects: 'Crist', and 'crowned Kyng'. The absence of connecting grammatical particle renders these phrases semantically equivalent, and as such, they define true kingship. Equally, at the end of the poem, the cleric refers to those saints who dwell with 'that crowned kyng that on cros dyed' (141). The demonstrative pronoun refers back to Christ, the crowned king of the opening line. The certainty and definition asserts that Christ is the 'siker example' of kingship (137). He is *the* crowned king and also the model of 'crowned kingness'. By comparison the only occasion when the earthly king is addressed as: 'Sir, crowned kyng, thow knowest well thyself' (51), the affirmative declaration is contextualised by a speech act whose illocutionary force may be construed as directive as much as representative.[71] The cleric's words frame the reality he wishes on the king, which is not necessarily concordant with the actual present state of the king's self- knowledge. Additionally, the statement is modified by the polyptoton of line 51, which emphasises the conditionality of the king's earning his name: 'Yif thou be chief Iustice, iustifie the trouthe'.

---

[71] This distinction derives from the work on speech act theory by J.L. Austin. The illocutionary force of a speech act is the action performed in utterance. The distinction between directive (illocutionary acts designed to get the addressee to do something, for example requesting, daring, suggesting, insisting) and representative (illocutionary acts that undertake to represent a state of affairs, e.g. stating, predicting, telling), is drawn from a summary of Austin's work in E.C. Traugott and M.L. Pratt, *Linguistics for Students of Literature* (New York, 1980), p.229.

The Crowned King is overtly concerned with the proper use of language. If the intention be honourable, then the expression is honest. Double meanings are not innately fraudulent; it is only their duplicitous use that makes polysemy dishonourable. Through juxtology, implicature and rhetorical figures the narrative demonstrates what constitutes a right use of language. One's behaviour must bear out the accepted understanding of one's name and one's words and heart must correspond. When the cleric shuns 'peynted pluralites' in favour of prose, he spurns not polysemy but paint. Figuratively, he speaks the truth.[72]

In *Richard*, there is also a clear distinction observed between intramental intention and physical language. In the parliamentary meeting in Passus IV, the fraudulent and incompetent speakers 'mafflid with the mouth and nyst what they ment' (IV 62). The physically indistinct sounds of their mouths arise from their ignorance of intention. In their failure to act on the responsibilities with which they have been entrusted, they demonstrate a mis-use of speech.

By contrast, in Passus I, the narrator acknowledges that he may inadvertently have written a 'word' that 'wrothe make myght' his 'souereyne that suget I shulde to be' (I 76-7). He prays to the king: 'To take the entent of my trouthe that thoughte non ylle' (I 79). Because his intention is one of loyalty and 'trouthe', he prays that the writer of the book be not blamed. If the words that he has written with the intention to 'mende' cause a reader to be aggrieved (85), then the reader should conduct himself better and 'blame not the berne that the book made,/ But the wickyd will and the werkis after'. (I 86-7). This defence of writing corrective poetry is very similar to Gower's in the Prologue to *Vox*. Indeed, Paul Miller has related it to the intention of satire expressed in Latin satirical theory.[73]

Whether or not the distinction between intention and physical form in *Richard* be influenced by academic discussion, it is a distinction often upheld by appeal to a common sense wisdom. The poem contains many examples of the misuse of physical language. In an emphasis similar to the concerns of *Confessio Amantis*, knights who are 'sad of her sawes' (III 201), who 'knowe well hem-self' (III 200) are spurned by the court in favour of 'flateris and fals men that no feith vseth' (III 198). So faithless

---

[72] cf. references in n.14.
[73] Paul Miller, 'John Gower: Satiric Poet', in *Gower's Confessio Amantis: Responses and Reassessments*, ed. A.J. Minnis (Cambridge, 1983), 79-105, p.86. While the opening of *Richard* does not show evidence of the headings of an intrinsic prologue, elsewhere in the poem, there are references to the 'matiere' of the writing. In contrast to *Crowned King*, there is more substantial evidence for some indirect influence of this academic literary theory in the narrator's defence of his poem.

are these retainers in matters of speech, that when they demand Wit's expulsion from court, their language is described with a verb more appropriate to hounds after prey than human beings: 'alle the berdles burnes bayed on him euere' (III 235). The courtiers banish Wisdom from court in a linguistic performance that obliterates the God-given distinction between human beings endowed with the power of rational speech, and dumb animals.[74]

Some of Richard's followers use physical speech which is inappropriate to their station. Those retainers, who wreak havoc by their lawless practice of maintenance to pervert the course of justice, prevent anyone speaking out against them. They 'carped to the comounes with the kyngys mouthe' (II 29). They speak with an authority that is not theirs to pronounce. The narrator has already criticised the king for 'partninge of youre powere to youre paragals' (I 158). The retainer's illicit ventriloquism licences bribery and corruption. In a similar fashion, the clerk who opens parliamentary proceedings: 'comsid the wordis,/And prononcid the poyntis aperte to hem alle' (IV 35-6). However, his outward 'comelich' adherence[75] to the procedure of parliamentary debate conceals a dishonest intention to use his speech to wheedle money out of the community: 'And meved for mony more than for out ellis/In glosinge of grette lest greyues arise' (IV 38-9). The chancellor's speech act defines him as one of those 'flateris and fals men that no feith vseth'.

At an earlier point in the poem, rather in the fashion of *The Crowned King*'s treatment of the names of 'king' and 'lord', the narrator questions the entitlement of some of Richard's followers to the name which they sought after. In commenting on how Richard's followers persuaded him to persecute his 'best frendis', the narrator writes:

> All that they moued or mynged in that mater
> Was to be sure of hem-self and siris to ben y-callid.   (I 190-1)

The followers have no entitlement to the 'sir' to which they aspire because their motivation is dishonest and selfish. A gap is exposed between the name of 'sir' and its proper application. The plural form 'siris' is a tiny detail which illustrates how the proper sense of the title 'sir' is dissipated if it is claimed or bestowed without due merit.[76]

[74] This is a point made by Gower, *Confessio Amantis*, VII 1509-13, quoted above.
[75] 'Comelich' suggests fitting, appropriate, see MED 'comli' 3b) and cf. *Richard* III 174: 'In comliche clothinge as his statt axith'.
[76] At I 144 the narrator refers to Richard's 'dukys' in an attack on Richard's liberal granting of honours often to men whom his critics thought most unworthy. The creation of de Vere marquis of Dublin in 1385 and his subsequent elevation to the dukedom of Ireland in 1386 drew scathing comments from Walsingham *Historia Anglicana*, II 140 and

While these lines show that names can be misapplied, elsewhere the narrative illustrates that a person may speak the truth without knowing it. This is evidenced in the case of the knights of the shire:

> But yit for the manere to make men blynde,
> Some argued ayein rith then a good while,
> And said, 'we beth seruantis and sallere fongen,
> And ysent fro the shiris to shewe what hem greueth,
> And to parle for her prophete and passe no ferthere,
> And to graunte of her gold to the grett wattis
> By no manere wronge way but if werre were;
> And if we ben fals to tho us here fyndyth,
> Euyll be we worthy to welden oure hire.'   (IV 44-52)

If the function of the representatives is to 'parle for *her* prophete' and to go no further, then this is rather a minimal activity which may take no regard of larger questions of right and wrong. This limitation apart, the direct speech is the truth. Habitually, however, the representatives use speech with the intention of blinding their addressees so that the proper signification of words is perceived as being 'ayein rith'. If those entrusted to 'shewe for the shire' are so incapable of determining truth from falsehood, such that in line 58 their information transforms 'good frendis' into 'foos'[77] then what hope is there for the institution of parliament to redress corruption?

This ineffectiveness is dramatised in a rather different point about language use in the simile which continues the sequence quoted:

> Than satte summe as siphre doth in awgrym,
> That noteth a place and no thing availith.   (IV 53-4)

These lines are indebted to a contrast between two different systems of mathematical signification. Roman numerals had no figure for 'nought', whereas the Arabic system did. This made a difference to the methods of computation.[78] While zero had no value in itself, its

---

148. At the September parliament of 1397, Richard created five dukes in a single day: Nottingham became duke of Norfolk; Derby (Henry Bolingbroke) duke of Hereford; Huntingdon earl of Exeter; Kent duke of Surrey and Rutland duke of Albermerle. The *Annales* comments that they deserved the title not of 'dukes' but of 'duketti' because the importance of the rank had been diminished by such an excessive act (p.223). While neither of these chroniclers are unbiassed observers, their comments provide an interesting parallel to the use of 'siris' in *Richard*.

[77] cf. Gower, *Confessio Amantis*: 'The wordes maken frend of fo/And fo of frend, and pes of werre/And werre of pes', VII 1574-6.

[78] The date of the introduction of zero in England is hotly debated, but Richard Steele notes that arabic numerals began to be common in the middle of the thirteenth century. The fact that Latin writers had a convenient way of writing hundreds and thousands without any cyphers probably delayed the general use of the Arabic notation, *Earliest*

presence was necessary in calculating the value of other numerals in the system.[79] In these lines from *Richard*, those who sit as a cipher corrupt the whole system of signification, or communication, because they 'no thing availith'. They stimie the computation for which the system of mathematics has been designed. Their individual and collective value remains 'nought'.[80] While they ought to enable the system to work in a mutually valuable fashion, they fail to bring value to the system by concentrating solely on their own empty significance.

Passus Two of the poem undertakes a thorough interrogation of the real significance of 'signs' and 'marks' in its criticism of the practice of awarding liveries.[81] Richard's retainers are very keen to 'schewe their signs' (II 34) but in a fashion which calls into question the validity of the whole signifying system. The narrative of this Passus is rich in wordplay as the narrator investigates the corruption that was caused by the 'many signes/ That ye and youre seruauntis aboughte so thikke sowid' (II 101-2). In his attempt to understand Richard's purpose, the narrator remarks: 'Thus were ye disceyued thoru youre duble hertis' (II 111). Here, as elsewhere in the Passus, e.g. II 43, there is a pun on 'hertis' as loyal retainers and as a metonym for the badges of the white hart which was Richard's personal sign.[82] 'Duble' refers to this double meaning. In one sense it means 'twice as much, great' and alludes to the excessive granting of badges, and in another sense it means 'false; deceitful'.[83] The juxtology of the line captures the essential truth that the excessive badges were innately fraudulent and transformed loyalty into deceit. While the retainers exhibit the duplicity of signs, and the excess of signifier over the signified, the narrator's critical use of polysemy demonstrates the truthful use of double meaning.

The narrator explicitly defends the use of polysemy as a truth-telling medium in a passage which simultaneously condemns the fraudulent and improper use of signs:

English Arithmetics (EETS ES 118 1922), pp.xvi-vii. 'awgrym' refers to the mathematical system known as 'algorism' as distinct from the mechanical 'abacist' computation. The use of zero in algorism enabled the columns used in abacist counting to be dispensed with; see pp.xiv-xv. (I am grateful to Anne Hudson for alerting me to this text).

[79] cf. Thomas Usk, *Testament of Love*, 72/82: 'Although a sypher in augrim have no might in significacion of it-selve, yet he yeveth power in significacion to others' cited in MED 'cifre' 1a) but it ought to illustrate sense 1b).

[80] MED 'cifre' 1a) 'the arithmetical symbol for naught'.

[81] With a rather different emphasis from mine, Nick Ronan has examined the treatment of 'signs' in *Richard*, see '1381: Writing in Revolt: Signs of Confederacy in the Chronicle Accounts of the English Rising', *Forum for Modern Language Studies* 25 (1989), 304-14, pp.313-4.

[82] MED 'herte' 3a) c) and 'hert'.

[83] MED 'double' 3a) and 6a).

So, trouthe to telle as toune-men said,
For on that ye merkyd ye myssed ten schore
Of homeliche hertis that the harme hente.
Thane was it foly in feith, as me thynketh,
To sette siluer in signes that of nought serued.   (II 41-5)

These are amongst the most elaborately punning lines in the whole poem. 'Merkyd' puns on the senses of 'provide with a badge', to 'stain or disfigure' and 'to take aim at'.[84] 'Myssed' has the senses of 'failed to find' and 'failed to hit'.[85] 'Schore' means 'twenty'; 'a total in a reckoning' and 'a mark on a tally stick'.[86] 'Hertis' has the double sense of deer and loyal retainer. Depending on how line 44 is stressed, 'feith' has two senses: 'then was it folly in the treatment of loyalty, as it seems to me', or 'then was it folly, indeed, as it seems to me'.[87] Line 45 anticipates the comment in Passus IV that signs and marks may have no value. 'Nought' picks up on 'ten schore' to suggest the arithmetic number zero and has the additional senses of 'a nothingness, non-existence and an insignificant person.[88] 'Serued' can be understood in a number of related senses. MED glosses 'serven' with 'nought' as 'to perform no service for' 1a). The verb can also have the sense of 'to serve as a knight or retainer'; 'to be subservient, obedient' and 'to be effective, useful'.[89] All of these senses are appropriate and are suggested by the elaborate wordplay of the previous lines. 'Serued' can also be understood as an aphetic form of the verb 'deserve' in the sense of earn, or merit.[90]

Over and above the particular criticism of liveries it addresses, the riddling of these lines may be read as mimetic of Richard's muddled policy. The narrator professes astonishment at Richard's motivation to unleash such chaos on the realm (II 109-110). The play of meanings suggests the lack of stability and control by which 'iche rewme vndir roff of the reyne-bowe/ Sholde stable and stonde' (III 248-9). Moreover, the instability of the linguistic sign is mimetic of the wavering loyalty that is earned by financial reward rather than unconditional allegiance. Values are turned topsy-turvey, a sense which is mirrored in the slide from 'ten schore' to 'nought' and the

---

84 MED 'marken' 3e); 4b) and 10a).
85 MED 'missen' 1a) and 3e).
86 MED 'score' 3); 2c) and 2a).
87 MED 'feith' 5a) and 8c).
88 MED 'nought' e); b) and d).
89 MED 'serven' 5a); 8a) and 16).
90 MED 'serven' (v) 2). The lines are mixture of puns, e.g. 'schore' and 'hert' and play on the range of collocability of a word, e.g. 'nought' and 'serven'.

disparity between 'siluer signes' and nothing. The perversion of financial value and the disruption of the currency is enacted in displacing the value of linguistic signs in the economy of language. In the passage on overdressed courtiers in Passus III, there is a similar equation between the perversions of linguistic and economic currencies.[91] The sum of this wordplay in Passus Two is that Richard's conduct in granting such liveries was injurious and incompetent. But as a consequence of the polysemous verbal texture, the narrator is able to 'telle the trouthe' that this was but the outward sign of a much more deeply-seated political disarray and distortion. The excessive 'signs' signal a malaise more far-reaching than a single misguided act of regal policy.

This technique of illustrating political instability through linguistic play is endemic throughout the poem. *Richard* capitalises on a tradition of political verse which puns on the cognomens of important figures. The work known as *The Prophecy of John of Bridlington* provides a useful case study of this poetic practice.[92] This anonymous Latin poem was dedicated to the young Humphrey de Bohun and internal evidence suggests that the commentary which accompanies the prophecy in some manuscripts was written shortly after the poem between November 1362 and April 1364. It has been argued that John Ergome was the author of the commentary but there is debate over whether he is also the author of the poem.[93]

While pretending to antedate events forseen, *Bridlington* is a historical retrospect of English affairs during the reign of Edward II. The second preface to the poem reads almost as an instruction manual of ways to encode subversive political meaning in poetry. The writer explains that the reading of his book is not a straightforward

---

[91] see III 138-41: 'For they kepeth no coyne that cometh to here hondis/ But chaunchyth it for cheynes that in chepe hangith/And settith all her siluer in [seintis] and hornes/ And for-doth the coyne and many other craftis' and 147-51: 'That hongith on his hippis more than he wynneth/And doughteth no dette so dukis hem preise/But beggith and borwith of burgeis in tounes/Furris of foyne and other felle-whare/And not the better of a bene though they boru euere'.

[92] The work is collected in Wright, I 123-215.

[93] The points in this paragraph are drawn from Thomas H. Bestul, *Satire and Allegory in Winner and Waster* (Nebraska, 1974), pp.62-4; M.J. Curley, 'The Cloak of Anonymity and *The Prophecy of John of Bridlington*', *MP*, 77 (1980), 361-9; A.G. Rigg, '*John of Bridlington's Prophecy*: A New Look', *Speculum*, 63 (1988), 596-613. The popularity of the work can be seen from its citation in closely contemporary chronicles, e.g. Usk, p.149, 171-3, *Annales*, p.407, *Eulogium*, III 391 and *Historia Anglicana*, II 270. There are 37 surviving manuscripts and there were some distinguished owners, including Humphrey de Bohun, John Erghome, prior of York Convent, William Rede, Bishop of Chichester (1368-85), see S.H. Cavanaugh, *A Study of Books Privately Owned in England 1300-1450* (unpublished PhD thesis, University of Pennsylvania, 1980), p.109, p.305, p.705.

process[94] and proceeds to list ten ways of concealing references in a prophecy. They encompass a striking range, but my concern here is with the first two categories. The first shows how a nickname may refer to a person in some way that is appropriate to his characteristics; thus the king of Scotland may be designated by the crab to recall his sideways political movements. Some incident from their lives, or peculiarity in manners, person, surname or arms, may give grounds for the second category of signification. A surname may give rise to a pun, e.g. 'penetrans' for Percy and so too, might his coat of arms, e.g. grey lions for the earl of Hereford.[95]

These, and other techniques are used plentifully by the writer of *Richard*, and they are also to be found in other closely contemporary works.[96] I shall focus on one example. At III 105, the narrator alludes to the execution of Richard Fitzalan, earl of Arundel, on Tower Hill in 1397. Froissart records that his son-in-law, Thomas Mowbray, earl of Nottingham, and earl Marshal of England, bandaged Arundel's eyes before the execution.[97] The line in *Richard* refers to this, and through its wordplay, evokes the unnaturalness of Mowbray's action:

[They] monside the marchall for his myssedede,
That euell [coude] his craft whan he [cloyed] the stede.   (III 105-6)

There is a pun on 'marchall' as Earl Marshal, and horse doctor,[98] and 'stede' as the cognomen of the earl of Arundel[99] which shows that the actions of Thomas Mowbray violated the principles of natural order. Instead of healing the horse, as a true horse doctor should, he lamed it.[100]

In the same Passus, the narrator puns on the word 'pikis' to make the point that overdressed courtiers violate principles of natural hierarchy and order. Wit is finally ejected from court by the porter: 'The porter with his pikis tho put him vttere' (III 232). 'Pikis' has the double sense of

[94] 'qui est obscuris et prophetalis, quia dat alia intelligere quam termini secundum communem usum loquenti signficant', Wright, I 125.
[95] ibid., p.126.
[96] e.g. Gower's *Chronica Tripertita* and *On King Richard's Ministers*, Wright, I 363-65. These are straightforward examples; the extent to which other contemporary poems make use of these types of techniques remains to be explored. I explore the use of political wordplay in *Richard* and *Mum* more fully in my unpublished D.Phil thesis (1989), pp.57-86.
[97] *The Chronicles of Froissart*, transl. J. Bourchier, ed. G.C. Macaulay (London, 1913), p.656, cf. Walsingham, *Historia Anglicana* II 225, who also states that Mowbray was present at his father-in-law's execution.
[98] MED 'marshal' 1a) and 4).
[99] See notes to *Richard*, III 26-7, in *The Piers Plowman Tradition*, p.271.
[100] I explore the articulation of the theme of the violation of natural order in *Richard* and *Mum* more fully in *LSE* (1992).

'spiked weapons' and 'piked shoes'.[101] Shoes with long exaggerated points became fashionable amongst the nobility in the late fourteenth century. That the porter wears them illustrates how hierarchy in dress has been subverted with inferiors copying the fashion of their betters.[102] The pun exposes court decadence, and how its outward opulence masks inward unmannerliness. Quite literally, Wit is kicked out of court. A pun has been described as anarchic because it refuses hierarchy or stability of meaning[103] but the pun in III 232 asserts the need for exactly those values.

At other points in the poem rather different types of wordplay work to a similar purpose. At I 142, the narrator criticises the extortion practised by the king's purveyors:

> And as tyrauntis, of tiliers token what hem liste,
> And paide hem on her pannes whan her penyes lacked.   (I 141-2)

The pun on 'paide' as a 'financial payment' and 'to strike a blow'[104] is emphasised by the chime of 'pannes' and 'penyes'.[105] The purveyors' distortion of commerce by breaking the law is reflected in the linguistic commutation, and also by the anti-pun[106] on 'paide' in the legal sense of making amends or restitution.[107] More of these legal puns are examined in Chapter Five.

In Passus IV, the rhetorical figure of anadiplosis[108] (though used with the two words written 'mete' which were originally distinct),[109] illustrates a different kind of corruption. After the chancellor's speech, the narrator writes:

> And whanne the tale was tolde anon to the ende,
> Amorwe thei must, affore mete mete to-gedir,
> The knyghtis of the comunete, and carpe of the maters.   (IV 39-41)

These lines allude to the type of corruption in which legal cases were corrupted by treating interested parties to lavish entertainment and hospitality. The narrator has already criticised this practice overtly:

---

[101] MED 'pike' 1a) and 5a).
[102] Hoccleve makes the same point in his denunciation of the fashion for long sleeves, *Regement*, 435-41.
[103] Shoaf (1988), pp.44-5.
[104] MED 'paien' 3) and 6b).
[105] Pararhyme is explored in *Piers* in Schmidt, pp.67-75.
[106] Schmidt investigates anti-puns in *Piers*, pp.116-7.
[107] Alford, p.107.
[108] Where the last word(s) of one clause or sentence become(s) the first of the one following, Vickers, p.491.
[109] OE 'metan' (vb) 'to meet' and OE 'mete' (n) 'food'.

For mayntenance many day well more is the reuthe!
Hath y-had mo men at mete and at melis
Than ony cristen kynge that ye knewe euere. (III 312-4)

It is a practice alluded to in the portrait of the Franklin in *The General Prologue*, especially the comment that in his own 'contre', he was a St Julian (340).[110] In Passus IV of *Richard*, the narrator capitalises on the fact that the verb 'mete' in the sense of 'come together' and the noun 'mete' in the sense of 'meal', are homophones.[111] The anadiplosis of line 39, with the clashing stress of marked alliterative staves around the caesura, emphasises the way that sharing food becomes blurred with the sense of modifying one's opinion. Entertainment and coming to a legal decision ought to be separate activities but the oral repetition of line 40 suggests that they have colluded. This suggestion is enhanced by the anti-pun on 'mete' as an adjective in the sense of 'fitting, appropriate' (MED 1a). The 'fitting' of evidence that this line suggests is a fix, however, that is quite inapppropriate. Once again, a play with semantic boundaries reveals a serious intent to expose the transgression of legal limits.

One final example from *Richard* shows how the narrator also uses wordplay to illustrate the right relationship of words and the realities to which they correspond. In the opening lines of the poem, the narrator professes his loyalty to Richard: 'All myn hoole helthe was his while he in helthe regnid' (I 26). In the a-verse there is a play on the range of collocability of 'hoole': 'undivided, whole', and 'healthy'.[112] The conjunction 'while' makes the loyalty and health of the narrator dependent on the king's own health. Through the wordplay, the positions of subject and ruler are fused and the link between 'hoole' and 'helthe' suggests that allegiance can be due to the king only so long as he assures his subjects' well-being by ensuring his own. Here, wordplay demonstrates the right relationship between words, while the polysemy also hints at the dangers that will befall a king if he neglect the right relationship to his subjects. From these examples, the relationship between 'signes' and 'soth' in *Richard* is very similar to that traced in *Crowned King*. If the intention be loyal, then double meanings can expose duplicity. But if the outward physical language is unmatched by honourable or competent intention, then the incongruity may result in social instability.

Mum follows a very similar pattern. In two crucial passages, the defence of truthtelling poetry is framed within an appeal to legitimate

[110] The legal sense of 'contre' is the jury consisting of the inhabitants of a certain district, Alford, p.36.
[111] MED 'meten' (4)1c) and 'mete' (n) 3a).
[112] MED 'hole' (adj.2) 5); 'hole' (adj.2) 1).

intention. At line 74, the narrator warns of the dangers of slander if telling the truth is conducted without sincere intention and careful practice: 'for though thy tale be trewe thyn tente might be noyous'. At line 1305, the beekeeper assures the narrator that it is lawful for him to attempt to redress corruption through bookmaking and bids him 'to change not' [his] 'intent'. These passages are discussed more fully in Chapter Five. Elsewhere, the narrator bids the reader to read his accusations in the spirit in which they are intended:

> Now take my tale as my intent demeth,
> And ye shal wel wite I wil thaym no mischief
> By my worde ne by my wille as wissely [for] sothe. (466-8)

This appeal to intramental intentions and the sincere wish that both word and will are 'sothe', and have the sole function of reform, contrasts strongly with the incompetent, or fraudulent advice which the narrator encounters at other points in the poem.[113] Mum's first speech is summarised by the narrator: 'And euer he concludid with colorable wordes' (286).[114] This description calls attention to the fraudulent, chameleon-like nature of physical language and contrasts with a truthteller, who has the responsibility of 'the soeth to seye that sitteth in his herte' (283).[115]

In *Mum* there is a clear concern that physical speech be grounded in honest action and that it be proportionate to one's status and social responsibilities. Parliament is described as the 'place that is proprid to parle for the royaulme' (1132). However, this appropriate forum for amendment and common interest has been bypassed because 'souurayns and the shiremen the sothe han eschewed' (1131) and instead of speaking out on important issues, they:

> . . .hiden alle the heuynes and halten echone
> And maken Mvm thaire messaigier thaire mote to determyne,
> And bringen home a bagge ful of boicches vn-y-curid,
> That nedis most by nature ennoye thaym there-after. (1137-40)

The failure of parliamentary representatives to speak in accordance with the proper function of parliament results in ill-health and disease. So too, does the improper use of speech by those who are not entitled to make criticism. The narrator states clearly that 'hit longeth to no laborier' (1462) to 'contre the king-is wil, ne construe his werkes (1459).

---

[113] cf. the beekeeper's advice to the narrator at 1203 to follow the sothsegger rather than those: 'that fikelly fablen and fals been withynne'.

[114] 'Colorable' puns on the colour of an object MED 2, and as a specious reason, 5b).

[115] cf. *Piers*, V.606: 'Thow shalt see in þiselve Truþe sitte in þyne herte'. In *Dives and Pauper*, flatterers are likened to the colour changing of the chameleon, II 223/37.

Such unlicensed language is 'lewed labbing' which the 'lande doeth apeire (1483).'[116] The chattering recalls the description of politically dangerous rumours:

> Lesingz been so light of fote, thay lepen by the skyes,
> And as swifte as a swalue sheutyng ovte at oones. (1402-3)

The personification of 'lesingz' into fleet-footed leapers, and the simile of the impulsive shouting of the swift swallow[117] emphasise the groundlessness of rumour. Physicality and insubstantiality are stressed in a description of sound which is a long way from the 'tente' and 'tale' 'temprid in oone' which characterises the ideal sothsegger envisaged at line 90.

This swift-shouting language also contrasts to the sober, measured speech of the beekeeper, the figure who becomes in effect the truthteller for whom the narrator has been searching. In an echo of Wit from *Piers*, he is described as 'sad of his semblant, softe of his speche' (963).[118] He is a 'semely' sage, whose appearance matches the honesty of his speech: 'his eyen were al ernest, eggid to noon ille' (960). He is a more fully drawn version of the actant Wit in *Richard*, who had 'awilled his wyll as wisdom him taught' (III 210), and who like the beekeeper matches physical appearance with true speech.[119] Both of these sages contrast to the figure of Elde in *The Parlement of the Thre Ages*.[120]

The beekeeper also stands in contrast to Mum. Save for a reference to his 'myter' Mum is not described physically. He has great verbal agility,

---

[116] Seditious rumours against Henry were persistent. In May 1405, the council instructed the sheriffs of all the counties of England to make proclamations against the circulation of lying rumours against Henry, *Cal.Close Rolls 1402-5*, p.515. A petition presented by the Prince of Wales to the Long Parliament of 1406 criticised those religious who persisted in sowing dissent amongst the king's subjects by spreading rumours that the late king was still alive, see P. McNiven, *The Burning of John Badby* (Cambridge, 1987), p.101, and for rumours persisting into 1407, p.145-6.

[117] The swallow derives its name from 'crienge' and is noted for its swiftness, Bartholomaeus, I 631-2.

[118] *Piers*, VIII 120: 'Sad of his semblaunt and of a softe speche'. Many B MSS read 'chere' for 'speche' but the reading of A and C MSS is 'speche'. cf. the description of the bird in *A Bird in Bishopwood*, 25: 'Sad in al semblant, sayd bot a lytyl' ed. Ruth Kennedy, 'A Bird in Bishopwood: Some Newly-Discovered Lines of Alliterative Verse from the Late Fourteenth Century', in *Medieval Literature and Antiquities*, edd. M. Stokes and T.L. Burton (Cambridge, 1987), 71-87.

[119] Wit is dressed not in fashionable clothes, but in garments which are 'holsum' and appropriate to the weather. In contrast to the beardless courtiers, he, like the beekeeper in *Mum* has a beard (III 212-15). His words and appearance are in accordance with the principles of natural law; see further, Barr (1992), p.56.

[120] D.K. Fry has analysed Elde's disgusting appearance and his factual errors, noting that he 'may supply corrective words, but hardly a corrective example', 'The Authority of "Elde" in *The Parlement of the Thre Ages*', in *Hermeneutics and Medieval Culture*, ed. Patrick J. Gallacher and Helen Damico (New York, 1989), 213-24, p.219.

however, such that, in a foretaste of the swift-leaping lies of 1402, we are told that he: 'couthe lye and laugh and leepe ouer the balkes' (808). Yet although he is the personification of the self-interested use of speech, at one point, in a manner reminiscent of the parliamentary representatives in Passus IV of *Richard*, Mum has a long speech in which he turns truthteller himself. He argues that if one sees corruption and fails to speak out to correct it, then one is as guilty as the perpetrator of the crime (750). His first example is Pilate, who:

> Wilned aftre watre to waisshe with his handes,
> To shewe hym by that signe, of the bloode-sheding
> Of Crist that vs creed and on the crosse deyed,
> His conscience was clensid as clene as his handes.
> Yit was he ground of the grame and moste guilty eeke.   (722-6)

In a misuse of signs which is reminiscent of the retainers in *Richard*, the outward sign proves to be contrary to the internal reality, Quite simply, Pilate washes his hands of the affair. The polyptoton of 'clensid' and 'clene' in 725 suggests that Pilate's conscience was cleansed only outwardly, just like his hands.[121] Such cleanliness is not next to godliness. At the conclusion of Mum's speech, the narrator comments:

> 'Now treuly,' cothe I, 'thy talking me pleasith,
> For thou has saide as sothe, so me God helpe,
> As euer sage saide sith Crist was in erthe,
> For thou has rubbid on the rote of the rede galle
> And eeke y-serchid the sore and sought alle the woundz.   (768-71)

The imagery of medicinal care shows that contrary to all expectation, Mum is able to accomplish a truthtelling of which the shire representatives are incapable. Like the ideal speech predicated of the sothsegger who is unable to 'speke in termes', Mum's castigation of those who eschew responsibilty for correcting crimes they witness, has a 'poynt' which 'priketh on the sothe'. Mum's avowed intention to dissuade the narrator from speaking 'sothe' is, in reality, one of the potent truthtelling speeches of the poem, and to add to the complexity, the speech uses wordplay to make the point that the double use of signs can be criminal.

This last point is one which has already been discussed as a feature of *Richard* and *Crowned King*. It is a feature no less widespread in *Mum*. We have already seen examples of it in the discourse of the academics, and further instances will be discussed in Chapters Four and Five. A few

---

[121] In his written defence of the charges against him, Walter Brut uses the example of Pilate to show, as in *Mum*, that priests should not kill anyone; *Trefnant*, p.324.

brief examples here will show how the techniques of wordplay already seen in *Richard* and *Crowned King*; techniques which recall the verbal texture of *Piers* are integral to the temper of *Mum*.

A tiny example at line 1124 demonstrates the attraction to wordplay precisely at the point where the narrator urges parliamentary representatives to speak out truthfully. Using once more an image of sores and boils, he exhorts the shire knights to burst the blisters to free poisonous anger: 'leste the fals felon festre with-ynne' (1124). There is a pun on 'felon' as a suppurating sore MED 'feloun' 2 and as a 'criminal' MED 'feloun' 1[122] which fuses the concepts of criminality and unredressed wrongs and suggests that keeping mum is antithetical both to the health of the realm and to the law of the land.

A rather different kind of wordplay suggests how the hearer of fraudulent discourse may be reduced to the kinds of impotent silence against which the poem inveighs. After discussions which were intended to clarify the relationship of mum and sothsegger, the narrator of *Mum* twice responds in astonishment and stunned silence:

> And stoode al a-stonyed and starid for angre. (351)
>
> And as I stoode staring, stonyed of this matiere. (578).

R.A. Shoaf has argued that in *The Franklins' Tale*, 'astonyed' means both astonished and 'turned to stone'.[123] That there is a similar pun on the root syllable of 'a-stonyed' in *Mum* is suggested by the description of one who stands silent when he should speak as one who 'stont stille as a stoone and no worde stire' (755), and of the narrator's self-description after he has witnessed the corruption of the mayoral banquet: 'I stoode stille as a stoone and starid aboute' (823). The effect of witnessing 'mumming' temporarily mums the narrator himself. Through the verbal play which records the astonished response to the misuse of language, he momentarily becomes implicated in the collusion that is described in the polyptoton between lines 818-19:

> But who-so mvmmeth a mayre to maynteyne his rente,
> Maniere were that the mayre shuld mvmme hym agaynes. (818-19)

The mutual criminality and complicity is mirrored in the self-reflecting language. Alongside the polyptoton of 'mvmmeth' and 'mvmme' (suggestively symptomatic of how mumming is contagious) is the ploce

---

[122] MED 'feloun' (2); 'feloun' (1). 'Feloun' as 'criminal' derives from OF 'feloneus' while the probable etymology of 'feloun' in the sense of boil is from Latin 'fel' meaning gall. MED expresses uncertainty about this, and also suggests that it could be a special use of 'feloun' (adj) in the sense of 'bad'.
[123] Shoaf (1988), pp.47-49.

of 'mayre', first in object, then in subject position. In addition, 'maynteyne' means both 'to pay for' and 'to support in a bad cause'.[124] 'Maniere', has the overt meaning of: 'a way of doing something', but there are anti-puns on 'a moral practice or principle' and 'proper conduct'.[125] Finally the device of antimetabole[126] links the two lines as a unit. It is this sort of double-dealing which reduces the narrator to 'stonyed' silence. But unlike the sothsegger whom he sees licking his wounds, having drunk a draught of 'dum-seede' (838-7), the narrator of *Mum* capitalises on this very doubleness in language to expose the duplicity of corruption.

To conclude this survey of wordplay in *Mum*, I should like to advert to the use of devices familiar from *Piers*, some of which I have already illustrated in relation to *Richard*. Pararhyme is used at 1236: 'But Mvm wol be no martir while mytres ben in sale' to suggest the incompatibility of martyrdom and simoniacal bishops. At line 681, in a direct verbal echo of a line which describes Mede in *Piers*, there is a chime on the two senses of 'goode': 'goodness', and 'material possessions': 'That Mvm hath a maister there men been of goode'.[127] As Schmidt has noted, this is an important site of play in *Piers* and it is used more than once in *Mum*.[128] At line 1718, it occurs together with a chime on 'kepe' which is accented by the ploce of the line: 'His custume was to kepe his good so lete vs kepe hit eeke'. The corruption of the executours is reflected in the perversion of 'kepe' from the sense of 'hoard' to 'take by force'.[129]

Another site of wordplay in *Piers* which is echoed in *Mum* is the comparison between the cross that was engraved on the backs of coins and the Christian cross of worship. In *Piers*, B XV 539-45, this play alludes to the corruption of spirituality by avarice:

> And now is rouþe to rede how þe rede noble
> Is reuerenced er þe Roode, receyued for [þe] worþier
> Than cristes cros þat ouercam deeþ and dedly synne.
> And now is werre and wo, and whoso why askeþ:
> For coueitise after cros; the croune stant in golde.
> Boþe riche and Religious, þat roode þei honoure
> That in grotes is ygraue and in gold nobles.

In Mum, this play is recast in lines on the avarice of the nobility:

---

[124] MED 'maintenen' 3b) and 2c).
[125] MED 'manere' 3a); 6) and 5b).
[126] The repetition of two or more words in inverse order, Vickers, p.492.
[127] MED 'god' n(2) 1a) and 12). cf. *Piers*, III 169: 'Swich a maister is Mede among men of goode'.
[128] See *Mum*, 413 and cf. n.31.
[129] MED 'kepen' 5a) and 3a) b).

How Couetise hath caste the knyght on the grene,
And woneth at Westmynstre to wynne newe spores,
And can not crepe thens while the crosse walketh.   (481-3)

'Crosse' puns on the cross-shape of spurs, the cross that was engraved
on the backs of coins, which is so mobile for business, and the Good
Friday ceremony of the veneration of the cross. The multiple meaning
shows how the values of knighthood, commmerce and spirituality have
become entangled. It is a play anticipated in the poem by line 66: 'the
colour of the crosse that many men incumbreth' and is reminiscent of, if
not indebted to, the lines on Coueitise in Passus XX of *Piers* who
'boldeliche bar adoun wiþ many a bright Noble/Muche of þe wit and
wisdom of westmynstre halle' (XX 132-3).[130]

As a final example from *Mum* we may note the use at 387 of a device
frequently employed in *Piers* – namely the anti-pun. The friars are
accused of going out into the world to live with lords: 'And with a
couetous croke Saynt Nicholas thay throwen'. The sense of 'croke' as a
'pastoral crozier', MED 'crok' 2b) is called up, but excluded, because of
the attributive adjective 'couetous'. Instead, the prevailing senses are:
'the devil's clutches' and 'stratagem, or trick'.[131] The latter sense
suggests the friars 'crooked' reading (MED 'acrok') – to go astray. The
link is reforged at line 784 when Mum warns the narrator: 'And come
not with clergie leste thou a-croke walke'. Once again, the anti-pun on
crozier foregrounds the way that instead of guiding the laity to spiritual
insight and behaviour, the contemporary clergy teach only crooked
paths which reflect their own distortions.

This advice from Mum is another example of his ability to use words
truthfully, despite his avowed intention to mislead and collude. It is
advice which might profitably have been given to the narrator of *Pierce
the Ploughman's Crede*, who walks 'a-croke' with all four orders of friars
until he finds the truth with Peres 'be the waie'. Twisting meaning is
frequently associated with fraternal discourse throughout the poem.
The friars are accused of beguiling the nobility with: 'glauerynge
wordes,/With glosinge of godspells thei Gods worde turneth' (708-9),
and that 'thei gilen hem-self and Godes worde turneth' (599).

Their financial corruption of the spiritual senses of words is conveyed
through their own double meanings. When the narrator first undertakes
to interrogate the friars:

. . .the[y] me fulle tolden
That all the frute of the fayth was in here foure ordres,

---

[130] The pun on 'noble' is discussed by Davlin, p.16.
[131] MED 'crok' 2b); 3) and 4a).

And the cofres of cristendam & the keye b[o]then,
And the lok [of beleve lyeth] loken in her hondes.   (28-31)

As in *Piers*, though in rather different senses, there are puns here on
'frute' and 'lok'.[132] 'Frute' functions in *Crede* as an anti-pun. The sense
which is called up but excluded is 'spiritual effect'; the sense of its later
use in Christ's words reported at line 151: 'by her fruyt men shall hem
ful knowen.' At line 29, 'frute' also carries the sense of 'income' to show
the distorted spiritual values of the friars.[133] The polyptoton of 'lok/
loken' of line 31 foregrounds the senses of 'key', alongside 'tax'. The
pun attests to the friars' appropriation of spiritual profits. Simultaneously, far from being a gift – one of the senses in which the word is
used in *Piers* – the financial profits of the faith are kept firmly secure,
locked in the hands of the friars.[134] 'Hondes' alludes ironically to the
stipulation in *The Rule of St Francis* that friars should not handle
money.[135] There is also in line 31 a pun on 'lyeth'. The Franciscan claims
overtly that the gift of faith is to be found in their hands, but 'lien' is a
homophone of the verb 'to tell a lie' and suggests that the fruit of belief
is capable of lying.[136] The suggestion of this sense foregrounds the fact
that the Franciscan's reported speech is a tissue of lies and half truths.

When the Franciscan begins his direct speech, he employs wordplay
to defame the Carmelites which is again reminiscent of an instance of
wordplay in *Piers*: 'With sterne staues and stronge they ouer lond
straketh' (82). The spiritual meaning of 'staues' as spiritual staffs of
guidance is called up, but excluded in favour of the sexual sense of erect
penises, a sense which 'lemmans' in line 83 clearly demands.[137] The pun
recalls the lines in *Piers* B Prol. 53-4: 'Heremytes on an heep with hoked
staues/Wenten to walsyngham, and hire wenches after'. In both poems,
the wordplay fuses the sexual with the spiritual to illustrate hypocrisy.

In *Crede*, not only do the friars twist the meanings of words to their
own advantage but they empty verbal signs of their spiritual meanings.

132 B IX 171 and I 202, cf. Davlin, p.62 and p.44.
133 MED 'frute' 4d) and 1b).
134 MED 'lok' n(2) 1a); 'lok'n(3) 2c) and 'lok' n(3) 2a). cf. *Piers*, X 320-1.
135 *Regula Sancti Francisci*, in *Monumenta Franciscana*, ed. Richard Howlett (RS 1882), II.68.
Wycliffite texts expose the friars' hypocrisy e.g. 'Frere, whi wole not summe of ȝoure ordre
touche siluer wiþ þe crosse and þe kyngis heed, as ȝe wolen touche a silueren spone and
oþere siluer?. . .& siþen ȝe wolen resceyue þe money in ȝoure hertis & not in ȝoure hondis,
it semeþ ȝe holden more holines in ȝoure hondis þanne in ȝoure hertis', *Jack Upland*, p.68/
322-9, and Matthew, p.49/29 where the friars are described as using a stick to count out the
money.
136 MED 'lien' v(1) 11a); MED 'lien' v(2), cf. line 49; 'And lieth on our Ladie many a longe
tale', which juxtaposes the friars' boasts with their lechery. 'lieth' puns on 'to tell a lie'
MED v(2) and 'to have sexual intercourse' v(1) 1b).
137 MED 'staf' 1d) and under 1c) 'hard or sturdy club'. The figurative sense of 'penis' is
not listed.

At the conclusion of the narrator's interview with the Franciscan, he receives the outward sign of absolution:

> And he sette on me his honde and asoilede me clene,
> And their y parted him fro with-outen any peine. (135-6)

The absolution offered by the Franciscans is as clean as Pilate's conscience in *Mum*. That the verbal and physical act is unaccompanied by inner spiritual meaning is suggested by the pun on 'clene' in the sense of 'innocent, guiltless' and 'void, empty'.[138] The narrator departs from the Franciscan in line 136 without any difficulty but also, more significantly, without any penance.[139] The discourse of the remission of sins is used without correspondence to the real state of affairs.[140]

This perversion of signs is commented upon explicitly both by the narrator and by Peres. The friars reverse the senses of signs, making financial substitution of the spiritual meaning so that God's word is indeed 'turned vp two-fold vnteyned vpon trewthe'. The narrator reels away in disgust at the Augustinian's version of the 'truth': 'Heere pride is the pater-noster in preyinge of synne;/Here Crede is coueytise; now can y no ferther (337-8). The rhetorical device of anaphora calls attention to the friars' vice of inverting the true meanings of words.[141]

Peres makes a similar accusation when he denounces the friars' misuse of the significance of outward signs by wearing habits whose colours make pretence to spiritual virtue:

> Thise tokens hauen freres taken but y trowe that a fewe
> Folwen fully that cloth but falsliche that vseth.
> For whijt in trowthe bytokneth clennes in soule;
> Yif he haue vnder-nethen whijt thanne he aboue wereth
> Blak, that bytokneth bale for oure synne,
> And mournynge for misdede of hem that this vseth,
> And serwe for synfull lijf; so that cloth asketh.
> Y trowe ther ben nought ten freres that for synne wepen,

---

[138] MED 'clene' 2a) and 3b).

[139] MED 'peine' 7b) and 1a).

[140] cf. Schmidt's comment (1983), p.140 that in *Piers*, the only guarantee that words will remain faithful is to use the phrase Trajan applies to himself: 'leel love and lyvyng in truthe' (XI 161). (Quoted from Schmidt's edition).

[141] This technique of inversion is analogous to the topos of renaming the sins which, as Kathleen M. Ashley has noted, was used by Lollard preachers as: 'an example of the perversions wrought by Antichrist and his followers, the clerks and friars who use "fals fablis" rather than plain Gospel', 'Renaming the Sins: A Homiletic Topos of Linguistic Instability in the *Canterbury Tales*', in *Sign, Sentence, Discourse*, 272-293, p.277. There is an example similar to *Crede* in *Jack Upland*, p.56/47-53 and also in *the Sermon of William Taylor*, ed. Hudson (1993), 419-23. Hudson notes, p.100, that this topos was used before the Lollards, and may have its ultimate source in Gregory, *Moralia*, xxxii.45 (PL 76.662). cf. discussion on the 'world upside down' topos in Chapter Two above, p.26.

For that lijf is here lust and thereyn thei libben
In fraitour and in fermori, her fostringe is synne.
It is her mete at iche a mel her most sustenaunce.
Herkne opon Hyldegare hou homlyche [ho] telleth
How her sustenaunce is synne; and syker, as y trowe.   (692-704)

The friars have taken tokens, both in the sense of 'assuming' them, or 'putting them on' and also in the sense of laying hands on them by force or artifice.[142] The 'misdede' of 697 is both the human sin for which the friars fail to weep, and their criminal act of the misappropriation of outward signs of holiness. For the friars, 'lijf' is 'lust'; 'fostringe' in the sense of 'nurture' is 'synne'. 'Sustenaunce' (702) is, for the friars, not spiritual, but bodily: 'mete' is physical food not holy nourishment.[143]

Spirituality sticks literally in the gorge of the bodily friars[144] a state of affairs which is encapsulated in an earlier comment by Peres, and which recalls a similar pun in *Piers Plowman*: 'And so thei chewen charite as chewen schaf houndes' (663). The paronomasia of 'charite' is similar to the line on the chaplains in *Piers* who: 'Chewen hire charite and chiden after moore' (I 193). In *Crede*, 'charite' describes the friars' persecution of such true livers as Walter Brut. Instead of dealing out holy love, both the friars in *Crede* and the chaplains in *Piers*: 'eat what other people give them and what they ought to give to others, but also destroy their own ability to love'.[145] Davlin also notes the ironic hint of Holy Communion in the phrase 'chewen charite'; where the communicant 'chews' Deus caritas. In *Piers*, this points up the incongruity of: 'curates communicating and thus taking "caritas" within them physically while "charite" is aweye' (I 190).[146] In *Crede*, the hint of the friars' uncharitable communion is followed by a disclosure of their zeal to persecute heretics by burning them and excommunicating them: 'to brenne the bodye in a bale of fijr,/ And sythen the sely soule slen and senden hyre to helle (667-8).[147] The mention of 'schaf' also calls up the 'grain/chaff' model of scriptural reading only to deny it.[148] The friars leave the grain of Walter Brut's 'sothe' and instead, gobble up the chaff like greedy hounds. Their

[142] OED 'take' 16a) and 2).
[143] The equation between spiritual disorder and the abuse of food recalls a similar theme in *Piers*, which is discussed by Jill Mann, 'Eating and Drinking in *Piers Plowman*, *E&S*, 32 (1979), 26-42 and A.V.C. Schmidt, 'Langland's Structural Imagery', *EIC*, 30 (1980), 311-25.
[144] *Piers*, X 67: 'God is muche in þe gorge of þise grete maistres'. Simpson (1986) notes how this pun creates: 'the collapsing together of properly distinct realms', p.173.
[145] Davlin, p.42.
[146] ibid.
[147] I discuss this passage further in Chapter Four, pp.109-110.
[148] The image derives ultimately from Matthew 3:12 (Luke 3:17). It is used in a variety of Middle English works, most memorably perhaps in the Nun's Priest's request to his audience to take 'the fruyt, and lat the chaf be stille'. (*NPT* VIII 3443).

misreading results in a misdirected 'sustenance' and 'fostringe,' and rather than acknowledging the truth of Brut's words, they 'awyrien that wight for his well dedes' (662).

The link between physical guzzling and spiritual emptiness recalls the description of the pinguid Dominican, who embodies the distinction between physical language and mental perception or intention. His face is as fat as a full bladder: 'Blowen bretfull of breth and as a bagge honged/On bothen his chekes' (223-24). The Dominican is full, not of spiritual 'bread', but of 'breath' – physical air without substance. He is puffed up with his own pride and gluttony. As his physique amply testifies, he is empty of 'charite', 'corpus' without Christ.

These last examples have shown that it is not only the speech of the friars which employs wordplay in *Crede* but also that of the narrator and Peres. The narrator and Peres use many of the same techniques characteristic both of *Piers*, and of the other poems in the *Piers* tradition in order to address corruption. In all of these poems pararhyme is used to link words as a means of testing the reality of the relationship between them. At line 574 of *Crede*, Peres questions the right of the friars to the academic title 'master' in the sense of Master of Arts:[149] 'And also this myster men ben maysters icalled'. 'Icalled' draws attention to the fact that the title 'mayster' is claimed by the friars, not one with which they have naturally been endowed.[150] The pararhyme of 'maysters' and 'myster' suggests that the true status of friars is that of humble artisans,[151] but as a result of their 'queynte' words and their pride, these 'myster men' have pronounced themselves 'maysters'.

A similar permutation of sound and sense occurs at lines 571-72, where Peres criticises how the friars grant absolution in return for money:

> But money may maken mesur of the peyne
> After that his power is to payen, his penance schal faile. (571-2)

---

[149] Matthew, 23:7-8 '[they love] to be called by men Rabbi. But be you not called Rabbi. For one is your master ; and all you are brethren' was often used to satirise the intellectual arrogance of the friars. 'Master' came to signify 'Master of Arts'. St.Francis exhorted his followers not to be called masters, (see Jill Mann, *Chaucer and Medieval Estates Satire* (Cambridge, 1973), p.39). In the *General Prologue*, Hubert is 'lyk a maister' (261) and in the *Summoner's Tale*, the friar accepts the title 'deere maister' from the sick Thomas (1781), but when the lord of the village uses the title to him, John quotes Matt. 23:7-8 to refuse it (2184-8). Wycliffite texts make extensive use of the comparison, e.g. *Tractatus de Pseudo-Freris*, Matthew, p.306/11-13: Friars read in God's law that they should not be made masters, but they sinfully covet it'. cf. *The Plowman's Tale*, 1115-24.

[150] cf. 'He mighte no maistre [ben] kald, for Crist it defended,/Ne puten [no] pylion on his piled pate' (*Crede*, 833-4) where baldness symbolises the natural state of the head (and suggests emptiness), which the outward show of learning, symbolised by the priest's cap, attempts to cover up.

[151] cf. discussion of 'beggers brol' in Chapter Two, pp.35-36.

'Peyne' ought to have the strict theological sense of 'pena', punishment for sin, but in these lines, it is transmuted into 'payen'. Through the subtle sound change of the pararhyme, penance becomes payment and 'mesur' commuted from moderation into calculated covetousness.

Peres also attacks the friars for emptying words of their value when they are used to criticise their behaviour:

> Lakke hem a litil wight and here lijf blame,
> But he lepe vp on heigh in hardynesse of herte,
> And [n]emne the anon nought and thi name lakke
> With proude wordes apert that passeth his rule,
> Bothe with 'thou leyest, and thou lext' in heynesse of sowle.
>
> (538-42)

Line 542, with its polyptoton 'leyest/lext' echoes Wrath's boast about backbiting gossip in *Piers*, V 162-63: 'Of wikkede wordes, I wraþe, hire wortes made,/Til 'þow lixt!' and 'þow lixt!' lopen out at ones'. That Wrath casts himself as a friar seems not to have gone unnoticed by the writer of *Crede*. In these lines, the quotation of fraternal dissent in *Piers* is transformed into a context in which havoc is wrought with semantic values.

Lines 538-40 are linked by epanalepsis[152] but there is a subtle transformation of sense between the two 'lakke's. The first carries the sense of 'to blame, disparage', but 'lakke' in line 540 also carries the sense of 'to be absent'.[153] The response of a friar to criticism is to blot out the name of the corrector. In contrast to the invitation to the narrator to read his name for ever in a church window if he endow the convent with money (129), the return for amendment in these lines is to be struck out of language; to be named nothing. There is a pun on 'anon' meaning 'at once' and 'a non' in the senses of 'no person' and 'nothing'.[154] This is suggested by the presence of 'nought'; not just an empty signifier, but no thing. Line 540 is over-determined. With the pun on 'anon', there are two words for 'no one' and the synonyms of 'nemne' and 'name' provide two words with the sense of 'to signify'. The excess of signification exposes the emptiness of the friars' own signifying practices and their refusal to accept the senses of the words they hear. Further, in line 541, the chime on 'apert' in the senses of 'open, public' and 'bare' illustrates how the proud words of the friars are baseless.[155]

---

152 Where the final part of each unit of a pattern repeats the initial part, G. Leech, *A Linguistic Guide to English Poetry*, p.82.
153 MED 'lakken' 2a) and 1a).
154 MED 'anon' 1); 'non' 1a) and 1c).
155 MED 'apert' 4a) and 2).

They 'pass' the fraternal rule in the senses of breaking it; and exceeding its signification.[156] The polyptoton of line 542, especially given that it is in the friar's direct speech, suggests that his words are, in fact, emptier than the vacant space to which he would assign his critic. The wordplay of these lines illustrates that the fraternal attempt to hold the key to language, to have sole control of naming and cancelling names, is nothing more substantial than a kind of vaulting linguistic ambition which overleaps itself.

Towards the end of the poem, Peres explicitly accuses the friars of false linguistic ambition: 'the power of the Apostells thei pasen in speche' (711). In addition to the senses of exceeding the power of Apostolic speech, and breaking their apostolic commandment, is the sense that the friars simply skip over it, MED 'passen' 9). As such, they could hardly be further from the exhortations to true Christian eloquence which are pervasive in Wycliffite texts. Preaching is the most important activity of the apostles sent by God, and those who preach must live up to the standards of the apostolic life.[157]

Right from the start of the poem, the narrator searches for a teacher who 'fulliche folweth the feyth and feyneth non other (19); a desire which is reiterated throughout the poem, and is accompanied by a desire for 'full' language. The friars claim such plenitude: 'they me fulle tolden/That all the frute of the fayth was in here foure ordres'(28-9). In this instance, however, 'fulle' has the sense of 'too much, sated', rather than 'whole or entire'.[158] The Franciscans at 291: 'seyn that they folwen fully Fraunceses rewle' but their luxurious habits state the contrary. In this poem, whatever the friars 'seyn', and however 'fully' they say it, is (like the Dominican's ample cheek) 'blowen bretful of breth'.

Christ's sayings, however, are 'full' in the exemplary, charitable sense of the word. The adverbs 'fulliche', 'clenli', 'purliche' and 'clerli' are

---

[156] MED 'passen' 10c) and 11f).

[157] Preaching is seen to be the primary function of the priesthood in numerous Wycliffite texts. *De Stipendiis Ministorum* lists the qualifications for priests and states: '3e schullen fynde hem to lerne Goddis lawe, to knowe hou þei schulde serve God in holy lif, and techen oþere men þe gospel, to save here soulis þerbi. For þei neden to have bokis of holy writt, as þe bible and exponitouris on þe gospellis and pistelis, more than Graielis and oþere bokis of song; and ben more bounden to lerne holy writt, and preche þe gospel, and Goddis hestis, and werkis of mercy, þan to seie matynes and masse bi Salisbury uss. And in what place or werk þei plesen most houre God bi holy lif, and stiren men to kepe Goddis hestis, in þat place and þat werk þei profiten most to here maistris and alle Cristen men (Arnold, III, p.202). *A Schort Reule of Lif* enjoins priests to live: 'holili, passyng oþer in holy preyere and holy deseir and þenkyng, in holy spekyng counselyng and trewe techyng, and ever that Goodis hestis and his gospel be in þi mouþ, and evere dispice synne, to drawe men þerfro' (Arnold, III, p.205).

[158] MED 'ful' 2b) and 4).

used frequently to characterise the language of the bible and the authority of Christ or God:[159]

> God forbad to his folke and fullyche defended. (587)
>
> That Crist hath clerliche forboden and clenliche destruede. (147)
>
> That the gentill Iesus generallyche blamed.
> And that poynt to his apostells purly defended. (575-6)

All these adverbs are contested in the poem[160] but the friars' claims to teach or behave in their manner are quashed by the affirmations of the narrator and Peres that these are adverbs whose meaning is fully stated only when they are used in an exemplary apostolic manner. At 449-50, the narrator laments that in his search for an exemplary teacher: 'y can fynden no man that fully byleueth,/ To techen me the heyghe weie and therfore I wepe.' His addressee is Peres, however, who turns out to be the very teacher whom the narrator has given up hope to find, and it is significant that for all the wordplay that Peres uses to condemn the friars on their own terms, he is also at pains to stress the 'full', 'holl' and 'cler' teaching of Christ. In his rehearsal of the Creed at the end of the poem, the density of words for 'holly', 'fully', 'soth' and 'beleue' is unmatched in the English versions of the creed recorded in *The Lay Folk's Mass Book*.[161]

What emerges with some insistence in *Crede* is the claim to a full presence of meaning by those who speak the truth. Those who peddle falsehoods, namely the friars, empty words of their meanings or twist them into 'tales' which turn them on their heads. The claim to a legitimate full presence of meaning is also a claim to the apostolic use of language. Peres makes the source of this plenitude abundantly clear:

> God forbad to his folke and fullyche defended
> They schulden nought stodyen biforn ne sturen her wittes,
> But sodenlie the same word with her mowth schewe
> That weren yeuen hem of God thorough gost of him-selue. (587-90)

This translation of Mark 13:11 is used to argue against the formal modes of learning practised by the friars, which in Lollard texts are often seen as tantamount to 'glosing'.[162] An infinitely more valuable, and powerful,

---

159 Often this authority is stressed by the addition of the words 'himself' in contrast to the 'they seyn' of the friars, e.g. 'Sithen Crist seyd hym-self to all his disciples' (259).

160 I explore this more fully in Chapter Four.

161 In *The Lay Folk's Mass Book*, line 210 reads 'al holly' (text E) line 222 reads 'þo sothe to say' whereas in *Crede*, line 796b reads: 'hollyche he fourmede'; line 801b reads 'clerlye in trewthe'; 802b reads 'this is the holy beleue'; line 804b: 'this is fully the beleue'; 814: 'withouten any doute' and 816: 'hold this in thy mynde'.

162 Anne Hudson notes that Wyclif's objection to the 'private religions' was to their

form of discourse is the words which God himself inspires. William Thorpe, in the account of his investigation before Archbishop Arundel, cites exactly the same text at the point where Arundel bids a clerk read a homily of Chrysostom from a 'rolle' and asks Thorpe how he understood the statement that 'it is synne to swere wel':

> And certis I was sum deele agast to answere herto, for I hadde not bisyed me to stodie aboute þe witt þerof. But, liftynge vp my mynde to God, I preied him of grace. And anoon I þouȝte how Crist seide to hise disciplis 'Whanne for my name þe schulen be brouȝt before iugis, I shal ȝeue to ȝou mouþ and wisedom, þat alle ȝoure aduersaries schulen not aȝenseie'. (76/1706-10)

As in *Crede*, the phrase 'bisyed to stodie about þe witt þerof', contrasts to the language which is inspired by the Holy Spirit. It is this God-inspired speech that is the 'full' language endorsed by *Crede*. Apart from one line which praises the founding ideals of St Francis (511), it is only the teaching of the bible and the teaching of Peres, the exemplar of apostolic eloquence, which is afforded the status of 'fullness'. Such 'full' language is equivalent to 'fully the beleue' which Peres preaches in his recitation of the creed, and, as the next chapter will explore in more detail, it is a plenitude available only to a Wycliffite account of the truth.[163]

Peres' language lays claim to apostolic eloquence as a result of his charitable living. The first verb that he pronounces in the poem is 'lene'

---

absence of 'grounding' in the gospels, a complaint which is echoed in Latin Lollard sermons, which distinguish between 'discipulos fundatos in euangelica ueritate' and those 'qui magnificant suas tradiciones et filios suos. . .supra ueritates scripture sacre' (MS Bodley Laud Misc.200 f.50), quoted in Hudson (1988), p.349. In *Jack Upland*, the friar is asked: 'whi preche ȝe fals fablis of freris and feined myraclys, and leuen þe gospel þat Crist bade preche & is moost holsum lore to bodi & to soule, and so also oure bileue bi whiche oonli we moste be saued? Frere, whi hate ȝe þat þe gospel schulde be prechid to þe trewe vndirstondinge of Crist? & ȝe ben more holden þerto þan to alle þe rulis þat euer ȝoure patroun made, & ȝe winnen more wiþ "In principio" þan Crist & hise apostlis & alle þe seintis of heuene' (p.64/233-42).

[163] The Wycliffite text, *On the Sufficiency of Holy Scripture*, makes a distinction between three kinds of Holy Writ in order to show the difference between the eternal fulness of the meaning of the Gospel, and its physical manifestation in the world: 'On the firste manere Crist him silf is clepid in the gospel holy wryt, whanne he seiþ þat þe writynge may noȝt be fordon þat þe Fadir haþ halwid and sent into the world. On the secounde manere holy wryt is clepid truþis þat ben conteyned and signyfied bi comyn biblis, and þes truþis may noȝt faile. On þe þridde maner holy wryt is clepid bookis þat ben writen and maad of enk and parchemyn. And þis speche is nouȝt so propre as the first and the secunde. But we taken of bileue þat þe secunde writ, of truþis writen in the book of lyf, is holy wryt, and God seiþ it, and þis we knowen by bileue. And as oure siȝt make us certyn of þat þing þat we seen, so oure bileue makiþ us certyn þat þes trewþis ben holy wryt. ȝif holy wryt on the þridde manere be brent or cast in the see, holy writ on the secunde manere may noȝt faile, as Crist seiþ' (Arnold, III, 186-7). This is discussed by Minnis (1975), p.15. See also Wyclif,

(445) as he offers to relieve the narrator's distress. Moreover, his corporeal words are fully commensurate with his intramental intentions. When the narrator suggests that Peres's criticism of the friars stems from a desire to revenge some grievance against them, 'to schenden other [schamen] hem with thi sharpe speche,/And harmen holliche and her hous greuen', (677-8) Peres denies the accusation emphatically: 'I praie the,' quath Peres, 'put that out of thy mynde./ Certen for sowle hele y saie the this wordes' (679-80).

Peres defends his intention. Unlike the friars, he is not concerned to harm, backbite, to slander or to speak fraudulently.[164] He speaks 'only for sowle hele'. Moreover, it is to the intention of spiritual health that Peres appeals at the end of the poem. I have already observed that the voice of the poem becomes monologic at this point, as Peres expresses his wishes that the friars will:

> . . .prechen in parfite lijf and no pride vsen.
> But all that euer I haue seyd soth it me semeth,
> And all that euer I haue writen is soth, as I trowe,
> And for amending of thise men is most that I write;
> God wold hy wolden ben war and werchen the better!   (835-9)

The overt intention of the writing is correction, and it is on this basis that its truth is asserted. While Peres asserts the full, intramental truth of his language, he concedes that full authority rests not with his own words and will but with those of God. Explicitly Peres disavows the pretences to 'maistry' for which he has so roundly castigated the friars, and concludes with a prayer:

> But, for y am a lewed man paraunter y mighte
> Passen par auenture and in som poynt erren,
> Y will nought this matere maistrely auowen;
> But yif ich haue myssaid mercy ich aske,
> And praie all maner men this matere amende,
> Iche a word by him-self and all, yif it nedeth.
> God of his grete myghte and his good grace
> Saue all freres that faithfully lybben,
> And alle tho that ben fals fayre hem amende,
> And yiue hem wijt and good will swiche dedes to werche
> That thei maie wy[nn]en the lif that euer schal lesten! AMEN.
>   (840-50)[165]

De veritate Sacrae Scripturae, I 22/16; 228/5; 283/3 and *Trialogus*, 64/14; 239/3 and *EWS* I 94/19 and 123/18 (I am indebted to Anne Hudson for these latter references).

[164] This contrasts to the narrator's observation about the speech of the Franciscan:'Here semeth litel trewthe:/First to blamen his brother and bacbyten him foule' (138-9).

[165] The reference to 'matere' suggests a distinction between intention or purpose, and the 'materia' of the work.

Crede advocates a model of language in which persuasive rhetoric is matched by the sanctity of living, and where the physical language and intramental perception and intention are congruent.

In *Crede,* and in the other poems of the *Piers* tradition, I hope to have shown that what at first sight appears an incompatibility between the appeal to a monosemic 'sothe' on the one hand, and the polysemy and performativeness of the poetic texture of the poems on the other, can be reconciled by appeal to a distinction between physical and intramental language which is found in various guises in a number of closely contemporary texts. Within such a framework, polysemy can function as the verbal expression of an intended truth. The poems' appeals to a stable, secular hierarchy[166] can be preserved intact from the linguistic anarchy that is threatened by the pun in particular, and the instability of the linguistic sign in general. Moreover, their mission to speak out unequivocally with the truth is not compromised by their perpetuation of the playful verbal texture of *Piers Plowman*. In their discussion of linguistic issues, and interrogation of semantic resources, they can be seen to perpetuate the seriousness of wordplay in *Piers Plowman*. They reveal truth by suggestive verbal connections, and expose the 'unleal' use of words though exploring, with 'pure' intent, the fraudulent use of plural sense.

As a rider to these conclusions, I should like to stress that the readings offered above are but one way of approaching the textual dynamics of the poems. Throughout, I have chosen to refer to declared narrative, rather than authorial, intentions in order to avoid an appeal to authorial intention which might suggest closure to other available interpretations.[167] Read through a different interpretative grid, it is comparatively straightforward to deconstruct the poems' avowed narratorial intention. My first four examples from the poems suggested ways in which the performativeness or polysemy of the poems gave rise to readings or senses which were incompatible with, or contrary to, some of the declared allegiances or standpoints of the poems.

Examples from the poems could be multiplied, and I shall not add to them here, except to note, in addition to my first four examples, that in the cases of *Mum* and *Crede* such deconstruction is afforded rich opportunity. It is, in both poems, a particular source of potential

---

[166] See Chapter Two, pp.23-27. This is discussed more fully in Chapter Five.
[167] I am influenced here by W.K. Wimsatt and Monroe C. Beardsley, 'The Intentional Fallacy' (first published 1946 and reprinted in 1949 in *The Verbal Icon* (Kentucky, 1954), pp.3-18; Roland Barthes, 'The Death of the Author', see Chapter 1, n.82 and Michel Foucault, 'What is an author?' in *Textual Strategies*, ed. J. Harari (London, 1979), pp.141-60.

collapse that the same terms license both speaking well and speaking badly. In *Crede*, 'full' is used both positively to describe apostolic 'graith', and negatively to denote the fraudulent antics of the friars. In *Mum*, 'fablen' is used positively to denote speaking the truth, and negatively, to mean false speech.[168] An analysis of these poems along the lines of Derrida's treatment of 'potion' in Plato, would shatter into tiny shards their appeals to monosemic narrative intention.[169]

To my mind, however, this would be an inappropriate model through which to read poems that so obviously address themselves to the current state of affairs in the real world. While, as I argued in the previous chapter, all of the poems express misgivings about the adequacy of institutional discourses, these are not the sum of language, but limited modes of expression. In contrast to *The House of Fame* where the indissolubility of the truth and the lie is framed within an investigation of the lack of authority in the world of literature, the poems of the *Piers* tradition mobilise what seem often over-kinetic linguistic resources to address questions of authority in the real world of secular politics and the church. It is with this in mind that it seems to me appropriate to attempt to knit up their 'signes' with their 'sothe'; to honour the social significance of their declared narrative intentions rather than consigning them to the self-reflexive swirl of a fictional house of twigs.

---

168 'Fable' and its derivatives are used to denote speaking truthfully at 41, 140, 145, and 1133; and to speak fraudulently at 264, 1203 and 1395.
169 In 'Plato's Pharmacy' Derrida observes that it is unclear what Plato is attempting when he writes down the words of the dead Socrates in order to attack writing. The intention is deconstructed by the fact that one meaning of 'pharmakon' in Greek is 'poison' and the other is 'medicine'. Is Plato trying to poison Socrates, or revive his authority? See *Dissemination*, trans. Barbara Johnson (Chicago, 1981), pp.95-119.

4

'Signes of the times': Contesting Sothe

'We knowen wel, ser, þat neiþer þe ne ony oþer bischop of þis
lond wol graunte to vs ony suche lettre of licence, but we
schulden oblischen vs to þou and to oþer bischopis bi vnleeful
ooþis, for to not passe þe bondis or termes which ӡe ser, and oþer
bischopis wolen lymyten to vs. And siþen in þese maters ӡoure
termes ben sumtyme to straite and sumtyme to large, we dur not
obleschen vs to ben þus bounden to ӡou for to kepe þe termes
which ӡe wolden lymyte to vs. . .'[1]

So runs William Thorpe's spirited riposte to Archbishop Arundel's
accusation that he is a 'lewed ydeot' for presuming to preach
without an official licence. Thorpe's complaint that ecclesiastical
authority limits preaching and teaching within 'bondis and termes' was
probably written in 1407.[2] By this date, prescriptions on what could, or
could not be said, within the terms of ecclesiastical authority were tight;
and with the eventual publication in 1409 of Arundel's *Constitutions*,
(drafted in 1407), they were to become even tighter.[3]

Even before it attempted to counter the subversive teachings of John
Wyclif, ecclesiastical discourse had placed 'termes and bondes' on those
who could speak and what they could discuss.[4] In May 1382, the

---

[1] *The Testimony of William Thorpe*, 46/753-60.

[2] For discussion of the date of the text, see p.lii. Within the text Thorpe dates the
conversation the 7th August 1407 (lines 166-69) and Hudson notes that there is nothing
that appears to refer to events post 1407, such as the publication of Arundel's *Constitutions*
in 1409, the presentation of the Lollard Disendowment Bill in 1410 or the Oldcastle rising
of 1413/14.

[3] *Conciliae Magnae Britanniae et Hiberniae*, ed. D. Wilkins (London, 1737), III 314-9.

[4] The restrictions on those entitled to preach, and the limitations to certain dioceses are
discussed by Alastair Minnis in 'Chaucer's Pardoner and the Office of Preacher', in
Intellectuals and Writers in Fourteenth Century Europe, edd. P. Boitani and A. Torti
(Cambridge, 1986), 88-119. Women were excluded from public teaching, monks and
layfolk could preach only with the special authority of the bishop. Minnis shows how the
Pardoner abuses his 'patente' by claiming falsely that it gives him the authority to preach.

Council of London condemned ten points drawn from Wyclif's teachings as heretical, and fourteen as erroneous. The condemnation of Wyclif's teaching that at the Eucharist material bread remained after transubstantiation limited (to use Thorpe's language) what could subsequently be discussed on the matter, and made the topic itself a dangerous site of enquiry. The tenth conclusion, which condemned as heretical the assertion that it is contrary to Holy Scripture for churchmen to have temporal possessions, rendered discussion which criticised the temporal wealth of the clergy potentially dangerous. The limitations imposed by the condemnations are both 'straite' in that they state categorically what must not be said, and also 'large' because the suppression of a particular opinion on a topic imperiled the safety of discussing the topic at all. At what point, for instance, can criticism of the abuses and excesses of the private religions be interpreted as concordant with the condemnation of the view that if anyone enters any private religious order he becomes more unable and unsuitable for the observance of God's mandates?[5]

The terms of the 1401 statute *De Haeretico Comburendo*, which made provision for the burning of heretics, created even stricter controls on what could be preached and written.[6] The introduction to the terms of the statute expressly draws attention to the fact that Wycliffites usurp the office of preaching, hold unlawful confederacies, conventicles and schools, and *make and write books* (emphasis mine). In order to check this attack on institutional authority, the statute decreed that no one could preach without the licence of the diocesan except the parish priest in his own parish and that no could express views, orally or in writing, contrary to the catholic faith. Anyone possessing books which promulgated Wycliffite ideas had to submit them to their diocesan within forty days of the promulgation of the statute.

These prohibitions are entirely consonant with Foucault's description of institutions and the discourses they generate; that they entitle certain

---

[5] From his denunciation of the 'sect' in *Confessio*, Prol. 349, Gower was no friend of the Lollards. *Vox Clamantis*, apart from Book I, was written before 1381, and hence before the Blackfriars Council, but some of the anti-clerical comment is close in temper to Wycliffite views which were condemned. In Book IV, Gower stresses that monastic orders are good in themselves but that there are many monks who betray the sancitity of their original foundation (IV 1-6). However, in his first criticism he shows how monasteries are ideal places to promote sensual pleasures (IV 25-38). Despite his caveats, this, and other comments on both the monks and friars could reasonably be interpreted as suggesting that these orders corrupt those who enter them. While the register of Bishop Thomas Polton of Worcester (1426-33) post-dates more stringent anti-Wycliffite legislation, the list of questions put to suspected Lollards includes: 'an aliquis qui ingreditur religionem priuatam qualemcumque, tam possessionatorum quam mendicancium, reddatur habilior et apcior ad obseruanciam mandatorum Dei', text quoted from Hudson (1985), p.134.

[6] *Statutes of the Realm* II 125-8; *Rot.Parl.* III 466-7.

speakers only, who must speak from legitimate sites, according to certain programmes of information.[7] Arundel's *Constitutions* limited speakers, sites and programmes even more rigorously than the 1401 statute. No one was to preach without a licence except a person privileged in law, and anyone suspended for preaching heresies or errors could not preach again until he had purged himself. If anyone preached in any church, graveyard or other place without such a licence the place would lie under an interdict. Preachers were prevented from condemning the failings of the clergy to an audience which comprised both lay and clergy. If any of the laity were present, criticism of clerical failings could not be undertaken and the preacher had to confine himself to criticising the offences of the laity.

The fourth constitution stated that discussion of the sacrament of the altar was confined to what had been resolved by Mother Holy Church, and the fifth, that masters teaching in arts of grammar were not to meddle with matters of the catholic faith, or expound holy scriptures, except the meaning of the text as had previously been the case. (By Thorpe's definition a very 'large' term indeed). The sixth constitution stipulated that no book or tract composed by John Wyclif or anyone else in his time was to be read, or taught anywhere without prior examination from twelve persons of authority from Oxford and Cambridge selected by the Archbishop. The seventh constitution prohibited the written translation of any text of Holy Scripture into English on a person's own authority, and the eighth stated that no one should assert anything contrary to the catholic faith beyond the necessary teaching of his faculty, in schools or outside.

So completely was the institution of the church unprepared to sanction any discordant voices within its terms, that alternative views were condemned to fall entirely outside what was possible in ecclesiastical discourse. Excommunication places a person outside the communications considered legitimate by Holy Church, including all the sacraments, and condemns them to negative semantic space.[8] The terms of the 1401 statute made provision for burning those bodies which were the sites of debate. Even before 1401 books which tendered views contrary to the Catholic faith, or which debated tendentious issues, were confiscated, and according to the writer of the *Opus Arduum*, burnt and destroyed.[9] In 1410 Wycliffite writings

---

[7] See Chapter Two, n.116.
[8] cf. discussion on the friars in *Crede*, 538-43 on pp.88-89.
[9] The relevant passage is quoted in Anne Hudson, 'A Neglected Wycliffite Text', (1985), p.53: '. . .per generalem mandatum prelatorum ad comburendum, destruendum et condemnandum omnes libros, scilicet omelias ewangeliorum et epistolarum in lingwa

were burnt at Carfax in Oxford in the presence of the chancellor of the university.[10]

These ecclesiastical provisions create a paradigm for the discourse appropriate to the true teaching of holy church.[11] Simultaneously, however, they categorize a 'reverse' discourse – namely that constituted by the beliefs and teachings of the Wycliffites.[12] The reverse discourse of Wycliffism is held in a kind of symmetry with the discursive practices of the institutionalised church. It is constituted by a resistance to the prevailing ideology that it seeks to challenge, on the same terms and on the same terrain.[13] Reverse discourse turns the same words, and often the same arguments, of the institutionalised discourse into a challenge.[14]

This conception of competing, or antagonistic, discourses is discussed by Pecheux, who argued that meaning exists antagonistically: it comes from positions in struggle so that 'words change their meanings according to the positions held by those who use them'.[15] Macdonnell has applied this theory to the writings produced in England between 1790 and 1830, in which the established church was opposed both by atheists and dissenting organisations. Her comments provide an interesting parallel to the relationship of institutionalised and Wycliffite discourse between 1382 and 1409. She discusses the words 'hymn' and 'salvation' and notes that in their dissenting contexts, the words 'hymn' and 'salvation' were brought down to earth and could take their meanings from atheist and humanistic positions. Words became a weapon of struggle. What might count as a 'hymn' became an issue of some importance'.[16]

This discussion of antagonistic discourses, and the struggle over the meanings of words can be very fruitfully applied to the competition

materna conscriptos. . .'. Hudson notes Knighton's account of the confiscation of books from William Smith of Leicester, II 313 (p.53, n.46).

[10] This is noted in Anne Hudson, 'Contributions to a History of Wycliffite Writings' (1985), p.3, drawing evidence from the account in Gascoigne, *Loci et Libro Veritatum*, ed, J.E. Thorold Rogers (Oxford, 1881), p.116.

[11] This point is based on the discussion in Kress, p.15. He shows how political movements generate texts which constitute paradigms of the discourse they want to promote. In forming such a discourse, the political movement can compete for power, and from a position of solidarity within the ranks.

[12] The term 'reverse' discourse is adopted from Foucault, who takes as his example the nineteenth century institutionalised investigation of homosexuality. This made possible the formation of a 'reverse' discourse, that of homosexuality, which was thus enabled to speak in its own behalf; see *The History of Sexuality: Volume 1: An Introduction* (1976) trans. Robert Hurley (Harmondsworth, 1979), p.101

[13] As discussed by Diane Macdonnell, *Theories of Discourse: An Introduction* (Oxford, 1986), p.117.

[14] Foucault, *The History of Sexuality*, p.101.

[15] Michel Pecheux, *Language, Semantics and Ideology: Stating the Obvious* (1975), trans. H. Nagpal, (London, 1982), pp.111-12.

[16] Macdonnell, p.24. See further, pp.24-27 and pp.45-8.

between the institutionalised church and Wycliffism over the control of meaning. Key tenets of Wycliffite thought struck at the heart of institutionalised control over discursive positions and practices. The concern that the bible be translated into English and made available to all[17] and the view that one need not necessarily be ordained priest by holy church in order to preach[18] shattered the clerical stranglehold on religious language. The definition of true holy church as the congregation of the faithful predestined for salvation[19] seriously weakened the importance of the material church on earth as a site for authorised meanings. And the view that oral confession to a priest was unnecessary for true contrition de-stabilised and de-hierarchised one of the most important sacramental power structures of the church.[20] In face of these threats, the measures passed between 1382 to 1409 attempted to reconstitute ecclesiastical discourse as the only authoritative discourse and, within that, to regulate the meanings that could be expressed within certain sites of discussion.[21] Wycliffite discourse, therefore, was locked into an antagonistic struggle with the words and meanings of holy church. Often, the same words were used with contrary meanings depending on the discursive position from which they were used.

It is from within this framework that I should like to approach the existence of a Wycliffite sect vocabulary in two poems of the *Piers* tradition, namely *Crede* and *Mum*. In her paper on 'A Lollard Sect Vocabulary' originally published in 1983, Anne Hudson drew attention to certain words and phrases used densely and distinctively in Wycliffite texts.[22] Her starting point was the recurrent accusation by critics hostile to the Lollards between 1384 and 1525 that they used a distinctive language. Particularly important was the evidence of Henry Knighton, who in his chronicle wrote scathingly, but informedly, about important aspects of Wycliffism. Alongside the accusation that in public places the

---

[17] See *Biblical Translation*, in *SEWW*, pp.107-9.

[18] 'Þat þer schulde be bot oo degree aloone of prestehod in þe chirche of God, and euery good man is a prest and haþ power to preche þe worde of God', from *Sixteen points on which bishops accuse Lollards*, *SEWW*, 19/16-18.

[19] 'But, howeuere we speken in diuerse names or licknessis of þis holi chirche, þei techen nouȝt ellis but þis oo name, þat is to seie, "þe congregacioun, or gedering-togidir of feiþful soulis þat lastingli kepen feiþ and trouþe, in word and dede, to God and to man, and reisen her lijf in siker hope of mercy and grace and blisse at her ende, and ouercoueren, or hillen, þis bilding in perfite charite that shal not faile in wele ne in woo' ', *The Nature of the Church*, *SEWW*, 116/21-7.

[20] *The Twelve Conclusions of the Lollards* states that oral confession to a priest is a 'feynid power of absoliciun' which 'enhaunsith prestis pride', *SEWW*, p.27/115-6.

[21] This point derives from the discussion in Kress, p.15 on the consolidation of paradigmatic discourses in the maintenance of power structures.

[22] This is reprinted in Hudson (1985), pp.165-80. My present chapter is substantially indebted to this paper.

Lollards barked like dogs with unwearying voices, is that, astonishingly, they adopted one mode of speech and doctrine: 'conformitate unius loquelae'.[23]

In examining the substance of this, and other remarks by Knighton, Hudson located a sample group of words and phrases consistently used in Lollard texts. The sample included the following: 'trewe men'; 'knowun men'; 'blabber'; 'cautel'; 'clowtyd'; 'colour' (sb. and vb.); 'contrary' (vb); 'covent'; 'found' (sb. and vb); 'gab' and 'gabbyng'; 'glose' (sb. and vb.); 'ground' (sb. and vb.); 'impugn'; 'jape' (sb. and vb.); 'mannis lawe'; 'Goddis lawe'; 'obedience'; 'order'; 'rule', and interestingly, 'reverse'.[24]

What interests me about 'reverse', and indeed about the words that I have quoted from Hudson's sample, is that they are actively constituted in difference, and a difference that is antagonistic. A componential analysis of these words would show that in every case their meaning is substantially constituted by their antonym.[25] 'Trewe' has significance only with the predication of the existence of 'false'; and 'false' is used densely in Wycliffite texts to denote beliefs and practices contrary to Lollard views.[26] 'Covent' signifies in the context of non-exclusive gatherings; 'rule' calls up anarchy, and 'ground' what is 'ungrounded'. 'Ground' is found frequently in Wycliffite texts prefixed by the negative particle 'un'.[27] 'Goddis lawe and 'mannis lawe' stand in opposition as a pair, and the frequency of words such as 'contrary' shows how Wycliffite discourse is the 'reverse' discourse of ecclesiastical authority. What links all these terms is that they are factive and counter-factive.[28]

In discussing the density of these terms, Hudson warned of the dangers of assuming Wycliffite allegiances in texts which used these words because they could equally be found in orthodox texts, though not always in the same contexts.[29] It is, I think, because Wycliffite discourse is an

---

[23] Knighton II 186-7.
[24] This list is drawn from examples on pp.178-9.
[25] My point is based on the discussion of componential analysis in Leech, *Semantics*, pp.89-109.
[26] These words all form binary, as distinct from multiple, taxonomic oppositions. Taxonomic oppositions are discussed by Leech, pp.99-109. He uses the examples of 'dead' and 'alive' to discuss binary taxonomy, p.99.
[27] e.g. 'þei clouten falsehed to þe trouþe wiþ miche vngroundid mater', *SEWW*, p.118/108; cf. Matthew, p.337.
[28] I have adapted these terms from the discussion of verbs in G. Leech and M. Short, *Style in Fiction* (London, 1981), p.81. Factives presuppose the truth of what is being asserted; counter-factives presuppose the negation of what is asserted. In discussing sect vocabulary, Hudson raises the question of whether it represents anything more than the usual sectarian tendency to use words of approbation for themselves and for the views they approve, whilst using terms of reproach for their opponents, p.167.
[29] Hudson (1985), p.173. From my analysis of some items of this sect vocabulary in

antagonistic discourse, locked into the struggle of meanings with the institutionalised church, that so many of these words and phrases can be traced in orthodox texts, especially those which attempt to counter Lollard views. The terms of debate are shared and contested.[30]

To return to the 1401 Statute *De Haeretico Comburendo*, we might note that the Lollards are accused of preaching against 'God's law' under 'the colour of dissembled holiness'. They teach heretical opinions 'contrary' to the blessed determinations of holy church and they make 'unlawful' conventicles and confederacies.[31] Blamires notes that in his *Repressor* Pecock uses the vocabulary of his Lollard opponents against them rather than introducing terminology of his own.[32] This is not uncommon. In Hoccleve's poem on the Oldcastle uprising of 1413,[33] many items of sectarian vocabulary are used. Hoccleve writes out of difference in his comment that the Lollards have made a 'fair permutacion/Fro Crystes lore to feendly doctryne' (17) and concludes a stanza grounded in antitheses by saying that Oldcastle has gone 'fro light of trouthe vn-to dirke falsnesse'. (24). Other Wycliffite vocabulary turned on its head includes 'byleeue' (14);[34] 'obei' (60; 62; 114; 118; 133); 'ordeyned' (119); 'fals' and derivatives (279; 282; 327; 339 and 367); 'coloured' (281); and 'ground' (299). The whole poem is a neat example of reversing reverse discourse. It abounds in antitheses which take a number of rhetorical forms. In a resounding chiasmus, Hoccleve writes: 'the feend is your cheef and oure heed is god' (468).

Chaucer, Gower and *Dives and Pauper*, it is clear that there is neither comparable density to the usage in Lollard texts, and that the terms are not part of a binary taxonomy. Space prevents examining these in context or providing references for all the examples. To take as representative, 'ground' and 'found'; see Chaucer, *I Pars*, 605-10; *RR*, 5207; (ground) and 'founde': *I Pars*, 880-5; *E.Cl*, 61; *D.Summ*, 2103; *Dives and Pauper*, I 173/35/42; 174/50/ 68; 251/56; II 121/8/10; 138/28; p.195/82 ('ground'). In my reading of *Dives* I did not locate any examples of 'founde' in the sense of 'established'. Interestingly, on I 340, three examples of 'groundyd in Goddys lawe': /7/9/11/ are omitted in G in the context of discussing clerical and secular obedience. The same manuscript omits 'be fals feynyng' in the discussion of apparently contradictory bible passages, II 216/23. The same manuscript's omission of the material in square brackets in the following: 'Godis lawe is forȝetyn and defendyd þat men schul nout connyn it [ne han it in her moder tunge], II 64/ 69, suggests that these omissions may reflect recognition of a typically Lollard collocation.

[30] Hudson notes that the language of refutation may adopt the colours of the opponent to gain its end, p.173.

[31] *Statutes of the Realm*, II 126: 'contra legem divinam. . .sub simulate sanctitatis colore. . .ecclesie sacrosance contrarias'.

[32] *Repressor*, p.118; A. Blamires, 'The Wife of Bath and Lollardy', *Medium Aevum*, 58 (1989), 224-42, p.228.

[33] Thomas Hoccleve, *To Sir John Oldcastle* in *The Minor Poems*, ed. F.J. Furnivall and I. Gollancz, revd. J. Mitchell and A.I. Doyle (EETS ES 61, 73 1970), 8-24.

[34] This is a very common word in Wycliffite texts, standing either on its own or prefixed by true or false, see e.g. *EWS*, II 86/110; 135/8; 159/155; 328/6-7; 330/51; Cigman, 1.306; 2.676; 3.152; Matthew, p.19; 159; 207.

Examples of this kind of writing could be multiplied. Among the more interesting are the Latin verses preserved in MS Cotton Vespasian D ix fol 51a printed by Thomas Wright in his *Political Poems and Songs*. The first verse is written 'contra praelatos ecclesiae' and the second 'contra eosdem Lollardos'. The terms used in the first are picked up in the second and reversed so that, for instance, the church prelates who are 'idola causa dolorum' become the Lollards' 'errores' which are 'in mundo causa dolorum'. The 'ingrati Giesitae Simone nati' become 'ingrati maledicti, daemone nati'. The first verse concludes by setting those who have temporal power, symbolised by the sword, against the prelates, and the second concludes by juxtaposing the defenders of the faith, symbolised by fire, against the Lollards.[35] The verses constitute a symmetry of reverse discourses.

There are a number of Lollard and orthodox texts which exist in a similar symmetry. *The Twelve Conclusions of the Lollards*, which were affixed to the doors of Westminster Hall during the session of Parliament in 1395, owe their survival to the activities of their opponents. There is a Latin version preserved in *Fasciculi Zizanorum*, and Roger Dymmok's *Liber contra duodecim errores et hereses Lollardorum*, which was written expressly to confute the *Conclusions*, preserves versions of them in both Latin and English.[36] *Jack Upland* was answered by *Friar Daw's Reply*, which re-uses not only the questions, but also Lollard vocabulary against itself.[37] *Daw's Reply* was itself answered by *Upland's Rejoinder*. A Latin version of the questions in *Jack Upland* was also answered by William Woodford's *Responsiones ad Quaestiones LXV*.[38]

A number of Lollard texts are grounded on the principle of reversing the discourse of Holy Church. The *Sixteen Points on which the Bishops accuse Lollards* lists sixteen articles which bishops use as the basis for accusing people of Lollardy and then proceeds to defend them.[39] The

[35] 'Qui reges estis, populis quicunque praeestis,/Qualiter his gestis gladios prohibere potestis' and 'Qui pugiles estis fidei populisque praeestis,/Non horum gestis ignes prohibere potestis', Wright, II. 128.

[36] The *Conclusions* are printed in *SEWW*, pp.24-29 and their preservation in *Fasc.Ziz* and Dymmok is noted on p.150.

[37] *Jack Upland, Friar Daw's Reply and Upland's Rejoinder*, ed. P.L. Heyworth, (London, 1968). Examples of reverse sect vocabulary include 'foundid' (85; 116; 274; 447) 'grounded' (15; 264; 282; 287; 'feyne' (84; 527; 772). At 578 Daw says: 'Alas Iak, for shame, whi art ʒou so fals/Forto reuerse þi silf in þin owne sawes'.

[38] The text is preserved in MS Bodley 703, see Hudson (1988), p.146 and printed by E. Doyle, in 'Bibliographical Notes on William Woodford OFM', *Franciscan Studies*, 43 (1983), 23-187, pp.120-87.

[39] The text is printed in *SEWW*, pp.19-24. Hudson notes that there is a parallel for these model answers in Arnold, III 455-96 and wonders whether they may have been intended for use in Lollard schools, p.145. In *Premature Reformation*, Hudson discusses the device of dialogue in Wycliffite texts, especially those which set up straw men which are knocked down by the superior strength of Lollard argument, pp.222-4.

examination of Walter Brut and his written defence of the charges against him show how the ecclesiastical examination of suspected Lollards proceeded by debating whether certain propositions were true or false. At the end of the examination there is a list of conclusions drawn from Brut's written defence which are condemned either as erroneous or heretical. Many of these conclusions repeat those of the 1382 Blackfriars Council. In a number of cases, the condemnation concludes with phraseology which shows how Brut's opinions reverse the discourse of Holy Church: 'dicere oppositum est erroneum. . .cuius contrarium affirmare est her-eticum. . .asserere oppositum est hereticum'.[40]

The Testimony of William Thorpe uses this reverse discourse rather ingeniously. The questions and accusations put by Arundel against him are used as the basis for displaying the central tenets of Lollardy in Thorpe's replies.[41] At the end of the testimony Thorpe describes the interview in words which fully draw attention to the way in which the opposing discourses have been schematically juxtaposed: 'for as a tree leyde vpon anoþer tree ouerthwert on crosse wyse, so weren þe Archebischop and hise þree clerkis alwei contrarie to me and I to hem' (2245-7). This is true both of the way that Thorpe's replies reverse the content of Arundel's accusations and questions, and also of the way that the archbishop's recourse to documents to authorize his points is answered by Thorpe not with reference to material books in his hand, but with his knowledge of Holy Writ and learned teachers thereon, and in one case, through apparent inspiration of the Holy Spirit.[42] It is by no means the case that Thorpe occupies the subservient position in the interrogation. Contrary to the usual subject positions which are encoded in interview discourse,[43] Thorpe often gets the upper hand, most memorably perhaps in his scriptural outwitting of Arundel in what comes across as a hapless attempt on the part of the Archbishop to justify the playing of bagpipes on pilgrimage (1332-42). Towards the end of the account Thorpe takes over the position of interrogator and forces Arundel to answer for his views. He also quotes texts in Latin and requires Arundel to declare them openly in English.[44]

[40] Quoted from the fourth, p.361; twentieth, and twenty second conclusions, p.363.
[41] Hudson notes, p.lv, that in the early trials of William Swinderby and Walter Brut, the suspect was given the opportunity to set out his arguments in full; but that this was done by inviting them to set down their ideas in writing, and these were answered by a number of orthodox texts.
[42] For Arundel's use of written documents, see lines 622-24; 928; 1697-1700. Thorpe's recourse to inspiration of the Holy Spirit is at 1705-11, and cf. my earlier discussion, pp.90-91 above.
[43] For an analysis of the characteristics of this, see N. Fairclough, *Language and Power* (London, 1989), pp.18-19 and pp.43-49.
[44] See p.55 and pp.86-7.

This text is a clear example of the contest over words and how they change their meanings according to the position from which they are used. Sectarian vocabulary is bounced back and forth between the disputants. For example, in the contest over tithes, Thorpe remarks that many priests 'contrarien' the teaching of St Paul. In a paraphrase of Acts 20: 28-35, he states that, whatever the dignity or 'ordre' of a priest, if he does not follow Christ and his apostles in 'trewe prechinge of Goddis word', he is a priest only in name (1460-70). Arundel replies:

> Certis, þis lore contrarieþ pleynli þe ordynaunce of holy fadris, whiche haue ordeyned, grauntid and licencide prestis to ben in dyuerse degrees and statis to lyue bi tiþis and offryngis of þe peple. (1472-75)

The definitions of words and phrases are contested. For example, Arundel asks Thorpe what he calls 'holi chirche' to which Thorpe replies 'Crist and his seintis'. Arundel agrees that this defines holy church in heaven but asks what is holy church on earth. Thorpe's reply gives back the standard Lollard teaching on the congregation of the faithful in heaven, who are 'sadli groundid vpon þe corner-stoon Crist'. Arundel remarks to his clerks that Thorpe's heart is 'traueilid wiþ þe deuel', which emboldens him in his 'erroures and eresies' (pp.51-2). Never the twain shall meet!

A very similar kind of discursive contest operates in both *Crede* and *Mum*. What I shall argue in the rest of this chapter is that both of these texts are organised on narrative principles of discursive competition. These correspond to ecclesiastical and Lollard positions, and reflect the wider context of reverse discourses which I have outlined above. In both poems sectarian vocabulary marks the areas of debate and words are used as weapons in a contest of meanings. As part of my discussion, and to provide a focus for my illustrative examples, I shall show that when quotations, or echoes of collocations from *Piers Plowman* are used in *Crede* and *Mum*, in this new ecclesiastical context, their political resonance is radically altered. This reflects the fact that the anti-Wycliffite measures passed since the writing of *Piers* circumscribed what could be said about Christian doctrine and church practices.

I have argued elsewhere that *Mum* contains a topical reference to Arundel's *Constitutions* and the later exemption of the friars from their terms. This conclusion is based on a reading of a criticism against the friars in lines 409-10: 'Whenne thay stirid a statute in strengthe of bilieue/That no preste shuld preche saue seely poure freres'.[45] The

---

[45] 'The Dates of *Richard the Redeless* and *Mum and the Sothsegger*', *N&Q*, 235 (1990), 270-5.

sentiment and position of these lines is consonant with the denunciations of Arundel's *Constitutions*, and the later exemption of the friars from their terms, which are found in works with demonstrable Lollard allegiances.[46] It is also consonant with the import of the narrative sequence at the end of the poem in which the narrator, at the beekeeper's request, takes out a bag of books and reads from their contents. A very important feature of this bag is that it had previously been confiscated by Mum and his confederates. It is not simply a result of alliterative expediency I think, that Mum is associated with mitres (1236), and that earlier in the poem he uses his mitre to menace the narrator: 'Mvm with his myter manachid me euer' (579). 'Manace' is used with some frequency in Thorpe's *Testimony* to describe Arundel's behaviour.[47]

In my view *Mum* actively comments on ecclesiastical persecution, both in the passages just quoted, and in the list of punishments which are cited as ready for those who are prepared to speak the truth:

> And yf a burne bolde hym to bable the sothe
> And [mynne] hym of mischief that misse-reule asketh,
> He may lose his life and laugh here no more,
> Or y-putte into prisone or y-pyned to deeth
> Or y-[brent] or y-shent or sum sorowe haue. (165-9)

Although line 169 reads 'blent', blinding was never a legal punishment, and the correction in the manuscript to 'brent' restores sense to the line. As David Lawton has noted, the list of punishments bears striking resemblance to the measures of *De Haeretico Comburendo*.[48] As we shall see from a passage to be discussed below, the poet was writing after this measure had been passed, and the reference to burning for speaking the truth would have had particular resonance after William Sawtre's death at Smithfield, even though his death technically preceded the terms of the statute.[49]

Further to this, a section on how it is fitting for priests to listen to the truth rings rather hollow after the narrator has been silenced by a mitred Mum, for doing exactly that:

---

[46] e.g. *Lanterne of Light*, 17/26; 100/1. The *Constitutions* are also criticised unambiguously in the sermons of MS Longleat 4 which were written by a friar; see A. Hudson and H.L. Spencer, 'Old Author, New Work: The Sermons of MS Longleat 4', *Medium Aevum*, 53 (1984), 220-38, p.222 and p.234, n.12.

[47] *Thorpe*, 413; 447; 658; 820; 1693; 2079 and 'manassing' 2194; 2200; 2224; 2228; 2241 and 2243; cf. usage in Matthew, pp.37; 63; 94; 99; 234; 417; 461.

[48] David Lawton, 'Lollardy and the *Piers Plowman Tradition*', *MLR*, 76 (1981), 780-93, p.788.

[49] In the absence of a statute providing for this punishment his death took the form of a royal edict which applied specifically and solely to his case, see Peter McNiven, *Heresy and Politics in the Reign of Henry IV: The Burning of John Badby* (Cambridge, 1987), p.88.

For prestz been not perillous but pacient of thaire werkes,
And eeke the plantz of pees and ful of pitie euer,
And chief of al charite y-chose a-fore other;
Forto fighte ne to flite hit falleth not to thaire ordre,
Ne to prece to no place there peril shuld be ynne.
That proueth wel by parlement, for prelatz shuld be voidid
Whenne any dome of deeth shal be do there,
Al for cause thaire conscience to kepe vn-y-wemmyd.
A man may saye thaym the sothe sonest of alle,
Withoute grucche other groyn, but gete many thankes.
Thay moste bowe for the beste, God forbede hit elles,
To shewe vs exemple of suffrance euer. (702-13)

This is not a situation that has been evidenced in the poem up to this
point. The parish priest has been shown to be clearly in league with
Mum (630), and in one of his ironically truthtelling speeches (placed just
before the narrator's paradigmatic example of how priests should
behave), Mum warns the narrator to keep clear of the clergy and not to
attempt to criticise them: 'And carpe no more of clergie but yf thou
cunne leepe,/For and thou come on thaire clouche, thou crepis not
thens' (698-9). Mum's words gain in gravity when we recall remarks
made by the narrator on the insufficiency of the clergy to provide an
answer to his question about the distribution of tithes:

Thay haue a memoire of Mvm among alle other;
Ys more in thaire mynde thenne martires of heuene
That token the deeth for trouthe of tirantz handes.
But here a querele or a question quyk mighte thou make:
Martires had more might and more mynde eeke,
And couthe more on clergie thenne cunne now a thousand.
But thereto I answere as I am lerid:
Thou, lewed laudate, litel witte has.
Hit was for no cunnyng ne clergie nother
That thay chosid the deeth, but for derne loue
And kindenes to oure creatour that creed vs alle,
And for pure trouthe that thay taught [euer].
Propter veritatem dimittam omnem familiaritatem etc
This made thaym martires more thanne ought elles,
For clercz were not knowe by thaire clothing that tyme. (630-643)

In this passage, the virtues of martyrs are contrasted with the vices of
the contemporary church, and in the continuation of the passage these
vices are catalogued in a long list.[50] The characteristics of those who have

---

[50] Lollard texts often encouraged martyrdom, e.g. *EWS*, I 625/68-9; Matthew, p.21/25ff;
452/17, Arnold, p.179/25ff, pp.184-5 and *Plowman's Tale*, 248 which states that although
Christ bade his priests not to slay others, they should not themselves be afraid to die.

been martyred are spelt out explicitly: they are dissociated from Mum (630); they suffered death at the hands of tyrants (632); they are exempted from the 'worldly workes' of the clergy (643ff) and above all, they suffered martyrdom not for 'cunnyng ne clergie' but for love of God and for the 'pure trouthe that thay taught euer' (641). 'Trouthe', as we have seen, is a term actively constituted in difference. It is used by orthodox writers to signify the teachings of Holy Church and by Lollards to describe the teachings of Wycliffism. What is interesting here is that these lines stress that the non-intellectual teaching of truth is the most important motivation for martyrdom. The focus recalls the primacy of this preaching of the truth in Lollard texts.[51] Moreover, in the opposition set up in this passage between the contemporary church and martyrs, 'trouthe' is less available for signification from an orthodox position. In its question and answer structure, the passage reflects the competition for the truth, but I would argue that the description of the early martyrs of the church is paradigmatic of Lollard martyrdom in the face of current ecclesiastical persecution: death at the hands of tyrants for speaking the truth.

This reading is strengthened by a comment made by the beekeeper in his speech on contemporary corruption. He says that 'Mvm wol be no martir while mytres been in sale' (1236). The wordplay of the line emphasises the incompatibility between contemporary simoniacal bishops and martyrdom. This antithesis between martyrs and the institutionalised church clarifies the contest in lines 630-43 and marks out 'trouthe' as a word used from a position sympathetic to Lollardy.

The fundamental narrative strategy in *Mum* is to contest the reverse discourses of truthtelling (Sothsegger) and silencing truth (Mum). While the ambit of *Mum* is wider than the discussion of ecclesiastical issues, it is interesting that the contemporary church is explicitly associated with a 'mumming' discourse, while the truthtelling discourse is entirely secular. The beekeeper in the poem turns out to be the sothsegger for whom the narrator has been searching. His is the highest voice of authority in the poem. It is he who bids the narrator open the bag of books which mitred Mum and his confederates had confiscated. And it is he who makes the opposition between martyrs and mitres.

Although he is a sage by virtue of his age and honest living, the beekeeper is a member of the third estate. Most of his speech is taken up with exposing secular corruption, but also, despite his social position,

---

[51] The emphasis on preaching 'pure trouthe' in line 641 is central to Wycliffite definitions of the priesthood, e.g. Matthew, pp.56-7, p.111/9ff, p.188/1; Arnold, p.130/16ff; p.145/9, p.202-3, *Lanterne*, p.55/10ff; *Jack Upland*, p.64/232ff.

he criticises 'the perillous poyntz of prelatz' (1134) to the narrator in what would be an infringement of the sixth of Arundel's *Constitutions*. Moreover, the book which he bids the narrator compile from the confiscated bag also contains criticisms of the contemporary church. In its narrative strategies, then, *Mum* contests the discourse of ecclesiastical silencing with the discourse of speaking truthfully about clerical corruption. While the contest of Mum and Sothsegger is wider than the competition between orthodoxy and Lollardy, it is certainly, as I shall argue in more depth, one of its vital components.

In his tending of a garden, the beekeeper bears some resemblances to the figure of Piers Plowman, who in B versions of *Piers* explains the Tree of Charity to Will.[52] In his refereeing of rival discourses of ecclesiastical discussion, however, he is a far more radical figure than Piers because of the date of *Mum*, and the fact that his discussion appears to contest Arundel's *Constitutions*. While in *Mum* the beekeeper contains only hints of the presentation of *Piers* at one particular point in the poem, in *Crede*, the figure of Piers is actively adopted and redrafted.

Indeed, one of the most striking parallels between *Piers* and *Crede* is that the sudden, and unannounced, entry of Peres Ploughman into the poem recalls the way that at the end of Passus V of *Piers*, Piers abruptly pokes his head into the poem from an adjoining field and immediately commands a position of unquestioned authority. While the wastrels disobey his command, the pilgrims act according to his words, and even the knight defers to his teaching (VI 55-6). We have seen earlier how in the Pardon tearing episode Piers contests the meaning of the words on the pardon with a figure of institutionalised religion.[53]

As in *Mum*, the reprise of the figure of Piers in *Crede* is more radical than the original presentation. There are a number of reasons for this, but once more date is crucial. *Crede* must have been written after the trial of Walter Brut in 1393 since lines 657-62 refer to it. We know with certainty then, unlike our knowledge of *Piers Plowman*, that it was written after the uprising of 1381. As we have seen, John Ball's letters link revolt with Piers the Plowman, and in *The Dieulacres Chronicle* 'Per Plowman' is listed as one of the leaders of the uprising.[54] Not only had the name Piers Plowman been linked to serious civil dissent, but the chroniclers linked John Ball and the uprising to the seditious teachings of John Wyclif.[55]

[52] This is altered in C versions as Liberium Arbitrium takes over the role of instructor.
[53] See above, pp.33-34.
[54] *Dieulacres Chronicle*, ed. M.V. Clark and V.H. Galbraith, *BJRL*, 14 (1930), 164-81, p.164.
[55] See Thomas Walsingham, *Historia Anglicana*, II 322-3; *Chronicon Henrici Knighton*, II 151, 170 and *Fasciculi Zizanorum*, pp.272-4.

In this context, Piers Plowman is a somewhat explosive name to give to a figure who commands the authority exemplified by Peres in *Crede*. It is because of this, perhaps, that Peres seems anxious to deplore the upward social mobility of the 'brol' of beggars.[56] In ecclesiastical terms, however, Peres is a very radical figure indeed. That he contests the meanings of the friars with his own authoritative meanings is not in itself heretical at this date. However, the principle of discursive competition on which the entire poem is founded[57] occupies a site of interrogation perilously close to the tenth conclusion of Wyclif's which the 1382 Council condemned as heretical. It is also close to five others condemned as erroneous.[58]

What is not orthodox, furthermore, is Peres' explicit support for Wyclif and Walter Brut. Unlike *Mum*, Wycliffite allegiances are openly declared in *Crede*. At line 528, Peres invokes the truthtelling discourse of Wyclif against the 'fals' and 'feyned' discourse of the friars:[59]

> Wytnesse on Wycliff that warned hem with trewth;
> For he in goodnesse of gost graythliche hem warned
> To wayuen her wik[e]dnesse and werkes of synne. (528-30)

Wyclif is associated with 'trewth' just as, later, Walter Brut is associated with 'sothe': 'for he seyde hem the sothe' (658). This truth, however, is not what the institutionalised discourse of holy church was prepared to hear and so it mobilised its discursive practices against the 'truthtellers' to silence them. It is noteworthy that Peres describes both Wyclif and Brut as truthtellers who are persecuted by the church. He states that Brut was persecuted by the friars and called 'an heretike' who 'yeuele byleueth' (660). While Peres considers Brut's teaching evidence of 'well dedes' (662), the church wished to excommunicate him (664-69). In Brut's written defence of the charges against him, there is considerable emphasis on the way that the church should take no part in warfare, or legal prosecution resulting in death or excommunication.[60] One of the charges against Brut was that he upheld Swinderby's proposition that no-one can excommunicate anyone unless they have been first excommunicated by God.[61] Amongst the condemned propositions

---

[56] See earlier discussion, pp.35-37.
[57] Christina Von Nolcken, '*Piers Plowman*, the Wycliffites and *Pierce the Ploughman's Crede*', YLS, 2 (1988), 71-102.
[58] The fifteenth, twentieth, twenty second, twenty third and twenty fourth points.
[59] These are both words which are used with some frequency in Lollard texts, e.g. 'fals': Matthew, 8/24; 16/6; 26/31; 59/11; 122/9; Arnold, 6/6; 274/14; *EWS* I 245/26; 252/5 and *Jack Upland*, 54/3; 57/83 and 'feyned': Matthew, 9/21; 14/9; 18/4; 20/11; 117/1; Arnold, 110/8; 123/13; 368/28; *EWS*, I.231/102; 314/32; 557/30; *Lanterne*, 38/15; 59/14; *Jack Upland*, 64/233.
[60] See *Trefnant*, p.311, p.319 and p.324.
[61] *Trefnant*, p.281.

Signes and Sothe

drawn from Brut's writing were that is unlawful to pass judgment and that it is heresy to assert that condemnation by human law is concordant with the law of Christ and his gospel.[62]

Peres considers that Wyclif warned the friars 'in goodnesse of gost graythliche' (529), but the friars 'seweden his soule' and 'oueral lollede him with heretykes werkes' (532). The comments about both Brut and Wyclif expressly draw attention to the reverse discourses of Wycliffism and Lollardy. Truth is contested as heresy, and vice versa.[63] It also noteworthy that the word which Peres uses to describe the accusation of heresy against Wyclif is 'lollede'. The verb 'lollen', and the noun 'loller' are words which have a contested semantic history.[64] 'Lollen', in its most straightforward sense, meant 'to hang limply' and 'loller' some kind of wastrel who relied on others for support.[65] Whether or not these words are important in the developing sense application of the word 'lollard' to describe the supporters and followers of John Wyclif, there is certainly evidence that writers punned on 'lollen' to refer to 'Lollards'.

The clearest example of this is in a poem which was written after the Oldcastle uprising in 1413.[66] The poem is preserved in British Library Cotton MS Vespasian B.xvi. Robbins entitles it *Defend us from all Lollardry*. Lines 33-40 criticise the behaviour of 'An old castel' and the refrain of each stanza pillories either the 'lewde lust of lollardie'; the 'sory sekte of lollardie', or warns people to be wary of the 'bawde of lollardie'. Its allegiances are very clear cut. As a result it is uncontentious to detect a pun on 'lolle' and 'lollard' in this poem:

> To lolle so hie in suyche degre
> hit is no perfit profecie,
> Sauf seker sample to þe & me
> to be war of lollardie.
>
> The game is noȝt to lolle so hie
> þer fete failen fondement
> and yut is a moch folie
> for fals beleue to ben brent. (13-20)

---

[62] *Trefnant*, p.364, no. 24 and p.363, no. 20.
[63] In *The Premature Reformation*, Hudson quotes the following from Bodleian MS Eng.th.f.39 fol.44v: 'ȝif ony symple curat or prest or lewid man wolde reule hym and hise, to whom he is holden aftir the lawe of God, he shal be holden an eretik and rebel aȝens holi chirche', p.394.
[64] This is discussed in detail by Wendy Scase, *Piers Plowman and the New Anticlericalism* (Cambridge, 1989), pp.150-60. She relates 'loll' and 'loller' to the discussion of gyrovagues in the late fourteenth century English church and discusses the uses of these terms in *Piers* in light of the development of the term 'lollard' to refer to the followers of Wyclif.
[65] MED 'lollen' (vb) 1a) and 2).
[66] It is not a piece that Scase examines in her survey, so my remarks about the relationship of 'loll' and 'lollard' differ in emphasis from her analysis.

And, parde, lolle þei neuere so longe,
yut wol lawe make hem lowte. (82-3)[67]

The references to 'hie'; to the absence of sure footing, and the contrast between 'lolle' and 'lowte' make it clear that 'lollen' is used partly in its sense of 'to hang'. That 'lolle' is used to signify presumption which will soon be brought down to earth also suggests that the poet is punning on 'lolle' as the root of the name 'Lollards'. Punning on the sounds of two separate words is used as a satirical weapon. This is in keeping with the narrative technique of the poem which uses the reverse discourse of Wycliffism against itself. Distinctive 'sect' vocabulary is used in patronising or pejorative contexts. There are a number of references to 'fals beleue' (20; 129 and 135). Line 64 refers to the 'colour' of Lollardy and line 137 uses the phrase 'vnder colour of suiche lollyng'. Wycliffite diction is explicitly quoted at line 102: 'þei seien hit is but mawmetrie' and the verb 'iangle' (22) and the phrase 'bable þe bibel' (27) are used against the Lollards.[68]

It is entirely possible that this poem is written to 'quite' *Crede* and that the two poems may exist in discursive symmetry, though spread out over nearly two decades. This is how the later poem opens:

Lo he þat can be cristes clerc
And knowe þe knottes of his crede,
Now may se a wonder werke,
Of harde happes to take goud heede.
The dome of dethe is heuy drede
For hym þat wol not mercy crie;
þan is my rede, for mucke ne mede
þat no man melle of lollardrye.

I sey for meself, yut wiste I neuer
but now late what hit shuld be,
and, by my trouthe, I haue wel leuer
no more kyn þan my a, b, c. (1-12)

The disparaging comment that a cleric is now one who knows the 'knottes' of his creed, together with the reference to 'a.b.c', sound suspiciously like a swipe at the narrator's comments on his educational proficiency at the opening of *Crede*. The later poem reads as a triumphant vindication of holy church's suppression of a Lollard uprising, and it

---

[67] Robbins, 64/152-57.

[68] 'mawmetrie' is frequently used in Wycliffite texts to describe the liturgical practices of the contemporary church and to condemn the use of images. e.g. *Lanterne*, 18/8; 101/10; 132/19; Arnold, 293/37; Cigman, 8.298; 10.329. On 'bable þe bibel' cf. the reverse comment in the Lollard William Wakeham's claim (1437) that it is no better for laymen to say the paternoster in Latin than to say 'bibull babull', quoted from Hudson (1988), p.31.

would be appropriate in achieving those ends, to counter the equally defiant Wycliffism of an earlier alliterative poem.

Such a connection cannot ultimately be proved, of course, but the reverse discourse strategies of *Defend us from all Lollardry* provide a clear case of distinctive terms being used as weapons in ecclesiastical warfare, and that those terms include 'Lollard'. It is exactly this strategy which I see from the opposite position in the lines on Wyclif in *Crede*. Peres has stated that Wyclif warned the friars with truth, but that this 'graith' has been perceived by the church hierarchy as 'heretikes wordes'. To complete the semantic reversal, Peres describes the accusation made by church hierarchy with 'lollede'. From an ecclesiastical position, to accuse someone of lollardy is a shameful insult. But in this context in *Crede* the derogatory force of 'lollede' is seriously weakened by the fact that what appears to the church as 'heretikes wordes' are defended by Peres as 'the graith'. A word which was used by the institutionalised church to ridicule the Lollards is thrown back with contempt by a Wycliffite plowman.

These poetic reversals and counter reversals reflect the history of the word 'lollard' at this time. Anne Hudson notes that its first recorded use in England was in 1382 when Henry Crumpe was suspended from academic acts in the university of Oxford for calling Wyclif's supporters 'Lollardi' directly after the Blackfriars Council had condemned Wyclif and his followers.[69] From the end of the 1380s 'Lollardi' was used to describe heretical suspects in official proclamations and records. As Anne Hudson has illustrated, in its early use the name 'Lollard' was intensely disliked by those to whom it was applied. She quotes from *Opus Arduum* and the sermons of MS Bodley 806 fol.70v: '3if a man or a womman do wel or speke wel, and gladly wolde plese God, þei ben contrarie to here dedis and so þei schornen such men and clepen hem Lollardis'. Later, however, the name became a badge proundly worn, as in a Wycliffite tract on biblical translation: 'þe most blessed Loller þat euer was or euer schal be was oure lord Iesus Crist, for oure synnes lollynge on þe rode tree'.[70] Like the modern semantic reversals of 'gay' or 'black', the term 'lollard', which in institutionalised discourse signified an authoritarian dismissal, or the marginalisation of persons or behaviour beyond the pale, was proudly reclaimed as a badge of identity in the discourse of solidarity.[71]

[69] Henry Crumpe was a member of the Blackfriars Council. His suspension is discussed in Hudson (1988[1]), p.87.
[70] CUL MS Ii 6.26 fol.60v. This discussion and quotations are drawn from Hudson (1988), pp.2-3.
[71] The comparison draws on the essays by Geneva Smitherman, 'White English in

We can see further evidence of this socio-linguistic outflanking in *Mum*. In the section of the poem about the friars, some crucial lines (crucial partly because they form a particularly knotty textual crux) use the word 'Lollardz' in ironic antithesis to 'lolle':

> The secund is a pryvy poynt, I pray hit be helid:
> Thay cunne not reede redelles a-right, as me thenketh;
> For furst folowid freres Lollardz manieres,
> And sith hath be shewed the same on thaym-self,
> That thaire lesingz haue lad thaym to lolle by the necke;
> At Tibourne for traison y-twyght vp thay were.
> For as hit is y-seide by eldryn dawes,
> 'That the churle yafe a dome whiche came by hym aftre'.
> Patere legem quam ipse tuleris. (415-22a)

These lines are a topical reference to the hanging of a group of Franciscan friars at Tyburn in 1402 for their part in spreading treasonable rumours (lesingz) that Richard II was still alive and was returning to wrest his throne from the usurping Henry Bolingbroke.[72] *Upland's Rejoinder* also refers to this event in a passage critical of the friars.[73] The passage in *Mum* recalls some lines from Ymaginatif's defence of learning in *Piers*, XII 190-1: 'That haþ take fro Tybourne twenty stronge þeues,/ Ther lewed þeues ben lolled vp; loke how þei be saued'. Ymaginatif points out that the benefit of clergy; knowing the heartening text 'Dominus pars hereditatis mee' has saved clerical thieves while unlettered thieves have been left to swing. The recall of this episode in *Mum* is ironic.[74] The friars, although they ought to be lettered, cannot read properly, and as a result they have been strung up on the gallows.

In contrast to the 'lolle/lollardry' antithesis in *Defend us from all Lollardy* and the pro-Wyclif context of 'lollede' in *Crede*, these lines in *Mum* are difficult to untangle. Lawton has stated that their sense is irrecoverable[75] Day and Steele, in the EETS edition, emended the MS reading 'manieres' (417) to 'names' following the gloss of the corrector.

Blackface or Who Do I Be?' and Edmund White, 'The Political Vocabulary of Homosexuality' in *The State of the Language*, ed. L. Michaels and C. Ricks (California, 1980), 158-68 and 235-46. Tony Crowley, in *The Politics of Discourse* (London, 1989) discusses how the term 'beyond the pale' is grounded in the distinction between the 'wyld Irysh' and the civilised language and government of the English 'pale', p.134. *Plowman's Tale* describes how the poor wretches who follow a simple faith, in contrast to the magnificence of the established church, are called 'lollers' (73).
[72] *Eulogium*, III 389-91.
[73] *Upland's Rejoinder*, 271-2.
[74] cf. the ironic recall of Ymaginatif's defence of learning in the lines on the university academics,: 'Sette the soeth-sigger as shorte as he couthe' (343) cf. *Piers*, XII 121-2: 'Forþi I conseille alle creatures no clergie to dispise/Ne sette short by hir science, whatso þei don hemselue'.
[75] Lawton *MLR*, 1981, 790-1.

They argued that the 'sense is clearly that the friars first gave the Lollards their names and now they must have the same name given to them'[76] The corrector has also marked 'folowid' for correction but the gloss is torn away. Day and Steele interpreted it as 'to give in baptism' from O.E. 'fullwian'. However, if we retain the manuscript reading 'manieres' and construe 'folowid' and 'shewed' (418) in their legal senses: 'folowid' to prosecute a case at law, and 'shewed' to lodge a plea before court,[77] then the wordplay on 'Lollardz', which must at this date refer to the Wycliffite movement,[78] and 'lolle' as the verb to hang, makes rather better sense. What the lines state cryptically and playfully is that the friars were the first to prosecute Lollard behaviour at law but since then they have themselves been the subject of a legal plea before court. The concluding proverb uses the word 'dome', judgment (422) and states that a judgment passed on the Lollards has rebounded on the friars' own heads.[79]

In recent history, this had indeed been the case. Of the seventeen doctors of theology present at the 1382 Blackfriars Council which condemned Wyclif's teaching, 16 were friars, four from each order.[80] In 1402, however, it was the friars who were on the receiving end of prosecution, being sentenced to hang for the crime of treason. In this passage in *Mum*, it is clear that 'Lollardz' (which is not altered by the corrector) is being used in an approving sense to write pejoratively about the friars. The name is contested and its original insulting connotations reversed to jibe both at the friars' foolishness in becoming involved in a treasonous plot, and at their claims to learning. The concluding proverb may be read as a clear indication that words are being used as weapons and that their values are reversed as they are thrown back and forth between one side and the other. As Friar Daw says in his reply to Jack Upland, 'Þis arowe shal turne aȝen to him þat it sent' (94).

---

[76] pp.112-3.

[77] MED 'folwen' 5c) and Alford, p.143.

[78] cf. *Crede*, 532. For full discussion, see Scase, pp.147-60.

[79] Variations on this proverb, that judgment, or cursing returns to one's own door, are recorded in Whiting, p.140 e.g. Chaucer, *The Parson's Tale*, 619: 'And ofte tyme swich cursynge wrongfully retorneth agayn to hym that curseth, as a bryd that retorneth agayn to his owene nest'. The proverb appears in English in John of Bromyard's *Summa praedicantium*, : 'Churl yewe then dom/and efte bi this dore ist com' ('Nocumentum', N.IV.); see S. Wenzel, *Mum and the Sothsegger*, lines 421-22', *ELN*, 14 (1976), 87-90. The Latin quotation, 'to suffer the same law which you have proposed. Seneca.' is not from Seneca, but from *Little Cato*, cf. *Minor Poems of the Vernon MS*, ed. Horstmann (EETS 117), p.560. It is also quoted by Bromyard in a development of the passage in which the English proverb is cited. Bromyard also attributes it to Seneca.

[80] cf. *On the Council of London*, which sides with Wyclif against the friars, Wright, I 253-63, p.259.

In both *Crede* and *Mum*, then, the name of the Lollard movement is a term contested between the discourses of authority and solidarity. *Mum* appears to quote lines from *Piers Plowman* at this point, but while 'lolle' is not a sign of unorthodoxy in Ymaginatif's defence of learning, in its new context in *Mum* it is radical. To reverse the term 'Lollardz' against the treasonable 'lesingz' of the friars defies the regulations laid down in *De Haeretico Comburendo*.

Crede was written before this statute was passed but its overt support for Wyclif post-1382 provides a useful control against which to measure the allegiances of other verbal strategies in *Mum*. While *Mum* contains no explicit Wycliffite teaching on the sacraments,[81] *Crede* is rather less guarded. At the end of Peres's rehearsal of the creed are some lines on the Eucharist:

> And in the [sacrement] also that sothfast God on is,
> Fullich his fleche and his blod, that for vs dethe tholede.
> And though this flaterynge freres wyln for her pride,
> Disputen of this deyte as dotardes schulden,
> The more the matere is moved the [masedere hy] worthen.
> Lat the losels alone and leue you the trewthe,
> For Crist seyde it is so, so mot it nede worthe;
> Therfore studye thou nought theron, ne stere thi wittes,
> It is his blissed body, so bad he vs beleuen.
> Thise maystres of dyvinitie many, als y trowe,
> Folwen nought fully the feith as fele of the lewede. (818-27).

At line 817 the printed edition contains 5 lines which are absent from both Trinity and Royal manuscripts:

> The communion of sayntes, for soth I to the sayn;
> And for our great sinnes forgiuenes for to getten,
> And only by Christ clenlich to be clensed;
> Our bodies again to risen right as we been here,
> And the liif euerlasting leue ich to habben. Amen.

---

[81] *Mum* as a whole fails to give any support to two immediately recognisable staples of Lollard thinking, the denial of transubstantiation in the Eucharist, and the view that contrition alone can make satisfaction for sin, without the need for absolution from a member of the institutionalised priesthood. That said, *Lanterne of Light* is a demonstrably Lollard work, and it equally is silent on these two points; see *Lanterne*, p.xv, though the text as it now stands is incompatible in this respect with the evidence of the trial of John Claydon before Henry Chichele in 1415. Ownership of *Lanterne* was the direct cause of Claydon's death, and the four friars who were set to examine the work produced a list of fifteen unacceptable statements expressed in it. One was the denial of transubstantiation; see Hudson, (1988), p.211. On pp.34-5 of *Lanterne*, in an enumeration of the five duties necessary for a priest, the free ministration of the sacraments is the fourth. While this does not afford it a position of priority, its validity is not questioned. With respect to *Mum*, it is useful to note that adherence to Wycliffite modes of thought did not necessarily entail subscription to the whole of a fixed code of essential beliefs, see Hudson, *Premature Reformation*, p.389.

Skeat believed that these lines were a forgery to cover up the printer's omission of some of the lines on the Eucharist and therefore included the lines in his text by marking them with italics and placing them within brackets. He noted, however, the absurdity of having 'Amen' in the middle of a sentence and that the lines produce a break in sense.[82] The textual disturbance at this point may be symptomatic of the fact that the lines contest the meanings of established orthodoxy.[83]

These lines in *Crede* attempt to deflect the accusations against Wyclif for his teaching on the Eucharist back on to the friars. The church had recently condemned Wyclif for his argument against the doctrine of transubstantiation. He stated that after consecration Christ's body is in the bread, but that the bread still remains on the altar. It is not changed into something else because there can be no accidents without a substance.[84] These lines in *Crede* suggest that it is the friars, not Wyclif, who are guilty of debating the sacrament. Lines 820-1 probably refer to the debate between the Dominican Aquinas and the Franciscan Duns Scotus over the mechanics of transubstantiation. Aquinas maintained that the outward manifestations of the bread and the wine were maintained by quantity, through which they received physical extension. Quantity replaced the original substance of the bread as the force that kept the accidents in being and the accidents of the bread were replaced by the substance of Christ's body. Scotus's view, which was accepted by Ockham and his followers, was that the substance of the bread and wine was annihilated to become Christ while the accidents remained through God's omnipotence. After transubstantiation, the bread and wine were accidents without substance because their original substance was now Christ's body. It was with this latter view that Wyclif was principally concerned.[85] *Crede*'s attribution of debate over the Eucharist to the friars is in itself an instance of reverse discourse.[86] It is a vernacular strategy which

---

[82] *Pierce the Ploughman's Crede*, ed. W.W. Skeat (EETS OS 30 1867), pp.54-5. The lines are also included in the edition of *Crede* by James Dean in *Six Ecclesiastical Satires* (TEAMS Michigan, 1991).

[83] Lawton has argued that these lines are authentic, (1981), p.784. They were not included in my edition of the text for the following reasons: the 1553 edition is not based on any of the surviving manuscripts, A.I. Doyle, 'An Unrecognised Piece of *Pierce the Ploughman's Crede* and other Work by its Scribe', *Speculum*, 34 (1959), 428-36. p.435; the lines interrupt the sense of the passage, and the fact that the 1553 edition omits lines 818-9 and 823-5 shows that there has been excision and interpolation.

[84] See A.Kenny, *Wyclif* (Oxford, 1985), pp.80-90.

[85] Gordon Leff, *Heresy in the Later Middle Ages* (Manchester, 1967), vol. II, p.551.

[86] Cf. the treatment of material bread after transubstantiation in *Vae Octuplex*. The writer gives the Wycliffite position and then says: 'but þe feend, siþ he was lowsud, haþ mouyd frerus to reuerse þis, and as þei seyn, þer newe seyntus and newe doctoures þat þei han,

contrasts the truth of Christ's words with scholastic interfraternal dissent, and as such, is consonant with the larger narrative strategies of the poem.[87] The passage is more radical than when Study in *Piers Plowman* satirises the friars' vain and academic questioning of theology, (X 72-3) or criticises the way that academic questioning leads people into false belief (X 117-18).[88]

As in *Crede*, *The Plowman's Tale* 1221-4, states that one should not strive to dispute the mechanics of the sacrament of the Eucharist. Wawn has noted of *The Plowman's Tale* that this is not an orthodox position.[89] Lawton comments that Lollards were condemned for saying that it did not matter how Christ's real presence entered the sacramental elements because the church's doctrine was exact and rigorously articulated.[90] We have seen above that the first three articles on which Wyclif was condemned in 1382 give a paradigmatic account of orthodox doctrine.[91]

The treatment of the Eucharist in *Crede* is evasive. It skirts the crucial question by remaining silent on whether material bread remains after transubstantiation. The injunction not to study thereon, nor stir one's wits recalls the citation in lines 578-90 of words from Mark's gospel, which, as we saw in the last chapter, were used by Thorpe to evade the question of whether it was lawful to swear upon a book.[92] While these lines in *Crede* do not set out an explicit paradigm of Wycliffite doctrine, in their attribution of queries about the nature of Eucharistic doctrine to the friars they contest the official discourse of holy church. It is a technique used also in the Wycliffite text *On the Leaven of the Pharisees* where the friars are accused of heresy for saying that the bread seen in

techen þat þis sacrament is an accident wiþowte suget', *EWS*, II.375/263-5. The target is the Ockhamist view of transubstantiation.

[87] The phrase 'matere is moved' (822) is used in scholastic debates when a particular question is addressed.

[88] *Piers*, X 72-3: 'Freres and faitours han founde vp swiche questions/To plese wiþ proude men syn þe pestilence tyme' and X 117-18: 'Swiche motyues they meue, þise maistres in hir glorie,/And maken men in mys bileue þat muse on hire wordes'.

[89] A.Wawn, 'The Genesis of *The Plowman's Tale*', *YES* 2 (1972), 21-40, p.32.

[90] Lawton, (1981), p.782. It was an item of belief on which Lollards were examined, e.g from Bishop Polton's register: 'In primis an post consecracionem sit in altari verum corpus Christi *et non substancia panis materialis neque vini*' (emphasis mine) quoted from Hudson (1985), p.133.

[91] Both Swinderby and Brut were charged with heresy for their views on the Eucharist, *Trefnant*, p.282. In Thorpe's *Testimony*, Thorpe cleverly outmanoeuvres Arundel's bludgeoning attempt to make him state clearly that after consecration, material bread remains on the altar. He states that his 'bileue' is simply Christ's words at the Last Supper, Matt, 26:26; Mark, 14:22; Luke, 22:19: 'Takiþ þis and etiþ of þis alle, þis is my bodi' (962-3). Arundel tries to get Thorpe to answer to the first three points of the 1382 condemnation of Wyclif's teaching, Thorpe states that 'material breed' is not written in 'holi writt' (952-3) and in answer to Arundel's next question, turns the tables on him by asking him to expound the meaning of Phil. 2: 5-6.

[92] See above, pp.90-91.

the priest's hands is neither bread, nor Christ's body. Like *Crede*, in its attribution of a heterodox view of the Eucharist to the friars, it contests institutionalised discourse.[93]

Rather more stark in oppositional terms is a contrast sustained throughout the poem between the 'fals' friars and the truth of criticisms sustained against them. Peres denounces the friars' hypocritical claims to a life of manual labour:

> Thei vsen russet also somme of this freres,
> That bitokneth trauaile and trewthe opon erthe.
> Bote loke whou this lorels labouren the erthe,
> But freten the frute that the folk full lellich biswynketh.
> With trauail of trewe men thei tymbren her houses,
> And of the curious clothe her copes thei biggen.   (719-23)

The false hypocrisy of the friars is contrasted with the honest labours of 'trewe men'. This appears to be similar to a contrast made in Anima's speech in *Piers* when he denounces the avarice of the contemporary church, particularly 'persones and preestes'

> That heuedes of holy chirche ben, þat han hir wil here,
> Wiþouten trauaille þe tiþe deel þat trewe men biswynken.
> They wol be wrooþ for I write us, ac to witnesse I take
> Boþe Mathew and Marc and Memento domine dauid.   (XV 487-90)

If Anima feared that a contrast between the corruptions of the contemporary church and the travail of 'trewe men' would anger the heads of holy church, then Peres ought to have been positively quaking in his mud-sodden shoes. Because of the 1382 Council and the outspoken support for Wyclif and Brut, the term 'trewe men' in *Crede* must be part of a discourse of solidarity with the Lollards. As Anne Hudson notes in her paper on Lollard sect vocabulary, it was the name which the Wycliffites used of themselves.[94] That 'trewe men' stands in opposition to the falseness of the friars strengthens this conclusion. Peres uses it to reverse the semantic values of the institutionalised church.

Such an interpretation of the lines in *Piers* is not so readily available, partly because of the absence of unequivocal support for Wycliffite opinions,[95] and partly because the date of *Piers* precedes any firm

---

93 Matthew, p.19.

94 Hudson (1985), 166-68.

95 The relationship of *Piers* to Wycliffite thought has been examined by P. Gradon, 'Langland and the Ideology of Dissent', *PBA* 66 (1980), 179-205; Lawton (1981); C. Von Nolcken, '*Piers Plowman*, the Wycliffites and *Pierce the Ploughman's Crede*', *YLS*, 2 (1988), 71-102, Hudson (1988), pp.398-408 and John Bowers, '*Piers Plowman* and the Police: Notes

drawing of boundaries between orthodoxy and heresy. Certainly, the lines in Passus XV of *Piers* could have been read by a later reader sympathetic to Lollardy as consonant with Lollard ideas, but at the time of their composition their orthodoxy remains an open question.[96] So far as contemporary records suggest, *Piers Plowman* escaped examination for heresy despite the fact that some of its discussion of the contemporary church fell into areas circumscribed by later anti-Wycliffite legislation.[97]

There is a further site of contestation in these lines in *Crede*. The friars are satirised for wearing russet. Russet was a kind of rough material worn by shepherds or labourers. It is because the friars' pampered lifestyle is so opposite to the life of manual labour that Peres denounces their use of russet garments. There is a further dimension to the accusation. Both Knighton and Walsingham, in passages hostile to the Lollard movement, state that Lollards wore russet garments.[98] Peres, however, reverses the terms of institutionalised discourse. He contrasts the hypocritical clothes of the friars with the honest garments worn by true followers of Christ; those who are 'trewe men'.

Throughout *Crede* other terms of Wycliffite discourse are treated in a similar fashion.[99] Space prohibits analysis of all of these and I shall focus on one instance of related terms in order to contrast them with *Piers* and *Mum*. In Wycliffite texts 'found', 'order' and 'rule' are all terms used to challenge the existence of the friars and possessioners on the grounds that they were not instituted by Christ when he sent out his apostles to teach. One of the clearest expositions of this is in *Jack Upland*:

Toward a History of the Wycliffite Langland', *YLS* 6 (1992), 1-50. In all cases, the verdict returned is of suspicious circumstances, but without proven evidence of guilt.

[96] Hudson notes of the lines on disendowment in B XV 500ff that calls for disendowment were not the peculiar prerogative of Wycliffism but the problem remains of whether after 1382 such blatant hostility could be interpreted as indicative of Wycliffite sympathies, (1988), p.406. Interestingly, XV 500ff. is retained in C without significant alteration (XVII 199 ff), while B XV 487-90 is cut. In CUL MS Dd.1.17, there is a 'nota' marked at XV 489 (Uhart, p.296).

[97] John Bowers (1992) has shown how annotations on copies of *Piers* can be interpreted as evincing support for passages that are closest to Wycliffite concerns. Lawton notes memorably that 'Lollards had Langlandian sympathies' (1981), p.793. Ownership of *Piers Plowman* does not indicate an exclusively heterodox audience, however, as various clerical owners cannot be identified as Wycliffites. For the question of audience, see J.A. Burrow, 'The Audience of *Piers Plowman*, *Anglia*, 75 (1957), 373-84 and A. Middleton, 'The Audience and Public of *Piers Plowman'* in Lawton (1982), pp.101-23.

[98] Knighton, II.184; Walsingham *H.A.*,I.324.

[99] e.g. 'beleue' (16; 802; 804); 'cautel' (303); 'fables' (274); 'fals' (97; 419; 484; 488; 616; 687; 769); 'feyne' (19; 58; 236; 273; 487); 'gabbynge' (275); 'glose' (275; 345; 367; 515; 585; 709); 'god's lawe' (21); 'iape' (43; 46); 'obedience' (71); 'ordeyne' (579; 610); 'ordynaunce' (245; 509); 'pore men' (217; 473).

Frere, of what ordre art þou and who mad þin ordre? What ben þi rulis
and who made þi cloutid rulis, siþ Crist made hem not ne noon oþer a
þousende yeere aftir þat Crist stiȝe into heuene? (58/103-6)[100]

The Wycliffite polemic *Fifty Heresies and Errors of Friars* uses a
combination of 'found' and 'rule' to question the institution of the friars
and to assert that their foundation was contrary to Christ's command:

> Freris seyn þat hor religioun, founden of synful men, is more perfite
> þen þat religion or ordir þo whiche Crist hymself made.
>
> (Arnold, I.367/1-3)[101]

This vocabulary is clustered in *Crede*, particularly in contexts where each
of the orders of friars compete with each other over the primacy and
perfection of their rule. First, 'founde':

> Oure ordir was [euelles] and erst y-founde.' (242)

> But felawe, our foundement was first of the othere,
> And we ben founded fulliche with-outen fayntise. (250-1)

> We friers be the first and founded vpon treuthe. (307)

> For-to all this freren folke weren founded in townes,
> And taughten vntrulie; and that we well aspiede,
> And for chefe charitie we chargeden vs seluen
> In amending of this men. . . (311-3)

> It is but a faynt folk i-founded vp-on iapes. (47)

> Sikerli y can nought fynden who hem first founded,
> But the foles foundeden hem-self freres of the Pye. (64-5)

> The fend founded hem first the feith to destroie,
> And founded hem on Farysens feyned for gode. (487)

> And Frauncis founded his folke fulliche on trewthe,
> Pure parfit prestes in penaunce to lybben,
> In loue and in lownesse and lettinge of pride,
> Grounded on the godspell as God bad him-selue. (511-14)

> For Fraunces founded hem nought to faren on that wise. (775)

The first block of quotations are the claims of the friars to authenticity,
primacy and perfection. The second block of quotations are the contestation of these claims in the voices of the narrator and Peres. In 511-14 and
775, Peres draws back from a full-blooded Wycliffite condemnation of all
the fraternal orders wholesale, in order to praise the founding ideals of St

---

[100] see also Matthew, p.2/6; 51/19; Arnold, 392/3; EWS, I 328/59.
[101] cf. Matthew, 51/18-19; EWS, I 295/84.

Francis. This is in line with Wyclif's initial admiration of the friars and his eventual revulsion at their contemporary practices.[102] Peres's attitude towards the friars is not consistent, however. While in these lines he exculpates the founding ideals of the Franciscans, elsewhere the very existence of all four orders is questioned.[103]

The contest over 'order' follows a similar pattern:

That all the frute of the fayth was in here foure ordres. (29)

Of oure ordre ther beth bichopes wel manye. (254)

And thanne oure prouinciall hath power to assoilen
Alle sustren and bretheren that beth of our order. (328-9)

Thei prechen in proude harte and preiseth her order. (370)

Neyther in order ne out but vn-nethe lybbeth. (45)

I trowe that some wikked wyght wroughte this orders
[Thorughe] that gleym of that gest that Golias is y-calde,
Other ells Satan him-self sente hem fro hell
To cumbren men with her craft Cristendome to schenden. (478-81)

Proue hem in proces and pynch at her ordre,
And deme hem after that they don and dredles, y leue
Thei willn we[xe]n pure wroth wonderliche sone. (523-5)

Here, the friars' pride in their order is contested by the narrator's opinions. He states that their order is singular, and hence contravenes all secular and ecclesiastical regulation, and that the fraternal orders were instituted by the devil. This is consistent with views found in Wycliffite texts.[104] Peres's comment (523-5) draws attention to the way that the friars contest criticism of their 'ordre'.

The contest over 'rule' has a slightly different format:

Seyn that they folwen fully Fraunceses rewle. (291)

Loke a ribaut of hem that can nought wel reden
His rewle ne his respondes but be pure rote. (376-7)

And Austynes rewle thei rekneth but a fable. (466)

---

[102] Wyclif originally supported the friars because of the closeness of their founding ideals to Apostolic poverty. But after the friars' denunciation of his views on the Eucharist, he turned against them. In *Trialogus* he bitterly attacks the friars, calling them greedy, idle, blasphemous seducers and hypocrites and forms the acrostic CAIM from the initials of the four orders, see further below. Between 1382 and 1384, Wyclif waged war against the friars in a flood of pamphlets and sermons, Kenny, pp.93-4, and A. Gwynn, *The English Austin Friars in the Time of Wyclif* (Oxford, 1940), pp.211-76.

[103] In lines 482-7, Peres says that the friars were founded by the devil. These lines are discussed below.

[104] e.g. *SEWW*, 75/4; 89/1-8; Matthew, pp.48-9 and pp.268-9.

Fynd foure freres in a flok that folweth that rewle,
Thanne haue y tynt all my tast touche and assaie. (536-7)

With proude wordes apert that passeth his rule. (541)

Bagges and beggyng he bad his folk leuen,
And only seruen him-self and hijs rewle sechen. (600-1)

But now the harlottes han hid thilke rewle,
And, for the loue of oure lorde haue leyd hire in water. (781-2)

The second block of quotations represent Peres's and the narrator's criticism of the friars' claims about the holiness of their rule. The first quotation is spoken by the narrator but represents the indirect speech of the Franciscans. What is ingenious in *Crede* is how the contest over these key terms of vocabulary is not simply a case of the friars versus Peres, and the narrator; the friars contest the significance of these terms amongst themselves and their squabbling helps to dissipate the claims to truth that such authenticating terms are intended to sanction.

As a result of Peres's concessions to the founding ideal of the friars, this sect vocabulary is not contested so damningly to the total disadvantage of the friars as it is, for instance, in *Jack Upland*. However, it is interesting to compare with *Crede* the usage of these same terms in *Piers Plowman*. There are six instances of 'found' in the B Text in the context of discussing the friars. These could, to a reader with Wycliffite sympathies, appear to use sect vocabulary as terms in a discourse of solidarity.[105]

None of the examples from *Piers* makes an explicit contrast between the founding of the friars and Christ's ordinance for the church. However, Anima's comment that friars and monks were: 'founded and feefed ek to bidde for oþere' (XV 325) and, more especially, his statement that Paul the hermit 'foundede freres of Austynes ordre or ellis freres lyen' (XV 289), questions the contemporary practices of these religious in a way that interrogates their foundation rather sharply. It is interesting that the b-verse of 289 is contested in manuscript witnesses. B manuscripts omit it completely.[106] Most interesting is that these lines are revised in C. There is an addition when Liberium Arbitrium queries the Austin's claim: 'yf frere Austynes be *trewe*;/For he *ordeynede* þat *ordre*

---

[105] My list does not include XX 383 where the sense of Conscience's comment: 'þat freres hadde a fyndyng þat for nede flateren' is difficult to construe. It is unclear what provision is intended and 'nede' in the b-verse may be heavily ironic.
[106] The contest over the b-verse of B XV 289 may be one fought more in the twentieth century than in the fourteenth. There is no annotation at this point in the manuscripts but the b-verse is written in another hand and ink in MS Bm. The reading in Kane Donaldson is based on the C revision, p.551. Schmidt does not include the b-verse at XV 289. There is a variation in the a-verse, as MS F substitutes 'fraunces' for 'Austynes'.

or elles þey *gabben'* C.XVII.15-16. I have emphasised sect vocabulary because so far as my manual search shows, this is the densest concentration of sectarian vocabulary at any point in *Piers*. CUL Ff 5 35, a manuscript with a very small amount of medieval marginalia, has a 'nota' against line 15.[107] If these lines in *Piers* were divorced from context, they could be slipped very easily into a Wycliffite text on the 'pseudo-freres' without obvious sign of disjunction.

There is also a tiny contestation of 'found' in the closing Passus of the poem. At XIX 325, Grace's provision for the establishment of a true apostolic church is described as a 'good foundement'. This refers explicitly to the physical foundations which Grace lays. In Passus XX 295, by contrast, Envy's provision for the friars to learn Philosophy is couched in the words 'he fond hem to scole'. A true foundation is contrasted with one that is less reputable. The degree of comparison is important. While a Wycliffite reader could interpret these lines as a damning contrast between the fraternal orders and the apostolic church,[108] such an interpretation is without the assistance of the clear discursive frame of contrast that is provided in *Crede*. Moreover, at the time of writing these lines, while the fraternal criticisms form a topic of discussion that had fallen under ecclesiastical control, they do not expressly contradict the specific resolutions of either the Council of London, or the 1401 statute *De Haeretico Comburendo*.

It is also worth noting the high density of 'founde' and its derivatives in *Crede* compared with these few examples from the very much longer text of *Piers*. While the sectarian vocabulary which is used in *Piers* could be construed along sectarian lines, its comparative infrequency does not suggest that it was a cornerstone of composition grounded on the opposition of key terms. The same is true of 'order' and 'rule', especially the former. In Passus XX, Nede asserts that:

> Monkes and Moniales and alle men of Religion,
> Hir ordre and hir reule wole han to a certein noumbre
> Of lewed and of lered; þe lawe wole and askeþ
> A certein for a certein, saue oonliche of freres. (XX 264-67)

While 'ordre and 'reule' are frequently found together in Wycliffite texts, here in *Piers* their juxtaposition is in the context of satirising the sheer number of friars, not their institution *per se*. The lines are part of a well-established topos of anti-fraternal satire, without particular

---

[107] Scase, p.95.
[108] 'Scole' is often used in Wycliffite texts as a derogatory reference to academic learning, Hudson (1988), p.226. cf. earlier discussion of *Mum* in chapter 2, pp.44-47.

oppositional Wycliffite emphasis.[109] Interestingly, the use of 'ordre' closest to the verbal texture of Wycliffite texts is the following, which if divorced from context, could be mistaken for lines from *Crede*:

> Was noon swich as hymself ne noon so pope holy
> Yhabited as an heremyte, an ordre by hymselue,
> Religion saunȝ rule and resonable obedience;
> Lakkynge lettrede men and lewed men boþe.   (XIII 283-6)

This does not describe a friar, of course, but Haukyn the Active Man.[110]

Other examples of 'ordre' in *Piers* are uncontentious.[111] In the case of 'rule' the lines about Haukyn are, once again, closest in verbal texture to Wycliffite thought. In none of the ten other instances in the B Text is 'rule' part of an oppositional vocabulary. The overwhelming use of this word is in contexts where a speaker castigates the religious for not adhering to their rule.[112] This is not the same as insisting that their rule contravenes Christ's ordinance. The clearest example of the difference in emphasis can be seen from the use of 'rule' in one of the most radical passages in *Piers Plowman*, Clergy's warning that a king will come and disendow the religious:

> Ac þer shal come a kyng and confesse yow Religiouses
> And bete yow, as þe bible telleþ, for brekynge of youre rule,
> And amende Monyals, Monkes and Chanons,
> And puten hem to penaunce, Ad pristinum statum ire.   (X 322-25)

The passage continues with the comment that friars will find in their refectory a key to Constantine's coffers and the prophecy that the abbot of Abingdon will receive a knock from the king.[113] Radical though this passage is, it is different in temper from Wycliffite calls for disendowment. There is no suggestion in the use of 'rule' that the foundation of

---

[109] William St Amour's tract *De Periculis* was influential in forming the topos, based on Wisdom 11:20, 'thou hast ordered all things by measure and number and weight' that the friars were without number. See Scase, pp.35-37 and quotation of the relevant parts of *De Periculis*, pp.186-7. See also P. Szittya, *The Antifraternal Tradition in Medieval Literature* (Princeton, 1986), pp.224-30.

[110] It is possible that this reflects the link between lay vagrancy and religious mendicancy that Scase has charted as a new anti-clerical polemic, pp.64-79, though Haukyn is not part of the discussion here.

[111] From the B version, see Prol. 58, VI 72; VII 193 (Schmidt) and XX 265. The conjunction of 'frere and faitour' in VI 72 has been examined by Scase as part of a new polemic between lay vagrancy and religious mendicancy, pp.69-72.

[112] In B texts see V 45; X 297; 299; 323; XII 36; XIII 285; XV 87; XV 100; XV 317; XIX 423; XX 247.

[113] The passage is transposed in C to form part of Reason's sermon in Passus V 168-72. 'Reule' is unaltered but the Abbot of Abingdon is changed to the 'abbot of Engelonde' (176).

the religious was against Christ's ordinance, and indeed 'rule' is the only example of sect vocabulary in the entire passage.[114]

It is in this context, and against the model of *Crede*, that it is useful to review the use of the same vocabulary in *Mum*. In his comments on the monks and friars the poet explicitly contrasts those orders of religion founded by God with those imposed on the contemporary world by man:

> Thenne passid I to priories and personages many,
> To abbeys of Augustyn and many hooly places,
> There prestz and prelatz were parfitely y-closid
> To singe and to reede for alle cristen soules.
> But for I was a meen man I might not entre;
> For though the place were y-pighte for poure men sake
> And eeke funded there-fore yit faillen thay ofte
> That thay doon not eche day do beste of alle.
> Mutauerunt caritatem in cupiditatem. Sapiencia.
> For the [fundacion as] the fundours ment
> Was groundid for God-is men, though hit grete serue.   (536-45)

Despite the possessioners' priories, parsonages and abbeys being called 'hooly places' (537), any impression of holiness is soon dispelled. The porter 'of his goodnesse' forcibly ejects the narrator from the abbey because he has no goods to contribute to the comforts of the place. The sense of 'hooly' is thus called into question. While orthodox anti-clerical satire often criticised the worldliness of the monastic orders, the comments in *Mum* have a distinctive slant. The use of the word 'parfitely' in 537 is questioned by the monks' subsequent treatment of the narrator. As a result, its antonym 'inparfitely' is called up – a resonance which brings the sense of the lines close to the type of comment in Wycliffite texts which state that enclosure is contrary to God's law:

> And, as Ierusaleem was wallyt aȝenys Crist and hise apostles, so þese religiows today ben wallyd aȝen cristene men. But þis wal is mennys fyndyng, hepyd wiþowten charyte, for hit is noo charyte to leue þe ordre þat Crist ȝaf and to take þese stynkyng ordres.   (*EWS*, I 328/55-9)

This sermon clusters sect vocabulary in a fashion similar to that in *Mum*. In contrast to the infrequency of its use in *Piers*, lines 541-5 in *Mum* contain six examples of sect vocabulary: 'poure men'; 'funded'; 'fundacion'; 'funders'; 'groundid', and 'God-is men'. The clustering of this vocabulary, together with the ironic use of positive words such as 'hooly' and 'parfite' enable these lines to be read as part of a discourse of

---

[114] There is a rather interesting use of 'Caym' (X 334) which will be discussed below.

125

solidarity with Wycliffite thought.[115] Furthermore, it is worth noting that this is one of the occasions that the 'dowel' triad is quoted from *Piers*.[116] The comment that the friars do not 'do beste of alle' in this new context in *Mum* shows how words and phrases from *Piers* take on a new political resonance in this later poem.

The anti-fraternal satire in *Mum* is also distinctive:

Thenne ferkid I to freres, alle the foure ordres,
There the fundament of feith and felnesse of workes
Hath y-dwellid many day, no doute, as thay telle. (392-4)

Thay prechen alle of penance as though [thay] parfite were,
But thay proue hit [in no] poynt there thaire peril shuld arise.
Thaire clothing is of conscience and of Caym thaire werkes,
That fadre was and fundre of alle the foure ordres,
Of deedes thay doon deceipuyng the peuple,
As Armacanes argumentz, that thaire actes knewe,
Provyn hit apertly in a poysie-wise;
For of Caym alle came, as this clerc tolde.
For who writeth wel this worde and withoute titil,
Shal finde of the figures but euene foure lettres:
C. for hit is crokid [for] thees Carmes thou mos take,
A. for thees Augustines that amoreux been euer,
I. for thees Iacobynes that been of Iudas kynne,
M. for thees Menours that monsyd been thaire werkes. (491-504)

The friars' claim to the 'fundament of feith' is challenged by the 'no doute, as thay telle' and the true nature of this foundation is revealed in the later passage which states unambiguously that Caim was founder of the friars. The narrative principle of the passage is to make a positive statement about the friars and then to reverse it.[117] Preaching of perfect penance is overturned by the fact that the friars fail to demonstrate it. The clothing of the friars is a token of conscience but their works are those of Cain.

The remark about clothing jibes at the supposed sanctity of the fraternal habit in a distinctively Wycliffite manner.[118] More conclusively Wycliffite is the use of the Caim acrostic. There appear to be no

[115] The distinctiveness of the sect vocaulary is emphasised if we contrast this passage with a similar moment in *The Simonie*, A 127-32: 'For is þere come to an abey to pore men or þre/ And aske of hem helpe par seinte charite/Vneþe wole any don his ernde, oþer ȝong or old/ But late him coure þere al day in hunger and in cold/And sterue/Loke what loue þer is to God whom þeih seien þat hii serue'.

[116] Other instances in *Mum* where the dowel triad is quoted are: 276; 772; 982; 1170; 1258 and 1278. In *Crede* the only possible reference is at line 95.

[117] This strategy is used throughout the Wycliffite text *How Satan and His Children Turnen Werkis of Mercy Vpsodom*, Matthew, pp.210-18.

[118] e.g. *Jack Upland*, 60/137-9. Jack asks why the friar wears such fine and precious clothes. The only reason for doing so is vainglory and yet the friars say they are beggars.

instances of the acrostic outside Wycliffite texts.[119] Interestingly in B versions of *Piers*, in the lines on disendowment in Passus X, Clergy states that before the Abbot of Abingdon is dispossessed: 'Caym shal awake/Ac dowel shal dyngen hym adoun and destruye his myȝte' (X 334-5). In C the reference to Caym is deleted and the b-verse 'as cronicles me tolde' is substituted (V 178). Even while the lines in B are not expressly about the friars, and the reference to Caym does not use the acrostic, perhaps by the writing of C, the cryptic comment was considered dangerous.

Wyclif had linked the friars with Cain in his *Trialogus*.[120] In *Mum*, the acrostic is attributed to Richard Fitzralph, Archbishop of Armagh. He was a vigorous opponent of the friars and, in one of his London sermons in 1357, said that the friars were hypocrites who followed the errors of Balaam and the way of Cain.[121] The texts of these sermons were circulated widely. Whether or not the attribution in *Mum* be based on familiarity with these sermons, it is interesting that Fitzralph is quoted as authority in this context. Frequently in Wycliffite texts, Fitzralph, along with Grosseteste is cited as a learned authority, or even a saint.[122] The conjunction of the Caim acrostic, the reference to Fitzralph and the use of 'fund' reverses the claims of the friars to sanctity in a distinctively Wycliffite manner. The lines suggest that the friars are not founded by God, and moreover, that they are outlaws. The use of Caim in Wycliffite texts reverses the ecclesiastical judgment on Lollardy as unlawful by branding representatives of the institutionalised church with the name of the first criminal; an outlaw from God's chosen people.[123]

One last example from the anti-fraternal section of *Mum* takes this last point further:

---

[119] cf. *Crede*, 486: 'Of þe kynrede of Caym he caste the freres'; *Jack Upland*, 58/86 where the friars are called 'Caymes castel-makers;' and the interpolation into *Upland's Rejoinder* at 374 which concludes: '& so þe deueyl & caym with judas ben ȝoure fadirs', p.171; *On the Leaven of the Pharisees*, Matthew, p.12/8, where the friars are called Cain's brethren and Robbins, 65/109-116: 'Thus grounded caym thes four ordours'. See also M. Aston, ' "Caim's Castles": Poverty, Politics and Disendowment' in R.B. Dobson, ed., *The Church, Politics and Patronage in the Fifteenth Century* (Gloucester, 1984), pp.45-81.

[120] J. Wyclif, *Trialogus*, ed. G. Lechler (Oxford, 1869), IV 33, p.362.

[121] Szittya, p.129.

[122] e.g. Arnold, p.281/13, p.412/22, p.416/20 and Matthew, pp.128/26.

[123] cf 'All þoo þat haue be and beþ, and schul be into þe Day of Doom, pursueris of true cristen peple, ben of þe generacioun of Caym; and alle þoo þat han be pursued for þe loue of God, and ben now, and schul be into þe Day of Doom, beþ of þe generacioun of Abel. And, as Crisostom seiþ, . . .þe cockel schal growe amonge þe good whete, into þe dai of ripe', Cigman, 2.699-705. Szittya comments that the friars are linked with Cain because he is the archetype of all those who wander without place or number within a divine order governed by the principles laid down in Wisdom 11:21, pp.229-30.

> I can not reede redily of what revle thay been,
> For hooly churche ne heuene hath not thaym in mynde,
> Saue in oon place thaire office and ordre is declarid,
> I sawe hit in a ympne and is a sentence trewe,
> And elles-where in hooly writte I herde thaym y-nempnyd.
> Auferte gentem perfidam. Credentium de finibus
> Deleantur de libro viuencium et cum iustis non scribantur.   (516-20a)

The obliqueness of these lines is in direct proportion to the sense they encode. What is in question is the friars' 'revle' (516) and 'ordre' (518). In order to unlock the sense of the passage, it is necessary to note the use of legal diction. 'Declarid' (518) has the legal sense of 'declaring law',[124] and 'sentence' the legal verdict in a court case,[125] The narrator cannot determine to which religious rule the friars adhere but states that their sect has been declared and judged to belong to one place. The judgment is supported by reference to external authorities which I believe to be authorial, and which decode the place for us.[126] The first quotation is from the hymn for the Vespers of All Saints, 'Placare Christi servulis'. It reads, 'he carries off the treacherous people (Of the believers in the Last Things)'. The second citation is from *Psalm* 68:29, 'Let them be blotted out of the book of the living and with the just let them not be written.' The 'oon place' (518) to which the friars are condemned is hell.

In light of this, the comment in 517 that neither holy church nor heaven is mindful of the friars is suggestive of the Lollard view that true holy church was not the material church on earth but the congregation of faithful souls predestined for salvation.[127] What these lines state, when they are decoded, is that the friars are outside the earthly church because they adhere to a rule not of Christ's making, and, as a consequence, they are excluded from the congregation in heaven.

This is one of the most radical positions in *Mum*. In answer to legislation which attempted to exclude Lollards from the communion of the church, the narrator of *Mum* rules the friars to be unlawful and no part of true holy church. Psalm 68:29 is worked into the alliteration of lines VI 75-77 in *Piers Plowman*.[128] In *Piers* the quotation is used to

---

124 Alford, p.42
125 MED 'sentence' 1a).
126 The quotations are discussed in Barr (1993), pp.42-3.
127 e.g. 'But, howeuere we speken in diuerse names or licknessis of þis holi chirche, þei techen nouȝt ellis but þis oo name, þat is to seie, "þe congregacioun, or gedering-togidir of feiþful soulis þat lastingli kepen feiþ and trouþe, in word and dede, to God and to man, and reisen her lijf in siker hope of mercy and grace and blisse at her ende, and ouercoueren, or hillen, þis bilding in perfite charite þat shal not faile in wele ne in woo'. ', *SEWW*, 116/21-6.
128 'Deleantur de libro viuencium; I sholde noȝt dele wiþ hem/For holy chirche is holde of hem no tiþe to aske/Quia cum iustis non scribantur. MS F adds 'scribantur in þe registre in hevene'.

128

identify the wastrels with those whose tithes are too unworthy for the church to receive. In *Mum*, the identical words endorse a rather different position, a theological position punishable at this time by death.

Finally, I should like to examine a passage on tithing in *Mum*, because although there are no examples of the sect vocabulary that I reviewed in *Piers*, it uses a quotation from a very important moment in that poem to reverse ecclesiastical discourse in a rather interesting fashion. The narrator goes to church and listens to a sermon preached from the pulpit in which the priest encourages his parishioners to make plentiful offerings to pay their tithes. The list of produce which the priest suggests they bring bears resemblances to the food which the folk bring to appease Hunger in Passus VI of *Piers*. This is an episode in *Piers* dominated by questions of honest labour, idleness and greed and these resonances are appropriate to the sequence in *Mum*. The narrator waits for the priest to say how the church intends to spend the proceeds:

> And euer I waitid whenne he wolde sum worde moeve
> How hooly churche goodes shuld be y-spendid,
> And declare the deedes what thay do shulde
> To haue suche a harueste and helpe not to erie.
> But sorowe on the sillable he shewed of that matiere,
> For Mvm was a meen and made hym to leue.   (613-8)

The suggestion in line 616 that the priest should earn his tithes through his deeds falls some way short from the Wycliffite view that parishioners had the right to withhold tithes from sinful priests,[129] but is still a more radical attitude to tithing than that in a manifestly orthodox text such as *Jacob's Well*: 'ye schul tythe truly, for to kepe you sekerly out of the artycle of cursyng', (p.37/5-6).[130] Church law made the payment of tithes obligatory. It was not conditional on the deserts of the recipient.[131]

In *Mum*, the narrator's stance towards tithing becomes more radical as the text progresses. The narrator spends seven years listening to sermons delivered by figures from the institutionalised church, but none of them discusses the matter of how the tithing should be spent. After an invective against the worldliness of the contemporary clergy, (630-51), and in the absence of any institutionalised solution, the narrator supplies his own answer to the question that has vexed him:

[129] This proposition was the eighteenth conclusion drawn from Wyclif's teaching which the 1382 Council condemned as erroneous. But some Lollard texts perpetuate it, e.g. Matthew, p.57/6-11; p.78/6-8, p.116/14-16; Arnold, p.126/34-6; 176/19-26.
[130] *Jacobs Well*, ed A. Brandeis (EETS 115 1900).
[131] See further Hudson (1988), pp.342-5.

For I am but lewed and lettrid ful lite,
And yit me semeth the sentence that I shewe couthe
And teche how the tithing shuld trewly be departid,
For in thre lynes hit [lith] and not oon lettre more.
Now hendely hireth how I begynne:
That ye clepe God-is parte lete God-is men haue hit,
Reseruyng for yourself sustenance for your foode,
And the ouerplus ouer that for ornementz of the churche.
Though this be shortly y-seide, yit so me God helpe,
Who-so had cunnyng and a clerc were,
Might make a long sermon of thees fewe wordes. (652-62)

There is an echo in line 655 of the tearing of the pardon scene in *Piers*, VII 111: 'In two lynes it lay, and noȝt a [lettre] moore'.[132] This recalls the interchange between Piers and the priest over the significance of the pardon sent by Truthe in which the 'little lettered' Piers challenges the priest's inadequate explanation of an institutionalised document. Similarly in *Mum*, although the narrator is 'lewed and lettrid ful lite', he pits his understanding against the learning of the church and offers his own explanation of how the tithes should be distributed.

The call to attention suggested by 'hireth' shows the narrator offering a rival sermon to that of the parish priest, not from a pulpit, but from outside the material church and within an alliterative poem. At first glance, the division of the tithes seems entirely orthodox. But the conjunction of 'ouerplus', 'ouer' and 'ornementz' in line 659 is rather interesting. According to Lollard teaching, the priest should have no 'ouerplus', let alone 'ouerplus ouer'. Many tracts, citing 1.Timothy 6:8: 'But having food and wherewith to be covered, with these we are content', state that any surplus should be given straight to the poor.[133]

One Wycliffite text, *De Officio Pastoralis*, outlines a distribution of tithes similar to that in *Mum*. In chapter seventeen, the writer states that the tithes should be used for: sustenance of the priest; the relief of the poor; the ornaments of the church and the upkeep of the church house.[134] The distribution is identical to that outlined in *Dives and Pauper*.[135] But the

---

[132] All B manuscripts read 'leef' at this point but 'lettre' is the reading in the C version.
[133] e.g. Arnold, p.475/30. See also Matthew, p.132/14-25. Wimbledon's *Sermon* criticises the clergy for wasting in their proud houses 'wagis that were sufficiaunt to hem' the 'ouerplus that nedy men sholde be susteyned by', ed. I.K. Knight, (Pittsburgh, 1967), p.76/248-55.
[134] Matthew, p.433/5-9.
[135] II 168. In answer to Dives's question whether it is lawful to withold tithes from priests who are openly sinful, Pauper says that it is lawful, but in that case, the tithe should be given to the priest's 'souereyn' (II 168/20-169/37). Given that this could be read as partial support for the 18th conclusion of Wyclif's condemned as heretical, and that the question: 'An decime dande personis ecclesie sint pure elemosine, et si parochiani possint propter peccata suorum prelatorum ad suum iudicium eas subtrahere vel auferre' was part of the

Wycliffite writer has already stated that this distribution is an example of 'mennus lawis' and concludes his account by saying that 'þis parting were ofte vnskileful & þus siche general lawe were nouʒt'. As we have seen 'mennus lawe' stands in discursive contrast to 'God-is lawe'. From a Wycliffite position, the distribution of tithes in *Mum* is not in accordance with the truth.

Criticism of church ornaments is a virulent strain of Wycliffite thought.[136] Priests are accused of conducting services with ostentatious practices and other ornaments which they have bought with poor men's goods. They allow dead walls to be covered in gold while poor men have naked sides.[137] In *Mum*, the phrase 'God-is men' (657) suggests the deserving poor, and in this context, I would argue that the emphasis on 'ouer' in conjunction with 'ornamentz' signifies excess. The narrative frame of the remark, with the echo of *Piers*, constitutes a challenge to the accepted teaching of the institutionalised church. If a reader sympathetic to Wycliffite discourse were to take up the narrator's invitation to make a long sermon out of his light words, the text produced would not look out of place in a Lollard sermon cycle. The lines contest the sermons licensed by the church; here, from the parish priest in his own parish, with the kinds of Lollard preaching which the church sought to suppress. It is in this context that we might recall Macdonnell's remark that, between 1790-1830, what constituted a 'hymn' was politically significant.

I have attempted to show in this chapter that *Crede* and *Mum* were written at a time when the ecclesiastical suppression of Lollardy generated two discourses, locked into reverse symmetry. The larger narrative strategies of the poems reflect the nature of this discursive struggle; Peres against the friars, and Mum against the Sothsegger. Representatives of the third estate command a position of authority in antithesis to members of the clerical estate. Ecclesiastical persecution is expressly commented upon in both poems, and from a position

episcopal examination of Lollards, Hudson (1985), p.135, it is perhaps understandable that in 1430 Bishop Alnwick confiscated a copy of *Dives* from Robert Bert, a chaplain at Bury St Edmunds. That the writer of the *Dives* was a friar and that in the same decade, abbot Whetehamstede, a pillar of orthodoxy, ordered a copy of *Dives* for the library at St Albans, is testimony of the dangers of touching on areas of debate circumscribed by ecclesiastical restrictions. The case of *Dives* is discussed more fully in Hudson (1988), 417-21.

[136] cf. *Crede*, in the lines on Blackfriars and 560-64. Attitudes towards church ornaments were interrogated in episcopal examinations, e.g.: 'An sancta crux sit adoranda et ymagines Christi, beate virginis et sanctorum sint cultu aliquo catholice venerande' Hudson, (1985) p.135.

[137] Matthew, p.91/27-34. For other criticisms see also p.69/4-17; *Lanterne* p.41/31-35 and Arnold, p.462/22ff.

favourable to Wycliffite views. Criticism of the contemporary church expressly confronts those measures which were designed to check it.

At the level of verbal detail, in keeping with other Wycliffite texts, both *Crede* and *Mum* use sect vocabulary as weapons in a discursive contest with the contemporary church. They reverse the meanings of words found in authoritarian discourse so that, in their new context, those same words become part of a discourse of solidarity. Where quotations, or echoes of *Piers Plowman* are used in these later poems, their political significance is altered because increasingly punitive ecclesiastical measures changed the significance of religious discussion. That *Mum* is more coded in its adoption of Wycliffite discourse may reflect the fact that expressing views on religious topics had become more dangerous since the writing of *Crede*. There is no evidence that either of these poems was examined for heresy. However, surviving copies are far from plentiful.[138] On these grounds, it is tempting to speculate that, unlike the friars in *Mum*, Arundel and his associates were actually rather good at reading 'redelles aright', and in a supreme gesture of reversing reverse discourse, suppressed these impertinent challenges to their authority.

---

[138] *Mum* survives in one copy only, and *Crede*, apart from a fifteenth century fragment, only in three sixteenth century copies. These are discussed in Barr (1993), pp.8-9 and p.22 and A.I. Doyle, 'The Manuscripts' in Lawton (1982), 88-100, p.98.

5

Legal Fictions

As a result of John Alford's *Glossary of Legal Diction*, we are now able to appreciate the density of legal reference in *Piers Plowman*. *Piers* emerges as a text whose mode of thought and argument is substantially indebted to legal procedure and vocabulary.[1] The same is true of the poems in the *Piers* tradition. *Richard the Redeless* and *Mum and the Sothsegger* are particularly rich in legal diction, but its use in *Crede* and *Crowned King* is also substantial. It is reasonable to contend that the pervasiveness of legal vocabulary in the tradition reflects, in part, the textual force of *Piers Plowman*. This chapter will examine the uses of legal diction in the tradition with reference to its density, its deployment in argument and metaphor, and finally, its role in defining the ethics of a truth-telling poetic.

Piers and its tradition are not unique in Middle English literature in using legal reference. Studies have shown that the works of Chaucer, the *Gawain*-poet, Henryson and Malory employ a variety of legal terms, motifs, procedures and arguments.[2] Blanch and Wasserman remark

[1] Other important studies have contributed to our understanding of the legal texture in *Piers*: John Alford, 'The Idea of Reason in *Piers Plowman*', in *MESGK*, pp.199-215; Anna Baldwin, *The Theme of Government in Piers Plowman* (Cambridge, 1981); W.J. Birnes, 'Christ as Advocate: the Legal Metaphor of *Piers Plowman*, *Annuale Medievale* 16 (1975), 71-93; P.M. Kean, 'Love, Law and Lewte in *Piers Plowman*', *RES* 15 (1964), 241-61; R. Kirk, 'Legal References in *Piers Plowman*', *PMLA* 48 (1933), 322- 27; James Simpson (1990), 43-60, and 'The Constraints of Satire in *Piers Plowman* and *Mum and the Sothsegger*', in *Langland, the Mystics and the Religious Tradition*, ed. Helen Phillips (Cambridge, 1991), 11-31 and Myra Stokes, *Justice and Mercy in Piers Plowman* (London, 1984).
[2] For a general summary see J.A. Alford, 'Literature and Law in Medieval England', *PMLA* 92 (1977), 941-51, and on Chaucer, R.J. Schoeck, 'A Legal Reading of Chaucer's *Hous of Fame*', *UTQ* 23 (1954), 185-92; Carter Revard, 'The Tow on Absolon's Distaff and the Punishment of Lechers in Medieval London', *ELN* 17 (1980), 168-70; on Malory, E.C. York, 'The Duel of Chivalry in Malory's Book XIX', *PQ* 48 (1969), 186-91, and 'Legal Punishment in Malory's *Le Morte D'Arthur*', *ELN* 11 (1973), 14-21; on Henryson, C. McDonald, 'The Perversion of Law in Robert Henryson's Fable of "The Fox, the Wolf and the Husbandman" ', *Medium Aevum*, 49 (1980), 244-53; and the *Gawain*-poet, J.A. Burrow, 'Two Notes on *Sir Gawain and the Green Knight*', *N&Q* N.S. 19 (1972), 43-5; R.J. Blanch and

that: 'medieval writers turn increasingly to an integration of legal and literary themes in order to underscore the spiritual role of law as an earthly representation of God's rule'.[3] As we shall see, this is certainly the case in *Piers*, but in the tradition, the emphasis is rather different. Apart from one sequence in *Mum* which I shall discuss below, the deployment of legal diction and motifs is distinctively social and political in temper. This is not unique to the *Piers* tradition, but it does mark a point of departure from *Piers Plowman*.

This socio-political emphasis in the integration of the legal and the literary can be seen in some of the earliest poems written in Middle English. One of the *Harley Lyrics*, the *Satire on the Consistory Courts*, presents a particularly interesting example because its main focus is on the oppression that is caused by the language of the law. The poem is the account of a single man who has been hauled up before the ecclesiastical court because he has unfortunately been caught in the act of fornication. In the first three lines of the poem, the speaker, who associates himself with the 'lewed', complains that no unlettered man can live in the land, however skilful he is with his hands, because of the way that the 'lerede' lead them:

> Ne mai no lewed lued libben in londe,
> be he neuer in hyrt so hauer of honde,
> so lerede vs biledes.   (1-3)[4]

The speaker is oppressed by the power of writing. He has his own natural language taken away from him. He complains that if he is caught with his lover, he will fall into the clutches of the learned and be compelled to 'lurnen huere lay/ant rewen alle huere redes' (5-6). The law will make him avow all kinds of oaths (11) with reference to 'heore boc ase vn-bredes' (12). Once in court, the speaker sees more than forty men in front of him ready to write down his offences: 'heo þynkes wiþ heore penne on heore parchemyn' (25). The frequent mention of parchment and writing in this poem is all at the expense of the plaintiff: 'ʒef y am wreint in heore write' (33). All of this writing, is, of course, in a language which the plaintiff cannot understand.[5] Even if it were in

---

J.N. Wasserman, 'Medieval Contracts and Covenants: The Legal Colouring of *Sir Gawain and the Green Knight*', *Neophilologus*, 68 (1984), 598-610; D. Everett and N.D. Hurnard, 'Legal Phraseology in a Passage in *Pearl*', *Medium Aevum* 16 (1947), 9-15; P.M. Kean, *Pearl: An Interpretation* (London, 1967), pp.185-96, and T.A. Reisner, 'The "Cortaysye" sequence in *Pearl*', *MP* 72 (1975), 400-03.
[3] Blanch and Wasserman (1984), p.598.
[4] Quoted from Robbins, no. 6, pp.24-27.
[5] The poem antedates The Statute of Pleadings of 1362 which was an important moment in the history of English as it stipulated that English was to be used for pleadings in the law

English, and not Latin, he would be unable to read it. When the woman is brought into the court, her language is described as 'shrieking' and 'screaming' and she refers to her own speech as 'gabbyng' (59-62). She protests that she does not wish to marry the man, but he is forced 'ase dogge' (82) to marry her in church. Their natural coupling in the fields is brought to book and amended by being institutionalised in a service of marriage. The language of the unlettered is silenced, or equated with noise, and the couple are forced to a union by two institutions from whose discourse they are excluded.

This social and institutional emphasis on legality and legal procedure is also characteristic of another early Middle English poem, namely *The Simonie*.[6] Embree and Urquhart have noted its institutional approach to evil in its classifications of sinners by legal rather than spiritual status (acountours, assisours, attorneis, baronage, cheiturs, corowners, gaþereris, southbailys and squierie).[7] In its exposure of institutional and legal corruption, the poem employs legal terms and procedures in a fashion that anticipates some of the manoeuvres in *Richard* and *Mum*. For instance, in a complaint that pleading will not be heard in court without corrupt payment, the A text reads:

> For if þere be in *countre* an horeling, a shrewe,
> Lat him come to þe *court*, his nedes for to *shewe*
> And bringe wid hem siluer and non oþer *wed*. (A25-7)

The words in italics are all part of a legal diction. Line 27 uses the sense of 'wed' as a legally binding pledge, or something deposited as security for payment, to show how in contemporary pleadings, such pledges have become not a surety for payment, but payment itself.[8]

In the C version of the poem, there is an extended section which criticises the way in which people are encouraged to bring lawsuits, not for their own benefit, but to line the pockets of the attorneys:

> *Attorneis* in *contre* wynneþ selfre for nowt
> Þei make men to bigynne *ple* þat neuer had it þow3t;
> Wan þei comeþ to þe rynge, hoppe if þei con.
> Alle þat þei wynne with *falsnes*, alle þat þei telle iwonne
> Ful wel.

---

courts; see *Statutes of the Realm*, I 375-76. The proceedings were still to be written up in Latin.

[6] cf. E.Salter, '*Piers Plowman* and *The Simonie*', *Archiv*, 203 (1967), 241-54 for a discussion of the relationship of these two poems.

[7] *The Simonie*, p.30.

[8] See Alford, p.166. 'countre' is a geographical district, a shire, Alford, p.36, 'court' the shire or county court, Alford, p.39 and 'shewe' to lay a complaint before court, Alford, p.143.

Ne tryst no man to muche to hem; þei be *fals* by *skyl*.

Such be þe men of þis world; *fals* in þe *bille*.
If eny man wolle his lyf in *trewth* and in *skel*
Let his fals neyȝbours and sewe not þe rowte
He may eche day of his lyf haue grete dowte.
For why?
þei schul al day be *endited* for *manslauȝter* and *robbery*.

Take þe *trewest* man þat euer in londe was,
He schal be *endited* for þing þat neuer was,
Itake and ibounde, a strong þef as he were,
And led to the kynges *prisoun* and lete hym lygge þere
And rote,
Oþer with a *fals enquest*, hang hym by þe þrote.   (C403-20)

Some of these terms are part of a general, rather than specialised, legal vocabulary,[9] but there are also a number of very specific legal terms, e.g. 'ple', (a plea in court), 'skyl' (a logical argument to prove a point) 'endited' (to charge with a crime) and 'enquest' (a trial by jury).[10] In a way that anticipates both *Piers* and poems in the tradition, the use of precise legal terminology lends authority to the criticism of legal corruption.

There are many examples of this in *Piers Plowman*. There are also passages where legal terminology is used to lend precision to the outlining of good legal conduct. I shall focus on one small passage, because it appears to have exterted textual force on *Richard the Redeless*.[11] In Passus I Holy Church preaches on the responsibility of each estate for preserving 'truthe'. Of the first estate she says:

Kynges and knyȝtes sholde *kepen* it by *reson*,
Riden and rappen doun in Reaumes aboute.
And taken *transgressores* and tyen hem faste
Til *treuþe* hadde *ytermyned* hire *trespas* to þe *ende*.   (I 94-7)[12]

All the words in italics have precise legal meanings. Some are common words which also have more technical senses: 'kepen' has the sense of 'to guard and protect laws, rights and property'; 'reson' here means 'equity or law'; and 'treuþe' the principle of right or justice.[13] The

---

[9] Arguably, 'fals', 'falshed' 'manslaughter', 'robbery', 'þef' and 'prisoun' are part of a general legal vocabulary that is accessible also to those not schooled in the law. Maintaining this distinction is not always easy. Alford discusses the problems of determining common from technical usage (pp.xi-xiii), and suggests that context should be the most important determining factor. In this instance in *The Simonie*, the context is undoubtedly legal, but only some of the vocabulary is technical.

[10] Alford, p.117, MED 'skil' (5), Alford, p.50.

[11] Other examples include II 102-7; III 315-22; IV 175-80; XI 125-36; XIX 247 and 451-64.

[12] Quoted from B but the lines are in all versions without significant alteration.

[13] Alford, p.77, p.134 and p.159. This example of 'kepen' is not included on p.77.

remaining words are technical: 'transgressours' is a Latin term meaning those who violate the law, which in the context of 'trespas', suggests an infringement which does not amount to treason or felony. 'Ytermyned . . .to þe ende' is a legal phrase which means to bring a legal case to a conclusion by pronouncing judgment.[14] The social responsibility of knights to preserve justice is couched in terminology which grants the speaker authoritative status on the subject.

There is a closely comparable example in *Richard*. In Passus Two, the narrator inveighs sharply against the practice of livery and maintenance, especially in the way that it corrupts the law. At line 67, the narrator stops his criticisms abruptly for fear that he is overstepping the mark, but Reason interjects to assure the narrator that what he is doing is for the good of the community and that he should continue.[15] Taking new heart from this reassurance, the narrator repeats his assertion that maintenance and livery should be kept out of legal proceedings, and goes on to outline the characteristics that a true, uncorrupted judiciary should possess:

> But ho-so had kunnynge and *conscience* bothe
> To stonde vnstombled and stronge in his wittis,
> *Lele* in his leuynge leuyd be *his owen*,
> That no manere mede shulde make him wrye,
> For to *trien a trouthe be-twynne two sidis*,
> And *lette* for no *lordschep* the lawe to susteyne
> Whane the pore *pleyned* that put were to *wrongis*,
> And I were of *conceill* by Crist that me boughte,
> He shuld haue a *signe* and sum-what be yere
> For to *kepe* his *contre* in quiete and in reste.
> This were a good *ground so me God helpe*!
> And a trewe *tente* to take and to yeue,
> [For] ony lord of this [londe] that leuerez vsith.
> But how the gayes han y-gon God wotte the sothe
> Amonge myghtffull men alle these many yeris,
> And whedir the *grounde* of [g]lifte were good other ille,
> *Trouthe* hathe *determyned* the *tente* to the *ende*,
> And *reson* hath *rehersid* the *resceyte* of all.   (II 81-98)

All the italicised words are examples of a legal diction. 'Conscience' is used in its legal sense of determining right from wrong; 'lele' means in accordance with the law; 'his owen' is that which belongs by law or justice to a person, and to 'trien a truthe' is to judge a true account or testimony.[16] The 'two sidis' are the opposing sides of a legal dispute;

[14] Alford, p.157, p.158, p.153.
[15] I discuss the significance of this below.
[16] Alford, p.34; p.86; p.70; pp.160-1; p.159.

'lette' is used here in the sense of 'to impede justice' and 'lordschep' in the sense of retinue. The retainers of powerful lords often tried to pervert the course of justice through bribery.[17] 'Pleyned' is from the verb 'pleinen' to make a legal complaint or accusation; 'wrongis' has the sense of actions defined by law as civil and criminal offences; 'conceill' means a body of legal counsellors or advisors, and 'signe' is the official badge of a notary.[18] 'Kepe', as we have seen from *Piers*, means to defend, and while 'contre' may mean judicial district, it can also mean 'jury', as in the quotation from *The Simonie*. From its collocation with 'kepe', I think that this may be its sense here, and that the line states that a judge ought to defend his jurors against intimidation.[19] 'Ground' is used in its specific legal sense as the basis of law, and 'so me God helpe' is an oath used in court which attests to the truth of one's testimony.[20] 'Tente' means the intention which motivates a person's actions.[21] 'Trouthe; 'reson', 'determyned' and 'ende' have the same legal senses as their counterparts in *Piers Plowman*, and indeed, this passage in *Richard* appears to be a precise verbal echo of Holy Church's outlining of legal responsibility in Passus I. 'Rehersid' means to recite aloud a plea or list of charges and 'resceyte' is glossed in the OED as having the legal sense of the admittance of a plea in a court of justice. I think that this may be the sense here, so that justice recites aloud a list of charges that have been admitted as a plea in court.[22]

I have quoted this passage and discussed the legal diction at some length in order to show that the density of legal reference is comparable to the verbal texture of *Piers Plowman*. In addition to the quotation of lines from Passus I, it is also noteworthy that, with the exception of 'ground' and 'resceyte', all the legal terms can be found in *Piers*. My other reason for quoting at such length is to show that these words have technical legal senses in what is unambiguously a legal context. Not only does this give the comments precision and authority, but it also shows that the poet is well aware of the legal meanings of words which can also be used in more general senses. This is important, because, as we shall see, as in *Piers*, such words are often used with precise meanings in *Richard* in non-legal contexts. To miss their legal significance, misses the particular focus of attention.[23]

---

17 MED 'side' 8b); Alford, p.87 and p.91.
18 Alford, p.117; p.169; pp.37-8 and p.144.
19 It could equally mean keep his judicial district in peace.
20 MED 'ground' 5c); Alford, p.146.
21 Alford, p.74.
22 Alford, p.130; OED 'receipt' 7d). This sense is not in MED.
23 This is a point made with respect to *Piers* by Alford, p.xii.

In *Mum* legal diction is equally dense. In the bag of books sequence, the narrator comments with notable precision on the corruption and inadequacies of the legal procedures of his day. Some of the books in the bag are themselves legal documents. There is an IOU, a writ, a last will and testament, a ragman's roll and a schedule.[24] One of the most detailed comments on the law is found in a frayed book cover, where both the rich and the poor are criticised for their continual resort to litigation, even when they have lost their case. The narrator criticises the loophole in the legal system which allows a plaintiff to appeal against a lost action, even if he has brought an action wrongfully. It is the expense which so angers the narrator, and he proposes a reform: that anyone who brings an action without good cause should have to pay a fine, and costs should be paid at the end of each action, rather than being postponed until the final appeal is heard. It is a dense passage, but it is worth quoting in full:

> For though men *pleede* and *poursuye* and in thaire *playntz* falle
> And newe thaym aftre *nonsuyte[s]* nynetene hunthred,
> Withoute *grovnde* or *guilte* but forto gete a bribe,
> Yit shal thay haue no *harme* though thay hurle euer.
> But shuld thay picche and paye at eche *pleynte-is ende*
> And compte alle the *costz* of men of court and elles,
> And taske al the *trespas* as *trouthe* wolde and *reason*
> Thay wolde cesse sum tyme for sheding of thaire siluer.
> I seye aswel of simple men that *suen* ayenst grete,
> And of the poure proute that *peyren* ofte thaire better,
> That *causelees accusen* thaym to king and to the lordz,
> As I doo of ducz that suche deedes vsen;
> For lordz and laborers been not like in *costes*.
> Hit wold pese the peuple and many *pleyntes bate*
> And chaunge al the *chauncellerie* and cheuallerie amende
> And ease be to euery man that been of euene states,
> And solas be to souurayns and to thaire seruantz alle,

[24] 'Papir' (1350) has the legal sense of a written promise to pay a debt, an IOU (Alford, p.108). The 'writte of high wil' (1498) is a legal document which inititates a criminal action, Alford, p.169; at 1697, there is a 'title of a testament'; a document recording a person's wishes on the disposition of personal property after death (Alford, p.153). It has a 'seel of th'office' (1699) because a will was authenticated with an official mark or seal, cf. Alford, p.142. The 'raggeman rolle' (1565) is a document recording accusations or offences. When justices heard and determined complaints in the shires, the testimony was recorded on rolls. The seals of the witnesses questioned were attached to these rolls by cutting the bottom edge of the parchment into strips, forming a tattered fringe. The inquisitors who carried these ragged rolls came to be known as ragmen and the term became attached to the rolls themselves and by extension to any document of a similar appearance (Alford, p.125). The 'rolle' at 1364 is a scroll containing legal documents and records of various sorts (Alford, p.138). Here, presumably the charter of endowment or account of bequests, and at 1734 the 'cedule' is a brief document attached to a roll or enclosed in a letter and usually containing a list of names or bill of particulars (MED 'cedule' 1b)).

And a miracle to meen men that *mote* lite cunne,
Were this oon yere y-vsid as I haue *declarid*, –
That of euery *writte* withoute *wronge* there were *amendes* made,
And paye for alle the *costes* at euery *pleyntis-ende*
And *tolle* for the *trespas* as *trouthe* wolde and *reason* –
The lawe wold like vs wel, and euer the lenger the bettre.
But pouaire of *prerogatife* that *poynt* hath *reseruyd*
That euery fode haue fredome to *folowe* vn-y-punysshid.
But *ciuile* seith vs not so that serueth for al peuple
That habiteth vndre heuene hethen men and other.
And Crist-is lawe-is y-canonized *canon*, yf thou loke,
And eeke the glorious gospelle *grovnde* of alle lawes,
Techeth vs a trewe texte that toucheth this ilke *matiere*;
    Nullum malum impunitum. euangelium
For in my *conscience* ne in my credo yit couthe I neuer vele
But that oure lawe *leneth* there a lite, as me thenketh.   (1594-1625)

Some of this vocabulary has already been introduced and so I shall concentrate on the new terms whose precise legal sense may not be immediately obvious. 'Pleede' is to plead a case at law; 'pursue' is to bring charges against and 'nonsuytes' are failures of a plaintiff to prosecute his claims or to provide sufficient evidence.[25] 'Harme' has the sense of legal damages; 'costz' are specifically legal costs; 'suen' means to make a claim at law, and 'peyren' to harm or damage, often by slander.[26] 'Causelees' means without ground for a legal action; 'bate' means to dismiss a case at law; and 'tolle' means to pay a tax or fine.[27] 'Mote' means to litigate; 'amendes' has the sense of legal redress, and 'poynt' means here a point of law, though elsewhere it often means an accusation or charge.[28] 'Reseruyd' means to secure a right by a formal stipulation, and 'prerogatife' is the special right granted by law to allow individuals who felt that they had been treated unjustly by common law, to take their cases to the equitable court of chancery (chancellerie).[29] 'Folowe vn-y- punysshid' means to prosecute at law without penalty; 'matiere' is a plea or petition, and 'leneth' has the legal sense of being partial, or showing bias.[30]

This must rank as one of the most detailed and pragmatic treatments of legal procedure in Middle English poetry. In its scope it is more focused and detailed than anything in *Piers*, despite the fact that the

---

25 Alford, p.117; p.123; MED 'non-suit' a).
26 Alford, p.68; MED 'cost' n.1) 1a); Alford, p.148 and p.7.
27 Alford, p.23; MED 'abaten' (3); Alford, p.156.
28 Alford, p.101; pp.5-6; MED 'pointe' 8).
29 MED 'reserven (vb) 3a and b); 'prerogatif' MED 1b) and Alford, p.26.
30 MED 'folwen' 5c); Alford, p.102; MED 'lenen' 2b).

majority of the legal terms are found in both poems.[31] The precision of the discussion is important, because we shall encounter some of this diction in other contexts in *Mum*. The passage also demonstrates the poet's familiarity with legal theory. He supports his point with reference to three texts: 'ciuile' or Roman law, which consituted the The *Digest* or *Pandects* of Justinian; 'Crist-is lawe-is y-canonized canon', which is ecclesiastical law, as laid down in the decrees of the popes and statutes of councils, specifically, Gratian's *Concordia discordantium canonum* or *Decretum*, and the Bible.

Earlier in *Mum* there are Latin quotations which are drawn from Canon Law which show that its author was familiar with the *Decretum*.[32] There is also a quotation from Justinian's *Institutes* at *Richard*, III 32, which, if I am correct in suggesting that these two poems had the same author,[33] shows that he was also familiar with the texts of Civil Law.[34] In this passage from *Mum*, there are specific texts which support the narrator's point that it is contrary to legal theory for everyone to have the freedom to prosecute a case at law without penalty. Civil law prohibits certain members of the community from prosecuting a case at law: minors; those serving in the army; magistrates; convicted criminals; those of insufficient means; magistrates; freedmen who wish to proceed against their patrons; anyone who accuses someone who is already the object of an accusation undertaken by a third party, and women.[35] A passage in the *Decretum* stipulates that clerics should neither bring proceedings in secular law courts nor be tried in them.[36] At 1623, the corrector has added a a Latin gloss from Innocent, *De Contemptu Mundi*, III.15, 'nullum malum impunitum euangelium' (No

---

[31] There is a similarly pragmatic passage at lines 743-758. Mum quotes the Canon Law text 'qui tacet consentire videtur' to show that witholding knowledge of a crime is itself a criminal offence. This text is also cited in *Dives*, II 211/11 and in the *Coliphazio* play in the Wakefield Pageants, lines 143-4. cf. 'qui non occurit, consentit erranti, *Dist. Grat.*, 83, c.5., Freidberg, p.294. Mum then cites an example from Land law to show that if the plaintiff fails to answer the charge then he can be convicted for perjury. The legal background is discussed in the notes to these lines in *The Piers Plowman Tradition*, pp.326-7.

[32] cf. n.31 and the Latin sidenote: 'Fauor et premium timor et odium peruertunt verum iudicium. Canon.' quoted at 1148: 'Patronage and fear, reward and hatred pervert true justice'. It is a summary of a chapter in canon law, *Decreti Secunda Pars*, Causa xi. Quest. III.c.lxxviii, Freidberg, I.665. I believe these Latin citations to be authorial; see Barr (1993), pp.42-3. *Dives* quotes the same text, II 248/1-3: 'Mannys dom is peruert þe foure þingis, as seith þe lawe, xi, q.iii: be dred, be coueytyse of ȝiftis, be hate, be loue'.

[33] Helen Barr, 'The Relationship of *Richard the Redeless* and *Mum and the Sothsegger*', *YLS*, 4 (1990), 105-33.

[34] 'Propter ingratitudinem liber homo reuocatur in seruitutem ut in stimulo compunccionis et in lege ciuili' (On account of ungratefulness, the free man is recalled into slavery according to the prick of conscience and civil law. There is nothing corresponding to this in *The Prick of Conscience*. The citation is from the *Institutes of Justinian*, I.t.16.i.

[35] Scott, *The Civil Law*, XI.18-19.

[36] Causa XI. Quest.1 c.xlvii; Freidberg, I.641.

evil should go unpunished).[37] This is a plausible candidate for the gospel text referred to by line 1623 as it paraphrases the sense of Matthew, 16:27 and 25:31-46, that at the Second Coming, all sins will be accounted for. It introduces a rather different emphasis to the argument, however, and it is possible that a text such as 1 Corinthians, 6:1-8, where Paul chastises the people of Corinth for going to law in the secular courts and bringing lawsuits against each other, may have been the writer's original intention. This is the text that is quoted in the *Decretum* to stipulate that clerics should not take any part in secular litigation.[38] Whichever original text was intended, this passage is remarkable for the meticulous criticism of contemporary legal procedure through reference to specific practice and actual legal texts.

This degree of legal familiarity is unmatched in *Crede* or *Crowned King*, but both of these poems make use of legal reference as part of the arguments they launch. In this respect, they are very close to the temper of *Richard* and *Mum*. I shall look at examples from *Richard and Mum* first, in order to provide a control against which to measure comparable instances in the other two poems.

Speakers within *Piers* often use detailed analogies from contemporary legal procedures to authorise their points of criticism. A clear example of this is in Trajan's speech in Passus XI. He argues that a priest who makes mistakes by missing parts out in reading the gospel, or in reciting services, is a fool. He prefaces his criticism with an analogy drawn from law:

> A *chartre* is *chalangeable* bifore a chief Iustice;
> If fals latyn be in þat lettre þe lawe it *impugneþ*,
> Or peynted *parentrelynarie, parcelles ouerskipped*. (B XI 303-5)[39]

A 'chartre' is a written document; 'chalangeable' means contestable, and 'impugneþ' means to call into question. 'Parentrelynarie' is 'between the lines', and 'parcelles ouerskipped' means the omission of sections of a legal document.[40] This legal introduction to Trajan's criticism of careless priests calls into question the validity of their place in the church. As a result the negligence of priests is put on a par with legal irregularity. Trajan continues his criticism by stating that the bishop who ordains such priests is as guilty as the priests themselves. His accusation continues the legal diction:

[37] cf. *Piers*, IV 143-4; cf. XVIII 390a.
[38] It is also the text quoted by Walter Brut in his condemnation of the contemporary church's persecution of heretics; Trefnant, p.311.
[39] This passage is not altered in C.
[40] Alford, p.25; p.24; p.72, and pp.109-10; p.109 and p.107.

Ac neuer neiþer is blamelees, þe bisshop ne þe Chapeleyn;
For hir eiþer is *endited*, and that [of] *'Ignorancia
Non excusat episcopos nec ydiotes preestes'*.   (B XI 315-17)

We have seen in the example from *The Simonie* that 'endited' has the legal sense of making an accusation against someone. Here, Trajan formally indicts bishops and chaplains with the charge that ignorance does not acquit them from blame.[41] His accusation bears some weight; he has earlier told the dreamer that it was only as a result of his 'loue and leautee and . . .laweful domes' that he was rescued from hell (XI 145). In this passage, it is the contemporary clergy who are on the receiving end of such 'laweful domes'.

The use of legal reference to define illegality is also used in secular contexts in *Piers*. The most obvious case is in the treatment of Mede. Mede is shown to corrupt law and legal procedure; in the words of the king, she 'ouermaistreþ lawe and muche truþe letteþ' (IV 176).[42] Mede's violation of the law is constantly defined by juxtaposing legal reference and procedure with the very principle that undermines it. Thus the marriage 'feffement' is made by False, (B II 73) and the standard opening of a charter of conveyance: *'Sciant Presentes & futuri &c'* (B II 74a) precedes the listing of the Seven Deadly Sins in the charter.[43] Because she is related to the king, Mede has violated the law of the land by not seeking his permission to marry, thus rendering the legal proceedings doubly invalid.[44] Amends for this perversion require the mobilisation of full legal powers, which is why Mede has to be tried in the King's court. Reason wins the case because of the justice of his claims and the King declares a legal sentence:

The kyng callede Conscience and afterward Reson
And *recordede* þat Reson hadde riȝtfully *shewed*.   (B IV 171-2)[45]

Interestingly, this legal *quid pro quo* strategy is exactly that which is used in Passus XVIII to prove Christ's right to the souls in Limbo. Lucifer, like Mede, has his wickedness defined in legal terms. He claims he was 'seised' with the souls in Limbo (XVIII 283) but, as Satan points out, he gained possession of the souls illegally, through guile, by

[41] 'Excusen' means to clear from a charge; Alford, p.53. The Latin text is a maxim of Canon Law; Alford, p.71.
[42] The phrase means to impede or obstruct justice; Alford, p.87.
[43] For the charter, see Alford, p.140. Stokes discusses the perversion of legal formality of this sequence, pp.106-8.
[44] See Baldwin, pp.31-3.
[45] 'Recorded' means to testify what had previously happened in court; Alford, p.127, Reson is the personification of justice, and 'shewed' means declared law; Alford, p.144. This passage is altered in C and line 172 is omitted.

deceiving Eve with words of 'treson' (XVIII 287-291).[46] Gobelyn endorses this: 'We haue no trewe title to hem, for þoruʒ treson were þei dampned'/'Certes I drede me' quod þe deuel, 'lest truþe do hem fecche' (XVIII 294-5).[47] Lucifer's legal claim is thus invalidated and the way is cleared for Christ to lay due legal claim to the souls. Discarding Lucifer's claim as invalid, Christ cites a series of laws which justify his own right to the souls in Limbo:

> It is noʒt vsed in erþe to hangen a *feloun*
> Ofter þan ones þouʒ he were a *tretour*.
> And if þe kyng of þat kyngdom come in þat tyme
> There a *feloun* þole sholde deeþ ooþer *Iuwise*
> *Lawe* wolde he yeue hym lif if he loked on hym.
> And I þat am kyng of kynges shal come swich a tyme
> Ther *doom* to þe deeþ dampneþ alle wikked,
> And if lawe wole I loke on hem it liþ in my *grace*
> Wheiþer þei deye or deye noʒt for þat þei diden ille. . .
> Nullum malum impunitum &c
> They shul be clensed clerliche and keuered of hir synnes
> In my *prisone* Purgatorie til *parce it hote*.   (XVIII 379-87; 390a-92)

The passage is full of legal diction[48] which frame three contemporary tenets of legal procedure: that one does not hang a felon twice, even if he is a traitor; that a king may decide to save the life of a convicted felon through exercising his prerogative, and that prison is a corrective institution which gives convicted criminals the opportunity to make amends for their crimes.[49] Just as in the Mede episode, illegality can be corrected only by due process of law: ' "Thus by lawe" quod oure lord, "lede I wole fro hennes/Tho ledes þat I loue" ' (XVIII 400- 1). Here, the political and spiritual realms are drawn parallel though a use of legal language which fuses the literal and the metaphorical.

Similar legal strategies are used in *Richard*, not in an attempt to expound spiritual doctrine, but to demonstrate true kingship and the right behaviour of a community. The stimulus for the poem is the deposition of Richard II and Henry Bolingbroke's accession. It becomes

---

46 This is discussed by Birnes, p.82.

47 'trewe title' means the legal right to the possession of property; Alford, p.155; 'treason' is an action of treachery, p.157 and 'fecche' means to recover what is rightfully one's own (p.56).

48 All the italicised terms are in Alford. Those whose technical meaning is not immediately apparent are: 'Iewis', which means judicial punishment or sentence (p.75); 'grace', which means a grace or favour as distinguished from right (p.66); and 'parce it hote' (until the word 'spare thou' commands an end) repeats a common formula in sentencings (p.108).

49 These are cited by Birnes, pp.82-5. The legal formality of Christ's reclaiming of the souls in Passus XVIII is also discussed by Baldwin, pp.69-74 and Stokes, pp.269-71.

clear that the narrator's sympathies are Lancastrian, and legal terminology is used both to endorse his position and Henry's legitimate right
to the crown. This is apparent as early as the Prologue, though the legal
connotations might easily be missed:

> Sodeynly ther sourdid selcouthe thingis,
> A grett wondir to wyse men as it well mygkth,
> And dowtes for to *deme* for drede comynge after.
> So sore were the sawis of *bothe two sidis:*
> Of Richard that regned so riche and so noble,
> That wyle he werrid be west on the wilde Yrisshe,
> Henrri was *entrid* on the est half,
> Whom all the londe loued in lengthe and in brede,
> And rosse with him rapely to rightyn his *wronge*.   (I 5-13)

While Richard was away on a military expedition in Ireland,[50] Henry,
whom Richard had exiled, landed back in England at Ravenspur with a
large army.[51] We have seen how earlier in *Richard*, 'bothe two sidis'
means the opposing parties in a lawsuit, and the use of the phrase here,
sets up the rival claims of both parties as if the narrator were
adjudicating a dispute between Richard and Henry. Henry is reputed to
have sent out circulars from Pontefract castle to all the towns of
England, setting out his own case against Richard,[52] and the narrator
suggests that the events were so extraordinary that it was impossible to
'deme' (i.e. to judge the relative merits of the case). This is ingenuous,
however, because, in these lines, the narrator does exactly that.

'Wronge', as we have seen, is a term of legal diction, meaning a
criminal offence.[53] Henry received a number of 'wronge's at Richard's

---

[50] 'the wilde Yrisshe' is a phrase used by Richard when writing from Dublin to the Duke
of York in 1395. He remarked that there were three kinds of people in Ireland, 'the wild
Irish, our enemies, the Irish now in rebellion and the faithful English', N.H. Nicolas, ed.,
Proceedings and Ordinances of the Privy Council (London, 1834), I.57-8. Richard made two
expeditions to quell the insurrections in Ireland, the first in 1395, and the second in 1399 to
avenge the death of Roger Mortimer, Lieutenant of Ireland, who was killed in an ambush
on 20th July 1398.

[51] Henry returned to England, probably at the beginning of July and eventually reached
Berkeley Castle in Gloucester at the end of July. In the course of his progress, he attracted
many supporters, while the duke of York, whom Richard had left as Regent, found it
difficult to raise an army. At the end of July, Richard returned from Ireland to Conway in
North Wales, and proceeded to Flint with the army which the earl of Salisbury had raised,
but desertions were frequent. He was either ambushed on the way and taken to Flint as a
prisoner, or, having arrived safely at Flint, submitted there to Henry. By the end of August
Richard was a prisoner in the Tower of London, while Henry, with his Lancastrian army,
marched into London in triumph at the beginning of September; see L.D. Duls, *Richard II
in the Early Chronicles* (The Hague, 1975), pp.152ff., and J.L. Kirby, *Henry IV of England*
(London, 1970), pp.53-59.

[52] *Chronique de la Traison et Mort du Richart Deux Roy Dengleterre*, ed. B.Williams (London,
1846), pp.180-2.

[53] cf. *Richard*, II 87, quoted above, p.137.

hands. In January 1398, Henry presented a petition to Richard accusing Thomas Mowbray, duke of Norfolk, of treason. The matter resulted in a trial by combat between the two men scheduled for 16th September 1398. Before the combatants met in battle, Richard, to the astonishment of the crowd, forbad the joust and imposed a ten year exile on Henry and life banishment on Mowbray. The *Annales* commented that Richard banished Henry without any legitimate cause and that his action was against all justice, military laws and customs of the kingdom.[54] Henry's father, John of Gaunt, died at the beginning of February the following year. In March, Richard announced that Henry's sentence amounted to life banishment, and that all the possessions of the house of Lancaster were forfeited to the crown. Before leaving England Henry had received express promise from Richard that he should enjoy his father's possessions should they fall to him during his absence.[55] The use of the word 'wronge' to describe Henry's side of the argument instantly invests him with 'right'. Even more categorically, 'entrid' is a term of legal diction, meaning the act of taking possession of lands and also the legal right to do so.[56] The term suggests that Henry is the lawful owner of England and thus, the throne.

The narrator's support for Henry is made even more explicit in Passus III. Here, the narrator employs an extended analogy of the behaviour of partridges to justify Henry's claim to the throne:[57]

> Thane cometh ther a congion with a grey cote,
> As not of his nolle as he the nest made,
> Another proud partriche and precyth to the nest,
> And preuylich pirith till the dame passe,
> And *sesith* on hir [sete] with hir softe plumes,
> And houeth the eyren that the hue laide,
> And with hir corps keuereth hem till that they kenne,
> And fostrith and fodith till fedris schewe,
> And cotis of kynde hem keuere all aboughte.
> But as sone as they styffe and that they steppe kunne,
> Than *cometh and crieth* hir owen kynde dame,
> And they folwith the vois at the frist note,
> And leueth the lurker that hem er ladde,
> For the schrewe schrapid to selde for her wombis,
> That her lendys were lene and leued with hunger.
> But than the *dewe* dame dineth hem swythe,
> And fostrith hem forthe till they fle kunne.
> 'What is this to mene, man?' maiste thou axe,

---

[54] *Annales*, p.226.
[55] *Cal. Pat. Ric. II, 1369-99*, p.425.
[56] Alford, p.51.
[57] cf. earlier discussion of the dangers of using this analogy, pp.54-55.

'For it is derklich endited for a dull panne;
Wherffore I wilne yif it thi will were,
The partriche propurtes by whom that thou menest?'
A! Hicke Heuyheed! hard is thi nolle
To cacche ony kunynge but cautell bigynne!
Herdist thou not with eeris how that I er tellde
How the egle in the est *entrid his owen*,
And cried and clepid after his owen kynde briddis. (III 45-70)

One partridge lays her eggs in a nest and incubates them, but she is then driven out by another partridge, the 'congion' who sits on the eggs until they hatch. But when the fledglings are strong enough, their true mother returns, and as soon as they hear her voice, they immediately desert the intruding foster-mother who never gave them enough to eat.

The true mother is Henry IV and the stingy foster mother is Richard II. Because this analogy is rather confusing, the narrator spells out its significance, and in line 69 equates the first partridge with the eagle, which was Henry's badge, and Henry's cognomen elsewhere in the poem.[58] The verb 'entrid' is used again with exactly the same legal force as in the opening lines of the poem, and the legitimacy of Henry's claim is secured by the addition of 'his owen'.[59] The phrase 'cometh and crieth' is an anglicisation of the legal phrase 'vint et clama' which was the terminology used when one came into a court and put forth a claim.[60] This fits perfectly the transferred political sense of the analogy because that was exactly what Henry did in staking his three-fold claim to the throne in the last Parliament of 1399.[61] Henry is described as the 'dewe' dame in line 60, an adjective which supports his legal right to the birds.[62]

By contrast, the illegality of Richard's claim is highlighted. The first partridge 'sesith' on the nest (49), but her claim to possession is shown to be no more lawful than Lucifer's claim to the souls in *Piers Plowman*.

---

[58] *Richard*, II 145; 176; 190; III 69; 74; 91; other poems refer to Henry Bolingbroke as the eagle, cf. *On King Richard's Ministers*, Wright, I.364; *On the Expected Arrival of the Duke of Lancaster*, Wright, I.368. See also *Chronicon Adae de Usk*, ed. and trans. E.M. Thompson (London, 1904), p.173. At *Richard*, III 74, Henry as the eagle flies higher than any other bird. Gower alludes to this in *Vox Clamantis* and uses it to symbolise the king pure in heart, VI.985-6.
[59] It means that which belongs, by law or justice, to a person; Alford, p.70. cf. II 83, quoted at p.137 above.
[60] Alford, p.31.
[61] 'I, Henry of Lancaster, chalenge this Rewme of Yngland and the Corone with al the membres and appurtenances als I am disendit be right lyne of the Blode comyng fro the gude lorde Kyng Henry therde and thorghe that ryght that God of his grace hath sent me, with helpe of my Kyn and of my Frendes to recover it; the whiche Rewme was in poynt to be undone for defaut of governance and undoyng of the gode lawes'; *Rot. Parl*, III.422-3.
[62] MED 'due' 2a) prescribed by law or custom.

Her act of taking possession has no legal authority. She is a 'congion' who seizes on the property which rightfully belongs to another, and she illegally takes possession of young birds by driving out their 'owen kynde dame' (55).[63] Just as Christ's claim to the souls in Limbo is proved by legal right, so too is Henry's right to rule the people of England. In the eyes of the narrator, Richard, like Lucifer, has no 'trewe title' to them.

Later in this Passus, the narrator describes the lawlessness of the band of retainers that Richard recruited from Cheshire. Richard began recruiting these men in 1387 and throughout the 1390s built them into a personal bodyguard, decorated with his white hart livery. When parliament opened in September 1397, Richard was protected by over 300 of these Cheshire archers. Because building work was in process in Westminster Hall, the parliamentary meeting was accommodated in a hall newly built for the session which had open sides. Usk, who was present at the parliament, records that the Cheshiremen were quite visible through the open sides and bent their bows whenever they thought any quarrel had arisen in the proceedings.[64] The Monk of Evesham comments that the hall was specially built for this purpose and that the Cheshiremen actually began to shoot but were restrained by the king.[65] Between January 1398 and early spring 1399, Richard was constantly accompanied by this retinue. Usk cites this as the chief cause of Richard's ruin, stating that these retainers oppressed the king's subjects with impunity. They beat and robbed them, he says, and committed murders, adulteries and other evils without end. Richard cherished his retainers so much that rather than listen to anyone who had a complaint against them, he would rather treat him as an enemy.[66]

In the passage in *Richard*, these retainers are described in legal diction which serves to highlight the way that they corrupted the law. The techniques used are reminiscent of the treatment of Mede in *Piers*. Indeed, there is a verbal echo of *Piers* at line 316. In *Piers* the line comes in the middle of Conscience's denunciation of the way that Mede motivates victualers to cheat the poor:[67]

> Tho ben men of this molde that most harme worchen.
> For chyders of Chester where chose many daies
> To ben of *conceill* for *causis* that in the court hangid,

---

[63] 'kynde' is used in the poem to denote behviour in accordance with principles of natural law; see Barr (1992).
[64] Usk, p.154.
[65] *Historia Vitae et Regni Ricardi Secundi*, ed. T. Hearne (London, 1727), p.134.
[66] Usk, pp.169-70. See also *Annales*, p.237.
[67] *Piers*, III 80: 'For þise are men on þis molde þat moost harm wercheþ'.

And *pledid pipoudris* alle manere *pleyntis*.
They cared for no *coyffes* that men of court vsyn,
But *meved many maters* that man neuer thoughte,
And *feyned falshed* till they a *fyne* had,
And knewe no manere *cause* as comunes tolde.
Thei had non other *signe* to *schewe* the lawe
But a preuy pallette her pannes to kepe,
To hille here lewde heed in stede of an houe.
They *constrewed quarellis* to quenche the peple,
And *pletid* with pollaxis and *poyntis* of swerdıs,
And at the *dome-yeuynge* drowe out the bladis,
And lente men leuere of her longe battis.
They lacked alle vertues that a juge shulde haue;
For, er a *tale* were ytolde they wolde *trie the harmes*,
Withoute ony *answere* but ho his lyf hatid.   (III 316-333)

'Conceill' means advice or legal counsel and 'causis' are legal suits or actions,[68] but this legal diction is used mockingly; we learn in the next line that the Cheshiremen pleaded piepowders in every action. The piepowder courts were set up to deal with matters arising out of fairs and markets. They were not hampered by the slow and technical rules of common law because they administered the law merchant. Interested parties were often accepted as competent witnesses, and as the courts were only in session for the duration of the fair, judgment was given without delay.[69] The narrator uses the different procedural rules of the piepowder courts as an ironic understatement. To plead 'pipoudris' for all 'pleyntis' is tantamount to disregarding proper legal procedure altogether.

We have seen earlier that 'mater' has the sense of making a plea, or puting forth a petition. However, the 'maters' moved by the Cheshiremen clearly bore no resemblance to those recognised by any court of law. 'Fyne' means final agreement or settlement,[70] but this is reached only as a result of criminality. Unlike the ideal judge in Passus II, who deserves to have a 'signe' (i.e. the badge of a notary), the only 'signe' which the Cheshiremen had to 'schewe' law[71] was a military headpiece worn instead of a lawyer's coif.

Lines 327-330 contain elaborate punning. 'Constrewed quarellis' in a legal sense means to fabricate an accusation, but there is also a pun on 'quarrel' in the sense of 'armed combat.'[72] The twin sense is brought out by the punning in the following lines on 'poyntis' as legal charge or

68 Alford, p.38, and p.23
69 L.B. Curzon, *English Legal History* (Plymouth, 1979), 188-9.
70 Alford, p.59.
71 cf. discussion of *Piers* IV 171-2 above, p.143.
72 Alford, p.35, MED 'querele' 2b and 2c).

accusation, and as the tip of a sword,[73] and 'leuere' as the bruises bestowed by cudgels, rather than heraldic badges.[74] The effect of this wordplay is to fuse the legal and the physical so that they become indistinct. In technique, it recalls the use of legal diction in Passus XVIII of *Piers*. Here, however, the sheer perversion of law, with the legal vocabulary emptied of any reference to lawful procedure, is also reminiscent of the treatment of Mede. In the last two lines of the quotation, we learn that the Cheshiremen would judge damages prior to the plaintiff's opening appeal, and without any defence in response to a charge or accusation.[75] Beneath the veneer of legal rectitude, this simply means that the Cheshiremen beat people up first and asked questions later, if at all. While this use of legal diction in *Richard* is without the spiritual sublimity of its counterpart in *Piers*, it is ingenious and trenchant in its new literary context.

There is one episode in *Mum* which approaches the fusion of the spiritual and earthly in a manner reminiscent of *Piers*. In his meeting with the beekeeper, the narrator asks where he can find a truthteller. Throughout the poem, speaking the truth is an activity associated with moral rectitude, and in the beekeeper's reply, it is associated with eternal Truth:

> Yn man-is herte his hovsing is, as hooly writte techet,
> And mynde is his mansion that made alle th'estres.
>   In corde fidelis est habitacio veritatis
> There *feoffed* hym his fadre freely forto dwelle,
> And put hym in *possession* in paradise terrestre
> Yn Adam oure auncetre and al his *issue* after.
> He spirith hym with his spirite that sprange of hymself
> To *holde* that habitacion and heuene afterwardes.   (1224-30)

I have discussed elsewhere how this sequence draws on ideas of natural law.[76] Here, I wish to note how when the beekeeper explains human psychology, he uses a complex allegorical argument which depends on procedures of land law. Truth has been enfeoffed by God with an estate where he is entitled to two dwelling places: the heart and the mind.[77] This God-given estate was Adam, and since then, Truth has been

[73] MED 'pointe' 8 and sense 11a.

[74] cf. the similar pun on physical beating and livery in the religious lyric *Wofully araide*, in *A Selection of Religious Lyrics*, ed. Douglas Gray, (Oxford, 1975), pp.26-7.

[75] 'tale' is the plaintiff's account in a legal suit; Alford, p.151, 'harmes' means damages; cf. Alford, p.68 and 'answere' means a defence in response to a charge or accusation; Alford, p.6.

[76] Barr (1992).

[77] 'feoffed' means to put in legal possession; Alford, p.57. An enfeoffment could take the form of a written document.

granted possession of Adam's successors in the earthly paradise.[78]
Possession of the estate by enfeoffment gives Truth physical occupation
of the estate, but not ownership.[79] That rests with God and thus the
beekeeper avoids stating that humanity is self-sufficient for good.
Through the inspiration of the Holy Spirit, Adam is entitled to hold
earthly paradise, and afterwards heaven, in fealty to his landlord, who
is God.[80] The sequence suggests that God has naturally endowed
humanity with rational behaviour which directs it to good and,
ultimately, to heavenly reward. The sequence is reminiscent both of
Piers's description of the dwelling place of Truth in Passus V: 'Thow
shalt see in þiselue truþe [sitte] in þyn herte/In a cheyne of charite, as
þow a child were' (V 606-7), and of the Castle of Caro passage in Passus
IX, where God's gift of everlasting life to humanity is couched in a legal
image: 'And þus god gaf hym a goost of þe godhede of heuene/And of
his grete *grace graunted* hym blisse/ Lif þat ay shal laste, and al his *lynage*
after' (IX 47-49).[81] The echoes of *Piers* in *Mum* are not just to a type of
diction, but to the metaphorical potential of its literary use.

This is seen further in the continuation of this sequence. Having
outlined the source of Truth within humanity, the beekeeper explains
why humans often behave in a manner contrary to the rational principle
with which they have been naturally endowed:

> For Mvm hath a *man* there, and is a muche shrewe,
> Antecrist-is angel that eche day vs ennoyeth.
> He dwellith faste by the dore and droppeth many wiles
> Yf he might wynne ouer the walle with a *wronge entre*.
> He debateth eche day with Do-welle withynne,
> And the maistrie among and the *mote* wynneth,
> And shoueth the sothe-sigger into a syde-herne,
> And *taketh* couetise the keye to come ynne when hym liketh.
> Thenne dreede with a dore-barre dryueth oute the beste,
> And maketh the sothe-sigger seche a newe place,
> And to walke where he wol withoute on the grene
> Til sorowe for his synnes *seese* hym agaynes
> And the *tenaunt* a-tourne to *treuthe al his life*. (1254-66)

The sequence is influenced by the closing stages of *Piers*, and the Barn of
Unity scene is translated into a struggle between good and evil in the
heart.[82] Humans do not always behave in accordance with rational truth

---

[78] 'issue' has the sense of offspring and legal successors in office; Alford, p.74.
[79] 'possession' has the sense of 'seisin'. Possession of the estate by enfeoffment is not
equivalent to ownership; see Curzon, p.313.
[80] 'holde' has the sense of holding an estate from a feudal lord (MED 'holden' 7b).
[81] 'Lynage' means 'issue, descendants'; Alford, p. 89.
[82] 'coueitise' is one of the assailants of the Barn of Unity in *Piers*, XX 296.

because the combined forces of sin, motivated by Mum, commit a crime against God's act of tenancy. The truthteller is dispossessed from man's heart because Mum's servant commits an act of unlawful entry, covetousness gains the key by fraud and dread evicts the rightful tenant by criminal force.[83] However, penitence allows the lawful keeper of the place to regain possession of the tenancy for life.[84]

At 1258, 'Do-welle' is the most explicit recall of the Dowel triad from *Piers*. Here, it is associated both with Truth and with speaking the truth. The use of legal imagery to explain human psychology maps out a picture of human behaviour which is fully consonant with the principles of legality. An analogy is drawn between the the moral sin which breaks God's law and the criminal violation of land law. Behaviour which is in accordance with Truth obeys the rules of contemporary legal procedure. Conduct which breaks contemporary law is associated with Mum.

This is an equation which runs throughout the poem. We have seen earlier that Mum is allied to the contemporary church. We have also seen that in his treatment of the friars, the narrator puts them on the wrong side of the law. He refers to their hanging at Tyburn for treason; associates them with Cain, the first criminal and outlaw, and passes judgment on them.[85] The techniques that are used here are reminiscent of Trajan's use of legal procedure to expose the negligence of some contemporary clergy. I argued in the previous chapter that the political significance of *Mum*'s ecclesiastical criticism is more radical than in *Piers*, and this applies also to the use of legal diction within the anti-fraternal passages. The entire section on the friars is framed as though the narrator is putting them on trial, and as we have seen, at the end of the case, he finds them guilty and sentences them to everlasting perdition.

This is how the narrator introduces his journey to the friars:

> Thenne ferkid I to freres, alle the foure ordres,
> There the fundament of feith and felnesse of workes
> Hath y-dwellid many day, no doute, as thay telle.
> I *frayned* thaym faire to fele of thaire wittes,
> And *moeuyd my matiere* of Mvm, as ye knowe,
> And of the soeth-sigger in fewe sho[r]te wordes.
> To euery couple I *construed my caas* for the nones,
> Til the cloistre and the quyre were so *accorded*
> To yeue Mvm the maistrie withoute mo wordes.   (392-400)

---

[83] 'man' (1254) means vassal; Alford, p.96, 'wronge entre' (1257) means unlawful entry; cf. Alford, p.51 and p.169. 'taketh' (1261) has the sense of 'appropriate property unlawfully'; MED 'taken' (vb) 3a) c).

[84] 'seese' is from seisin, to put in legal possession, Alford, p.141. ' al his life' recalls the legal phrase 'terme of your lifes' at 205 to indicate life tenancy; MED 'lif' 2b).

[85] See earlier discussion, pp.113-115 and 126-28.

In the course of lodging his plea against Mum, the narrator cross-examines the friars, and explains his case to them. The friars concur in judging the case in favour of Mum.[86] This verdict allies them with criminal behaviour, and the narrator gives us the substance of his cross-examination by proceeding to indict them of various crimes. He introduces his comments against the friars as a series of four 'skiles' or 'poyntes' (405; 408; 415; 434). We have already seen that these have the technical legal meanings of a logical point to prove an argument and an accusation. Each of the narrator's 'poyntes' against the friars, is a criminal charge against them.

Within this judicial framework, he accuses them of various offences. Some of these have already been noted, and I shall take just one more example to show the deftness with which legal diction is used in this part of *Mum*:

> The fourthe *poynt* is fructuous and *fundid* al in loue:
> Whenne freres goon to chapitre for charite-is sake,
> Thay casten there the cuntrey and coostz aboute,
> And parten the prouynce in *parcelle-mele*
> And maken limitacions in lengthe and in breede,
> Til eche hovs haue his owen as hym aughte.
> Thenne hath the limitour *leue* to lerne where he cometh
> To lye and to licke or elles lose his office;
> But sum been so *courtoys* and kinde of thaire deedes
> That with thaire charite thay *chaungen* a knyfe for a peyre,
> But he wol *pille* ere he passe a *parcelle* of whete
> And choise of the chese the chief and the beste.   (434-45)

The sense of 'poynt' (434) as a legal accusation is emphasised by 'fundid' in the sense of furnishing witness or proof.[87] 'Parcelle-mele' has the legal sense of an allotted share, as of an estate, and 'leue' (440) has the sense of formal permission, but the succeeding lines show that the friars' division of the countryside is anything but legal.[88] 'Courtoys' (432) recalls the noun 'curtesie' which can mean a sum of money or other recompense which is given above the stated terms of a contract or agreement.[89] The friars' 'curtesie' is inverted. What is given above the terms of the agreement is given not by the friars, but to them. The friars give one knife and receive two.[90] The use of 'courtoys', and 'chaungen',

[86] MED 'frainen' 3c) means to question someone in court, to move a matter means to put forth a petition, Alford; p.102; to construe a case means to construct a case against someone (p.35), and 'accorded' means to concur in a judgment; Alford, p.1.
[87] Alford, p.59.
[88] Alford, p.109; MED 'leue' (n)2 1a).
[89] Alford, p.41.
[90] cf. *The Orders of Cain*: 'For if he gife a wyfe a knyfe/ þat cost bot penys two,/Worþe ten knyues, so mot I thryfe,/he wyl haue er he go', Robbins; 65/69-72.

which has the legal sense of an exchange of goods for profit,[91] serves to define the friars' criminality. Their sense of 'charite' inverts its true meaning. This contradictoriness is encapsulated in the next line by the juxtaposition of the antithetical legal terms 'pille' (robbery) and 'parcelle' (an allotted portion).[92]

This ironic use of legal diction serves a number of purposes. It defines the friars' illegality, both in terms of the contemporary church and in terms of their relationship to secular authority.[93] It also illustrates the double-dealing of the friars. They cheat their own rule, the people whom they encounter, and they manipulate the meanings of words to their own advantage. It is not surprising that the narrator sums up his sentencing of the friars by saying that they were *'alied* to Mvm in many maniere wises/And eeke ful *partie*, as *prouyd* by thaire wordes' (529-30).[94] By using the imagery of opposing sides in a lawsuit, the narrator states that the friars are in league with Mum, and ultimately with Antichrist.

Legal opposition to the friars is a narrative strategy also used in *Crede*. As in *Mum*, the narrator undertakes a cross-examination of them:

> But to many maner of men this *matter* is asked,
> Bothe to lered and to lewed that seyn that the[y] leueden
> Hollich on the grete god and *holden* alle his heste[s];
> But by a *fra[y]nyng* for-than faileth ther manye.
> For first y *fraynede* the freres and the[y] me fulle tolden
> That all the frute of the fayth was in here foure ordres. (24-29)

The narrator raises the issue of the friars' claim to sanctity as if it were a legal case ('matter'). But the friars' claim to keep faith with God's commandments is not borne out by cross-examination. Their pretense to legality is exposed by the legal inquiry of the narrator. In his attempt to persuade one of the fraternal orders to teach him his creed, the narrator uses legal diction to frame his remarks:

> And therfore, for Cristes loue, thi *councell* y praie.
> A Carm me hath *y-couenaunt* the Crede me to teche;
> But for thou knowest Carmes well thi *counsaile* I aske. (37-39)

> And an Austyn this ender daie egged me faste;
> That he wolde techen me wel he *plyght me his treuthe*. (239-40)

'Councell' is often used in the sense of advice in a legal matter,[95] The Franciscan's response, however, is outside legal propriety. He defames

---

[91] Alford, p.52.
[92] Alford, p.115.
[93] I explore the implications of this in my conclusion, pp.168-70.
[94] 'alied' is an alliance between parties; MED 'allie' (n) 1a); cf. *Richard*, III.31. 'partie' is a group of persons involved on the same side in a lawsuit; Alford p.110.
[95] Alford, p.38.

the Carmelites by calling them 'yugulers and iapers', 'lorels and lechures' (43-4).[96] Legal terminology also works against the Carmelites here. A 'couenaunt' is a legally binding agreement between two parties, but despite the promise to the narrator, neither the Carmelite, nor any of the other orders of friars will teach him his creed. This is evidenced by the failure of the Augustinian to keep his word (240).[97] At lines 137 and 332, the friars enter a 'couenant' with the narrator in their promise to absolve him from sin. The only absolution that the narrator receives, however, is completely illegal:

> 'My soule y sette for thyn to asoile the clene,
> In *couenaunt* that thou come againe and katell vs bringe.'
> And thanne loutede y adoun and he me *leue* grauntede.   (332-3)

The Augustinian's 'clene' absolution is not pure, but empty.[98] Absolution ought not to be conditional on the narrator's gifts to the order. 'Leue' is used ironically in line 333. Its technical sense is dispensation from sin,[99] but, like the careless priests indicted by Trajan, here the use of legal vocabulary emphasises the friars' criminality.

As in *Mum*, antifraternal criticism is also couched as legal accusation. At 546, Peres turns to the narrator to ask him to endorse his previous remarks against them: 'Loke nowe, leue man beth nought thise i-lyke/ Fully to the Farisens in fele of thise *poyntes*?' Part of the effect of this legal diction is to turn the tables against the friars in a similar way to the reverse discourse strategies I examined in the previous chapter. The chief emphasis of Peres 'poyntes' is that the friars are unable to tolerate legal criticism of their own faults:

> '*Proue hem in proces* and pynch at her ordre
> And *deme* hem after that they don and dredeles, y leue
> Thei willn wexen pure wroth wonderliche sone.   (523-5)

Peres aligns his truthful criticism of the friars with legal procedure.[100] Their response, however, is anger, and they proceed to accuse honest men unjustly. The lines which follow state that they responded to Wyclif's true criticisms with false accusations. Throughout the poem,

---

[96] cf. 138-9 where the narrator explicitly says of the speech of the Franciscan: 'Here semeth litel trewthe/First to blamen his brother and bacbyten him foule'. I discuss these lines below.

[97] Alford, p.39.

[98] cf. the similar pun on 'clene' in *Crede* discussed on p.85 above.

[99] cf. Alford, p.88.

[100] 'Proue' means to give adequate legal proof; MED 'preven' 7); 'process' has the sense of a legal action; MED 'proces' 4a) and 'deme' means to judge in a court of law; Alford, p.44.

the friars' mutual calumny, and their predilection for ill-founded lawsuits and criminal persecution (655-6; 665-70), is contrasted to the legally valid charges of criminality brought by Peres and the narrator. Moreover, as the use of 'fraynyng' shows, under fictional cross-examination, the friars condemn themselves out of their own mouths.

It is in this light that I shall return to the issue of 'intent'. I have already discussed the passage where the narrator asks Peres why he is so harsh against the friars, and whether he is determined to revenge some grievance against them, 'to schenden other [*schamen*] hem with thi sharpe speche,/And *harmen* holliche and her hous *greuen*' (677-8). The words italicised are all drawn from legal definitions of defamation. It is an accusation of unlawful speech which Peres denies emphatically: ' "I praie the," quath Peres, "put that out of thy mynde./Certen for sowle hele y saie the this wordes" ' (679-80). Peres defends his intention as being fully proportionate to human and divine law. In contrast to the friars, he is not concerned to harm, backbite, to slander or to speak fraudulently. We might compare the narrator's observation about the speech of the Franciscan: 'Here semeth litel *trewthe*:/First to *blamen* his brother and bacbyten him foule' (138-9). Unlike the Franciscan, who speaks unjust slander, Peres speaks 'only for sowle hele'.

Legal diction is used at significant points in *Crede*. Its literary deployment adds another dimension to the narrative strategy of reversing reverse discourse. The friars' use of legal terms is shown to be criminal, and the language of one institution, namely the legal system, is used to sentence the members of another, namely the fraternal orders of the church. Ultimately, however, the legal propriety of a truth-telling discourse of alliterative poetry, fictionally voiced by the 'lewed', exceeds both.

We can detect a similar strategy in *Crowned King*. For a short piece, there is a significant count of legal vocabulary. Before the clerk offers his advice to the king, the narrator rehearses the recent tax levy that has been imposed on the realm in order to finance Henry V's military campaign against the French:[101]

> Me thought y herd a crowned kyng of his comunes axe
> A soleyn *subsidie* to susteyne his werres,
> To be rered in the reaume, as *reson* requyred,
> Of suche as were seemly to suffre the *charge*;
> That they that rekened were riche by *reson and skyle*
> Shuld pay a *parcell* for here poure neighbowres;
> This *ordenaunce* he made in ease of his peple.   (35-41)

---

[101] cf. earlier discussion in Ch.2, p.43.

There is a cluster of legal terms here. 'Reson' has its legal sense of justice, 'skyle' has the sense of a legal argument, 'parcell' has the legal sense of an allotted portion, and 'ordenaunce' the legal sense of a decree. The diction suggests that the levy is in accordance with strict justice and equity, but this sits rather uncomfortably with the sentiments in the rest of the poem. Why, if this parliamentarily-agreed grant were so fair, and to the 'ese' of the people, does the clerk have to remind the king to take due cognisance of the 'loue' of his 'liegemen' (61) and the 'playnt' of the poor people (65), who sweat and labour for his food? If this 'ordenaunce' were truly equitable, surely such reminders were redundant? Equally, if this legal diction is to be taken at face value, it seems a little strange that the first thing that the clerk says, once he has been given permission to speak, is to remind the king of his duty to rule in accordance with 'trouthe' and 'reson':

> Than he said, 'Sir, crowned kyng, thow knowest well thyself.
> Thiself hast lyfe, lyme and lawes for to keep;
> Yif thou be chief Iustice, iustifie the *trouthe*;
> And rule the be *reson*, and vpright sitte.
> For that is a *poynt principall* – *preve* it who-so will –
> To be dred for thy *domes* [and dowted] for thy myght.   (51-56)

This reads like a gentle reminder to the king that in order to behave in accordance with his calling, he must pay full heed to the legality of his actions and defend the laws of the realm. While the preservation of justice is a commonplace in advice to princes literature,[102] it sits oddly with the topical precision of referring to the recent parliamentary ordinance in such legally precise language. Moreover, lines 53-5 suggest that the king himself may be legally examined on the question of whether he has fully obeyed the principles of law. While it is important for the king to be feared for his legal powers, it is equally desirable that the king exerts those powers in full congruence with what is just. The poem seems to have taken to heart lines from the B Prologue of *Piers*, which, it appears, the author of *Crowned King* knew in some detail: 'Dum rex a regere dicatur nomen habere/Nomen habet sine re nisi studet iura tenere' (Prol. 141-2).[103]

---

[102] e.g. Kail, III.11-15:
> 'Iustice in goddis stede is dight.
> Do euene lawe to fooll and wyse.
> Set mesure in euene assise,
> The righte weye as lawe ges.
> And lawe be kepte, folk nyl not ryse.'

Gower, *Vox*, VI 481-2; *Confessio* VII 2695-2701; *Mirour*, 24601-12; and Hoccleve, *Regment*, 2514-6: 'A kyng is made to kepen and maynteene/Iustice, for she makith obeisant/The mysdoers that proude ben & keene.'

[103] cf. discussion in Chapter Two, pp.28-9.

The role of the clerk in the poem, by contrast, is unequivocally in keeping with legal procedure. He asks the king for permission to '*shewe you my sentence*' (46). We have seen how both of these words have precise legal meanings, and I think that their technical legal senses of declaring judgment are appropriate here. In answer to the dubious legality of the parliamentary tax levy, the clerk offers his own view, one that is fully in accord with legal standards of propriety. He views the recent grant as the opinion of one side in legal dispute, and having paid due deference to legal procedure, proceeds to put, without slander or defamation, the side of the argument from the taxpayers' position. In all of his comments, the clerk delicately avoids the open confrontation or slander that is so characteristic of the friars in *Crede*. Instead, his words are gentle prompts which have the weight of an advice to princes' tradition behind them. Crucially, the speech of the clerk is offered within a legally-defined framework; he speaks only when he has been given leave by the king, and in his conclusion, he reverts to a position of deference: 'My liege lord, of this *mater y meve you no more*' (135). While it is possible to interpret this diction as part of a scholastic process of argument, to my mind it makes more sense of the narrative positions of the poem as a whole to construe it as the clerk's final words in a lawfully-worded petition.[104] In his commentary on the recent statute, the clerk is anxious not to overstep the law, but simultaneously, his own use of legal diction, both in his reminders to the king, and the framework of his own remarks, lightly questions the equity of the parliamentary grant. In *Crowned King*, truthtelling alliterative poetry is legally sanctioned to query the ordinances of the very institution that determines the law of the land.

This use of legal diction to legitimise poetry is central also to the poetic agendas of both *Richard* and *Mum*. We have seen how, in his treatment of the friars, the narrator of *Mum* turns prosecutor. Exactly the same occurs in *Richard*. At the beginning of the poem, the narrator sets up the rival claims of Richard and Henry and proceeds to adjudicate their legitimacy:

> Thus *tales* me troblid for they trewe where,
> And amarride my mynde rith moche and my wittis eke:

---

[104] Alford notes that the use of this phrase in *Piers* suggests mainly the practice of scholastic debate, but that the phrase also figures commonly in descriptions of legal suits (to move a debate; a plea etc). Technically a 'matter' is a proceeding commenced by a bill or a petition rather than a writ (p.102). Given that the clerk is addressing the king, who offers no reply, the setting in *Crowned King* is less one of scholastic debate, than of a petition presented to the king, by a spokesman for the larger commonwealth. As such, I think that the register of the phrase 'move. . .matter' is legal.

For it passid my parceit and my *priefis* also,
How so wondirffull werkis wolde haue an *ende*. (15-18)

The use of 'tales'; the plaintiff's account in a legal suit, 'priefis'; legal evidence or testimony, and 'ende' – to conclude a legal case, give judgment,[105] suggests he is presiding over a legal dispute whose outcome is not yet known. We know from the beginning of Passus II, however, that the poem must have been written after January 1400,[106] so this ignorance of events is a narrative fiction.

Even before Passus II, as we have seen, it is apparent that the narrator's allegiances are Lancastrian. What, in effect, transpires, is that the narrator puts Richard II on trial in his poem. Often, the narrator comments on the substance of his narrative with vocabulary that suggests he is putting forth a case at law, for example:

Of *maters* that I thenke to *meve* for the best. (I 171)

But for ye cleued to knavis in this *cas* I *avowe*. (I 199)

For the more partie I may well *avowe*. (II 37)

For *mater* that my mynde is *meved* in now. (III 2)

For a preuy *poynt* that persith my wittis,
Of *fauutis* I fynde that frist dede engendre. (III 111-12)

In all of these quotations, the narrator authorizes his criticisms by framing them with diction drawn from a legal context. As a result, his accusations against Richard and his misrule have full legal backing. In Passus I, he lists a catalogue of crimes against Richard for which he was deposed:

Of *alegeaunce* now lerneth a lesson other tweyne,
Wher-by it standith and stablithe moste –
By dr[e]de, or be dyntis or *domes vntrewe*,
Or by creaunce of coyne for castes of gile,
By *pillynge* of youre peple youre prynces to plese,
Or that youre wylle were wroughte though wisdom it nolde;
Or be *tallage* of youre townnes without ony werre,
By rewthles routus that ryffled euere,
Be preysinge of polaxis that no pete hadde,
Or be dette for thi dees deme as thou fyndist,–
Or be ledinge of lawe with *loue* well ytemprid.
Though this be derklich *endited* for a dull nolle,
Miche nede is it not to mwse ther-on. (I 96-108)

105 Alford, p.151, MED 'preve' 1c), and Alford, p.50.
106 'half a yere after' at *Richard*, II 17 is a reference to the Cirencester revolt of January 1400. For further discussion see Barr, 'Dates' (1990).

These offences correspond very closely to the list of crimes against Richard which were read out at the 1399 parliamentary assembly which deposed him. These 'gravamina', consisted of 32 articles of misconduct and the 'record and process' of this parliament was widely distributed by Henry and his supporters as propaganda. It was used by several of the chroniclers, and Adam Usk notes in his eye witness account of the parliament that all the crimes with which Richard was tainted, were reasons enough for setting him aside.[107] In these lines in *Richard*, the poet supplements the parliamentary accusations against the former king by indicting him for the same offences in his poem.[108] 'Endited' means both to compose and to charge with a crime.[109] The narrator sets himself up as Richard's prosecutor.

This narrative strategy smacks of presumption, but the narrator takes measures to clear himself of that charge before it can be brought. In the first Passus he makes his intention in writing the poem abundantly clear:

> It shulde not *apeire* hem a peere a prynce though he were,
> Ne *harme nother hurte* the hyghest of the rewme,
> But to holde him in hele and helpe all his frendis.
> And if ony word write be that wrothe make myghte
> My souereyne, that suget I shulde to be,
> I put me in his power and *preie* him, of *grace*,
> To take the *entent* of my *trouthe* that thoughte non ylle,
> For to wrath no wyght be my wyll neuere,
> As my soule be saff from synne at myn ende.
> The story is of non estate that stryuen with her lustus,
> But tho that folwyn her flessh and here frelle thoughtis;
> So if my *conceyll* be clere I can saie no more,   (I 73-84)

This is a passage that I examined in Chapter Three in the discussion of the narrator's intention. Here, I would like to emphasise how the narrator's anxiety to escape charges of defamation and slander is couched in legal diction. 'Apeire' has the sense of harming or injuring by slander; 'harme nother hurte' appears to be an anglicisation of the legal formula 'damage e huntage' in civil actions where claimants sought compensation for harm and shame, and 'grace' carries the legal emphasis of 'the power to show pardon or mercy'.[110] The narrator is

---

[107] Usk, p.181; *Rot. Parl.*, III.417-22.
[108] Apart from 'endited' the legal vocabulary here is general rather than technical. The narrator gives the king a lesson in lawful loyalty, criticises his illegal judgements, his robbery of the people, his harsh taxation (Alford, p.150) and his perversion of justice through partiality; favouritism towards one of the parties in a lawsuit; Alford, p.91.
[109] MED 'enditen' 1, and 4; cf. Alford, p.50.
[110] Alford, p.7; p.68 and p.66.

anxious not to overstep the bounds of his allegiance to his sovereign by writing anything that could be construed as defamation. His concern to legalise his writing can be seen from his declaration of just 'entent', and his appeal to legal advice, 'counceyll'.[111]

Half way through the poem, however, the narrator appears to have got cold feet about its legality. At this moment, rather in the fashion of Piers's abrupt, but authoritative, appearance in *Piers Plowman*, a speaker named Reason interrupts into the poem and bids him continue:

> But it longith to no liegeman his lord to anoye
> Nother in werk ne in word but if his witt faile.
> 'No, redely,' quod *Reson* 'that *reule I alowe*:
> Displese not thi *demer in dede ne in wordis*
> But if the liste for to lede thi lyf in dissese.
> But yif God haue *grauntyd the grace* for to knowe
> Ony manere mysscheff that myghtte be *amendyd*,
> *Schewe* that to thi souereyne to schelde him from harmes.   (II 67-74)

It is striking that the poem's recommission comes from a speaker who represents justice. Reason legalises the narrator's criticisms: 'reule I alowe' means to uphold a ruling as valid and binding; 'in dede ne in wordis' is a common collocation, which in this context, suggests a contrast between written evidence and uncorroborated testimony.[112] 'Grauntyd the grace' is a legal phrase meaning to bestow an indulgence or privilege as distinguished from a right, and 'schewe' has the legal sense of laying a complaint before court.[113] There could be no higher legal authority to legitimize truthtelling poetry than the personification of Justice. This interchange legalises the poem's project of laying out charges against those who have committed criminal offences against society. The purpose of such poetic prosecution, however, is not vindictiveness but 'mendes'. The poem is offered as legal redress for the wrongs that have been suffered, and as a model of correction to avoid future damage.

All these strategies are re-used in *Mum*, and in more expanded forms. Towards the start of the fragment, the definition of the ideal truthteller is a defence of corrective poetry:

> Yit is hit not my *cunseil* to clatre what me knoweth
> In *sclaundre* ne scathe ne scorne of thy brother,
> For though thy *tale* be trewe thyn *tente* might be noyous,
> For whiche thou mighte be harmed and haue that thou *serues*.
> For go to the gospel that grovnd is of lore,

---

[111] Alford, p.74 and p.38.
[112] MED 'allouen' 2a); 'reule' (n),4d); 'dede' 8a), and 5c).
[113] Alford, p.66 and p.143.

And there shal thou see thyself, yf thou can rede,
Whethir I wisse the wel wisely or elles.
He seith that thou shuldes the synne of thy brother
Telle hym by tyme and til hymsilf oon,
Yn ful wil to *amende* hym of his mysse-deedes.
Si peccauerit in te frater tuus corrige etc.
And yf he chargeth not thy charite but chideth the agaynes,
Yit leue hym not so lightly though he lovre oones,
But funde hym to *freyne* efte of the newe,
And haue *wittenes* the with that thou wel knowes,
And spare not to *speke*, spede yf thou mowe,
And he that moost is of might thy mede shal quite
For suche [soeth] sawes that sounen into good,
And of a *reasonable* man rewarde to haue.
For whenne thy *tente* and thy *tale* been temprid in oone,
And menys no malice to man that thou *spekys*,
But forto *mende* hym mukely of his misse-deedes.   (72-92)

There are many of the legal terms which we have seen in *Richard*: 'cunseil'; 'tale'; 'tente' and 'harmed'. There are also some new terms: 'sclaundre' is a false accusation, which the narrator is anxious to avoid; 'serve' has the legal sense of rendering judgment.[114] The narrator's point is that to bring a false charge against someone renders the plaintiff subject to the same legal process and sentence he initiates. What these lines state is that the intention and prosecution of corrective language should be fully in line with legal procedure.

The narrator authorizes his defence of corrective poetry with a citation from Matthew's gospel,[115] and continues by saying that if such truthtelling is prosecuted without slander, within the confines of the law, and still the defendant will have none of it, then a fresh course of action is necessary. The advice again makes free use of legal terms. The defendant is to be cross-examined once more ('freyne'); there should be a 'wittenes' present of proven good character, and the truthteller is bidden to 'speke' forth in the legal sense of 'plead'.[116] Such conduct will be rewarded according to justice. It is 'reasonable' because the pleading ('tale') and intention ('tente') are in harmony.

---

[114] Alford, p.140; MED 'serven' 14).
[115] Matthew, 18:15: 'But if thy brother shall offend against thee, go and rebuke him between thee and him alone. If he shall hear thee, thou shalt gain thy brother'. The Latin citation at line 81 quotes this text. Hoccleve offers similar advice in *Regement*:
> 'Of conceill and of helpe we be dettoures,
> Eche to other, by right of bretherhede;
> For whan a man y-falle in-to errour is,
> His brother ought hym conceille and rede
> To correcte and amende his wikked dede.'   (2486-90)
[116] Alford, p.146.

This is exactly the procedure which the narrator adopts in *Mum* in his cross-examination of all the estates of society, and the petition that his poem presents against their faults and offences. As we have seen in the case of the friars, he makes a list of their illegal activities and then passes judgement. Interestingly, as in *Richard*, a legal defence of truthtelling poetry, which proceeds from the mouth of the narrator, appears to be insufficient. Towards the end of the poem, the beekeeper, who, as I have said earlier, commands the highest voice of authority in the poem, and represents the truthteller for whom the narrator has been searching, recommissions the poem.

Having explained to the narrator where Truth is to be found, the beekeeper instructs him to write down his words:

> *Loke* thou write wisely my wordes echone;
> Hit wol be exemple to sum men seuene yere here-after.
> And *loke* thou seye euer sothe but *shame* not thy brother
> For yf thou telle hym trouthe in tirant-is wise,
> He wol rather wexe wrother thenne forto wirche after.
> But in a muke maniere thou mos hym *asaye*,
> And not eche day to egge hym, but in a *deue* tyme.
> Do thus, my dere soon, for I may dwelle no longer,
> But fare to my good frend that I fro come.
> I haue *infourmed* the faire loke thou *folowe* after
> And *make vp thy matiere*, thou mays do no better.
> Hit may *amende* many men of thaire misdeedes.
> Sith thou felys the fressh lete no feynt herte
> *Abate* thy blessid bisynes of thy boke-making
> Til hit be complete to clapsyng, caste aweye doutes
> And lete the *sentence* be sothe, and *sue to th'ende*;
> And furst *feoffe* thou therewith the freyst of the royaulme,
> For yf thy lord liege allone hit begynne,
> Care thou not though knyghtz copie hit echone,
> And do write eche word and wirche there-after.'   (1268-87)

There is the same concern to avoid slander and defamation ('shame') and, further, to be sure that the legal examination of the defendant ('asaye') takes place at a 'deue' time. [117]

The beekeeper's instruction to the narrator to make a book of his criticisms takes the form of a legal injunction.[118] He has given the narrator advice fully in accordance with legal procedure ('infourmed');[119]

---

[117] Alford, p.10; cf. use of 'dewe' in *Richard*, see above, pp.146-47.
[118] 'Loke' means to ordain or decree, Alford, p.89.
[119] MED records no legal senses in the entry for 'infourmed' but under 'informacioun' 1c, the sense of legal counsel or advice is recorded. *Doc* (1429) in Flasdieck *Origurk*, 75: 'He shall discontinue or make discontinue. . .the foresaide taile. . .as the councell of the foresaid Richart can best deuyse and gyff hym jnformacion.'

he bids the narrator to prosecute his case ('folowe) and assemble his petition ('matiere') in order to 'amende' criminal action. He warns the narrator not to stop writing his book by using the word 'abate', which is a legal term meaning to abolish or dismiss a case at law.[120] He must prosecute his case to the end and ensure that the sentence passed is true (1283). Finally, he is asked to 'feoffe' the king with a copy of the book. The book of poetry becomes part of a legal property transaction, by virtue of which the king is put in legal possession of constructive reform.

The parallel between writing a book of poetry and procedure in the lawcourts is sustained throughout. It is after this speech by the beekeeper that the narrator opens his bag of books and provides a bibliography of the offences they contain. This passage in *Mum* gives fullest expression to a founding tenet of all four poems in the tradition, namely that the writing of corrective poetry is a legal activity, and one that is analogous to prosecuting a suit at law and passing judgment on those found guilty of the charges against them.

In *Mum*, the beekeeper tells the narrator that if he follows his advice, he may 'do no better' (1278). This is an echo of the Dowel triad in *Piers*, but in turning to legal standards of propriety and truth to legitimise their poetry, the four poems in the tradition capture only part of the ethical temper of *Piers Plowman*. I gave examples earlier of the use of legal diction in *Piers*, and showed how in the case of Trajan, legal reference was used to endorse criticism against the church. He expressly uses the verb 'enditen'. But it is important to recall that Trajan is a pagan and that his view of correction may be limited. Other characters within *Piers* use terms of legal diction such as 'shewe', 'meven a matter' and 'prove' but with more of a scholastic than legal emphasis.[121] In contrast to their function in parts of poems in the tradition, in *Piers* these terms are not appropriated by speakers within the poem solely to press charges against persons or institutions. Significantly, in his meeting with the two friars, the dreamer disputes with them in a scholastic mode: ' "Contra!" quod I as a clerc and comsed to disputen' (VIII 20) but in contrast to *Crede* and *Mum*, there are no terms drawn from legal prosecution, cross-examination and sentencing.

---

[120] MED 'abaten' (3). The same word is used in *Richard*, III 307.

[121] See Alford, p.102. Examples of 'preved' which are more concerned to make a theological, rather than legal point include the narrator's comment that Reason's preaching 'preued' (V 13) that the recent pestilences were as a result of sin, and in the same context, the narrator uses the word 'matere' (21); cf. Will's retort to Scripture over predestination: ' "Contra!" quod I, "by crist! þat kan I wiþseye/And preuen it by þe pistel þat peter is nempned" ' (X 349-50); and his later sullen rebuke that he is no wiser for her long lesson: 'Where dowel is or dobet derkliche ye shewen./Manye tales ye tellen þat Theologie lerneþ' (X 378-9).

Trajan's view of correction is consonant with that expounded by Leaute in the same Passus. When Will expresses misgivings about criticising the friars, Leaute responds with a classic legal defence of satire:

> It is *licitum* for lewed men to *legge* þe soþe
> If hem likeþ and lest; *ech a lawe it graunteþ*.   (XI 96-7)[122]

James Simpson has shown how in this passage, Leaute's legal defence of satirical poetry from both canon and civil law is part of a long-standing Latin tradition.[123] However, as Simpson has well illustrated, this is not the end of the tale in *Piers*. The strict legal basis of satire is ultimately questioned within a theological framework. While such criticism may be lawful, in a poem which is so concerned to understand the relationship between justice and mercy, a legalistic poetic leaves no room for love.

This appears not to have been an issue for the poets in the tradition. In all four poems, criticism of contemporary society is grounded entirely within a legal framework. It is almost as if they had taken Leaute's defence of satire as a text 'to mayntene hir cause'. But while it is important to recognise that an important dimension of the ethical poetic of *Piers* is lacking in these later poems, the tradition is not concerned with the theological and spiritual issues that are so central to *Piers*. Their perpetuation of a poetic diction substantially grounded in legal reference, is further evidence that the tradition responded to *Piers* primarily as a social document, and continued its social poetic temper in their own works.

Within this narrower poetic, the tradition's literary adaptation of legal reference, motifs and vocabulary is very similar to the texture of many parts of *Piers*. Contemporary institutions and their representatives are measured against standards of legal propriety and truth. Legalistic inquiry and and lawful accusations expose corruption, hypocrisy and inadequacy. The parallels drawn between poetry and prosecution create a truthtelling medium which supplements the official discourse generated by established institutions. While in *Crede* and *Mum* the language of the law is used to sentence representatives of the church, elsewhere in

---

[122] 'licitum' means lawful, Alford, p.88. 'legge' means to state the ground of a legal defence and then support it, Alford, p.3; 'ech a lawe' refers to canon and civil law; Alford, p.81 and 'graunteþ' means to permit or allow; Alford, p.66. There is some textual disturbance at this point in B. The majority of B MSS read 'segge', or a variant form, for 'legge'. (Hm reads 'synge'), Kane Donaldson, p.422. This passage is altered in C XII 31-34 and lines 96-7 from B XI are absent.

[123] James Simpson, 'The Constraints of Satire' (1990), p.25. The argument of this paragraph is substantially indebted to this article.

Mum, Richard and *Crowned King*, legal language is used to expose the abuses of the legal system and the inadequacies of parliament and governmental procedures. The language of the law is used against its guardians.

In this respect, the poems in the tradition have travelled a long way from *Satire on the Consistory Courts*. I argued at the beginning of this chapter that this early poem showed how the 'lewed' were oppressed by the language of the law. Despite the fact that the unlettered are paradoxically given a voice, in that the poem has been written from their perspective, the supposedly 'lewed' speaker does not turn the tables on the courts of law by appropriating their language. In all four poems of the tradition, a non-institutionalised narrative voice speaks with full legal authority and, far from being oppressed by legal technicalities, presses them into literary service for their own ends. On this basis, we might collapse J.D. Peter's distinction between satire and complaint, and argue that in these alliterative poems, the satirical strategies produce a truthtelling poetry which is exactly one of 'complaint' in its legal sense.[124] While the poems in the *Piers* tradition are not unique amongst works in Middle English in their use of legal thought and expression, they must stand as some of the best examples of legal fictions.[125]

---

[124] J.D. Peter, *Complaint and Satire in Early English Literature*, (Oxford, 1956).
[125] cf. Owen Barfield, 'Poetic Diction and Legal Fiction, in *Essays Presented to Charles Williams*, ed. C.S. Lewis, (London, 1947), 106-27. Barfield constructs an analogy between metaphor, language and meaning: legal fiction, law and social life.

Conclusion

I have attempted to show that *Pierce the Ploughman's Crede, Mum and the Sothsegger, The Crowned King* and *Richard the Redeless* comprise a tradition of social poetry indebted to *Piers Plowman*. As a group, they can be seen to give a shape and coherence to the disparate early responses to *Piers* which are witnessed by the poem's appropriation by John Ball, and by textual interventions on the part of copyists, annotators and continuators. Taking impetus from the absence of a literary-fashioned author in *Piers*, the four poems form part of what I have termed a social literary tradition. This tradition contrasts with the self-conscious, and agonistic literariness of many of the works inspired by Chaucer.[1]

From close analysis of the four poems it is clear that their indebtedness to *Piers* is not simply a case of symbiosis of ideas, but demonstrable textual force. All four poems perceive the social significance of 'right' reading in *Piers* and perpetuate its importance. This is evidenced by their close attention to the precise meanings and connotations of the words and phrases from *Piers* which they quote. Moreover, they perpetuate the distinctly social alliterative temper of *Piers Plowman*. This sets them apart from the more formal poems of the classical alliterative corpus, as they, like *Piers*, use alliterative verse to supplement the institutionalised discourses of church and state.

This social temper is not plain, however, in the sense of being transparent or simple.[2] One of the ways in which *Piers* exerted textual force on these later poems was by demonstrating the serious and social consequences of wordplay. As in *Piers*, the texture of these new poems is linguistically self-conscious through dense play on the meanings and sounds of words. At first sight, this appears to contradict the tradition's condemnation of verbal subtlety and their professed aims to speak the

---

[1] *The Plowman's Tale* is an exception to this, and the anonymous *Partonope of Blois* is without the obvious signs of the anxiety of influence that characterise some of the works of Hoccleve and Lydgate.

[2] The 'plain style' is the term used by Turville-Petre (1977), p.59 to describe the poetic temper of the *Piers* tradition.

truth unequivocally. But it is clearly the narrative intention of these poems to demonstrate a right use of the manipulation of linguistic resources. In their ingenious, but socially responsible, use of the multiple valencies of 'signes', they defeat those who attempt to silence or to suppress 'sothe' by outwitting them at their own game.

This last strategy is used with particular emphasis in the two poems which expressly address ecclesiastical issues and controversies. In *Crede* and *Mum*, Wycliffite diction is used as a weapon in a discursive contest against the control of language and meanings by the institutionalised church. Within the poems, speakers, and the discourses they represent, compete for the truth in narrative manoeuvres which reflect not merely topical events but the ways in which recent legislation affected how religious topics could be discussed. Analysis of the re-deployment of words and phrases from *Piers*, and the reprise of episodes or figures in these later poems, provides an index of the way that words and expressions changed in political significance after the increasingly punitive condemnation of Wyclif's teachings.

In *Crede* and *Mum*, the interrogation of official church discourse is more radical and confrontational than the tradition's supplementation of secular institutionalised discourses. While all four poems supplement the legal and governmental institutions of their day, they write within a legally-sanctioned truth-telling temper. Each poem makes substantial use of legal reference and diction to legitimise their exposure of corruption or inadequacy in contemporary society. Poetic complaint and legal prosecution become synonymous.

Crede and *Mum* invoke the power of secular authority against the claims of the contemporary church in a manner which is in keeping with the emphasis of a number of Wycliffite texts.[3] In *The Plowman's Tale*, there is an appeal to the king and to parliament to redress clerical corruption,[4] and in *The Thirty Seven Conclusions*, a tract which might have been addressed to the Lollard knights,[5] the writer advises the king and representatives of the legal system on their role in the kingdom. They are required to compel men 'to entre mekeli into the kepinge of Goddis lawe'.[6] The text *Sex Raciones*, written probably between 1380 and 1409, lists six reasons to prove that it is the duty of the secular king to punish clerics who commit mortal sin. Five of the six reasons use clauses

---

[3] The support given to secular authority in Wycliffite texts is discussed by Hudson (1988), pp.362-7.
[4] *The Plowman's Tale*, 677-84.
[5] Hudson (1988), pp.214-7.
[6] *Thirty Seven Conclusions, [Remonstrance against Romish Corruptions]* ed. J.Forshall, (London, 1851)], p.27.

from the coronation oath, and words from the coronation service to demonstrate the author's case. The fourth reason argues that it pertains to the king to use a sword to destroy false clerics.[7]

In *Tractatus de Regibus*, the Lollard writer stresses that it is the responsibility of the king to make sure that the realm is not destroyed by the church,[8] and that it is essential that a king's subjects are utterly loyal to their sovereign.[9] As in *Jack Upland*, the friars are criticised because their singular vow of obedience to their order compromises secular allegiance.[10] Further, the king should take steps to ensure that people are not imprisoned for speaking the truth.[11] This is a view that is shared by the author of the *Thirty Seven Conclusions*.[12]

This plea to secular authority to defend the interests of the Lollards against the punitive measures of the corrupt contemporary church is seen perhaps most strikingly in the appeals of William Swinderby against his sentence of heresy in 1391. He sent a letter to the knights in parliament, urging them to consider whether his propositions deserved condemnation as heresy, and to promulgate his views in parliament 'to schewing of the trouthe and amendyng of holy chirche'.[13] He also sent a letter to the King's Council, appealing against his conviction, 'on cause is fore the kynges court in suche mater is above the bysshopes courte'.[14] This is an exemplary statement of the way that in all of these texts secular authority is mobilised against the power of the material church.

Legal authority provides the ultimate poetic authority in all the poems of the *Piers* tradition. This is consonant with the concern evinced in the poems for a stable secular hierarchy. In none of the poems is the questioning of civil authority radical. In supplementing the secular discourses of authority they query or castigate recent specific abuses: excessive taxation, the corruption of the legal system through livery and maintenance, and the inadequacies of parliamentary representation. But this interrogation of the honesty and efficiency of the institutions of

---

[7] See Anne Hudson, 'The King and Erring Clergy: A Wycliffite Contribution' in *SCH*, Subsidia 9 (1991), 269-78. The fourth reason is on p.276. The writer supports his case by referring to the point in the coronation ceremony where the metropolitan hands the king a sword and reminds him of his duty to defend the church and his people. Hudson notes, p.274, that the writer of the tract appears to have missed the irony that by quoting the words of the metropolitan, the secular ruler is endowed with authority by the Church.

[8] *De Regibus*, in *Four English Political Tracts of the Later Middle Ages*, ed. J.-P. Genet, CS, 4th Series, 18 (1977), p.14.

[9] *De Regibus*, p.6.

[10] *De Regibus*, p.10; *Jack Upland*, 57/72ff.

[11] *De Regibus*, pp.17-18.

[12] *Thirty Seven Conclusions*, p.149.

[13] *Trefnant*, p.278.

[14] *Trefnant*, p.272.

government and law lacks the desire to dismantle or deconstruct their establishment.

This concern for a stable, secular hierarchy is reflected in the traditions' explicit equation of right reading with correct social position. Within this firm framework, however, there is room for manoeuvre and flexibility. While the tradition manipulates a socially alliterative poetic to query the practices of secular government and law, it adopts legal language and procedures both to authorize its criticism, and to stay within the limits of the law. Similarly, on a smaller scale, the poems exploit linguistic devices such as puns which have the potential to destabilise linguistic hierarchy and deconstruct the very system of meaning in which they work. However, in keeping with the poems' predilection for overall legal restraint, this wordplay is kept within the bounds of addressing particular targets of criticism. Their declared intention is to use language as a rich resource of communication, not to collapse into anarchy the very system which makes meaningful communication possible.

I hope to have shown that it may be constructive to view these four alliterative poems as a *Piers Plowman* tradition. None of the poems is a slavish imitation of *Piers*; nor is any one of them simply a mindless pastiche of half-remembered borrowings.[15] Precise quotation and the reprise of themes, episodes and figures are re-worked intelligently into new poems which can stand independently from *Piers* and on their own terms. While none of the poems captures the affective, theological or spiritual dimensions of *Piers*, I would argue that this is best seen not as deficit, but as difference. The legal and political framework of each poem in the tradition is entirely apposite for the issues it seeks to address.

In tracing the contours of language in these four poems, I hope to have shown that it is neither a simplification to group these poems together, nor a misnomer to invest this classification with the name *Piers Plowman*. Their use of language and reflection of linguistic issues shows that they have much more in common than social and political interests which are graced with the occasional recall of phrases in *Piers Plowman*. As a group, they share a distinctive poetic which is sensitive to the texture of *Piers*, without being woodenly derivative. The prevailing temper appears to have been a collective effort to mobilise poetry in the search

---

15 David Lawton has described *Crowned King* as 'bland and mercifully brief . . .in which "speculum regale" barely rises into sense through unintelligent Langlandian pastiche'(1982), pp.9-10. While in scope it is obviously the least commanding of the poems in the tradition, I think that it represents an intelligent reading of *Piers*, and that the poem is rather deft in its questioning of the recent tax ordinance. Far from being a Shadwellian enterprise which cannot even make pretence to a faint meaning, the reprise of the opening of *Piers* in *Crowned King* is put to effective use. See further, Barr (1993), pp.30-35.

for truth and integrity. As such, I feel it appropriate to invest this corpus of poetry with the name, not of an author, but of a poem whose genesis and conclusions are still open to debate, and of an uncompromising labourer who hovers between fact and fiction.

It is my hope that the arguments and illustration in these pages have justified my act of literary colonisation.[16] While four alliterative poems have become annexed into the rather better known, and more powerful, territory of *Piers Plowman*, I see no reason for this to stand in the way of their forming simultaneous alliances with other literary works; indeed, I have sketched some interested parties in the course of this book. Obviously none of the poems in the tradition commands the literary puissance of *Piers Plowman*, yet in their idiosyncratic and intriguing ways, they are very much more than satellites to their source of inspiration. In considering the territorial implications of proposing the existence of the *Piers Plowman* tradition, I have been mindful less of the computer precision of modern cartography, as of the maps of much earlier times: at the top are whales, and at the bottom, cormorants, beakfull of fish. In between, is a subjective account of the lie of the land.

---

[16] I am referring here to the opening comments of Chapter One.

Bibliography

PRINTED PRIMARY SOURCES

The Anonimalle Chronicle, ed. V.H. Galbraith (Manchester, 1927).

Arnold, T., ed., *Select English Works of John Wyclif*, vol. III (Oxford, 1871).

The Poems of John Audelay, ed. E.K. Whiting (EETS 184 1931).

Augustine, *De Dialectica*, ed. J. Pinborg, trans. B. Darrell Jackson (Dordrecht, 1975)

Barr, H., ed. *The Piers Plowman Tradition* (London, 1993).

Bartholomaeus Anglicus, *De Proprietatibus Rerum*, transl. John Trevisa as *On the Properties of Things*, ed. M.C. Seymour, et al. (Oxford, 1975), 2 vols.

The Riverside Chaucer, ed. L.D. Benson et al. (Oxford, 1988).

Cigman, G., ed., *Lollard Sermons* (EETS 294 1989).

Conciliae Magnae Britanniae et Hiberniae, ed. D. Wilkins (London, 1737).

The Complete Works of Dante, ed. C.S. Singleton (Princeton, 1970-4).

Davies, R.T., ed., *Medieval English Lyrics* (London, 1963).

Dean, J., ed., *Six Ecclesiastical Satires* (TEAMS 1991).

The 'Gest Hystoriale' of the Destruction of Troy, edd. G.A. Panton and D. Donaldson (EETS 39 1869 and 56 1874).

Dieulacres Chronicle, edd. M.V. Clark and V.H. Galbraith, *BJRL*, 14 (1930), 164-81.

Dives and Pauper, ed. P.H. Barnum (EETS 275 1976 and 280 1980).

Dobson, R.B., ed., *The Peasants' Revolt of 1381* (London, 1970).

English Medieval Lapidaries, edd. J. Evans and M.J. Serjeantson (EETS OS 190 1933).

English Wycliffite Sermons, vols. I and III, ed. A. Hudson, vol. II, ed. P. Gradon (Oxford, 1983, 1988 and 1990).

Eulogium Historiarum, vol. III, ed. F.S. Haydon (RS 1863).

Historia Vitae et Regni Ricardi Secundi, ed. T. Hearne (London, 1727).

Fasciculi Zizaniorum, ed. W.W. Shirley (RS 1858).

Fitzralph, R., *Defensio Curatorum*, in *Trevisa's Dialogues*, ed. A.J. Perry (EETS 167 1925).

Freidberg, E., ed., *Corpus Iuris Canonici* (Leipzig, 1879-81), 2 vols.

The Chronicles of Froissart, transl. J. Bourchier, ed. G.C. Macaulay (London, 1913).

Gawain and the Green Knight, edd. J.R.R. Tolkein and E.V. Gordon, 2nd edn. ed. N. Davis (Oxford, 1967).

Genet, J.-P., ed., *Four English Political Tracts of the Later Middle Ages* (CS 4th Series, 18 1977).

Bibliography

The Complete Works of John Gower, ed. G.C. Macaulay (Oxford, 1899-1902), 4 vols.

The English Works of John Gower, ed., G.C. Macaulay (EETS ES 82 1901), 2 vols.

The Major Latin Works of John Gower, ed. and trans. E.W. Stockton (Seattle, 1961).

The Harley Lyrics, ed. G.L. Brook (Manchester, 1956).

Polychronicon Ranulphi Higden, ed. J.R. Lumby (Rolls Series 41 1871).

Hoccleve, T., *The Regement of Princes*, ed. F.J. Furnivall (EETS ES 72 1897).

——, *The Minor Poems*, edd. F.J. Furnivall and I. Gollancz, revd. J. Mitchell and A.I. Doyle (EETS ES 61, 73 1970).

Hudson, A., ed., *Two Wycliffite Texts* (EETS 301 1993).

Jack Upland, Friar Daw's Reply and Upland's Rejoinder, ed. P.L. Heyworth (London, 1968).

Jacobs Well, ed. A. Brandeis (EETS 115 1900).

Kail, J., ed., *Twenty Six Political and other Poems* (EETS 124 1904).

Kennedy, R., ed., 'A Bird in Bishopwood: Some Newly-Discovered Lines of Alliterative Verse from the Late Fourteenth Century', in *Medieval Literature and Antiquities*, edd. M. Stokes and T.L. Burton (Cambridge, 1987), 71-87.

The Lay Folks Mass Book, ed. T.F. Simmons (EETS 71 1879).

Lydgate, J., *Minor Poems*, ed. H.N. McCracken (EETS ES 107 1911 and OS 109 1934). 2 vols.

Kane. G., ed. *Piers Plowman: The 'A' Version* (London, 1960).

Kane G., and Talbot Donaldson, edd., *Piers Plowman: The 'B' Version* (London, 1975).

Knighton, H, *Chronicon*, ed. J.R. Lumby (RS 1889-95), 2 vols.

The Lanterne of Light, ed. M.L. Swinburne (EETS 151 1917).

Matthew, F.D., *The English Works of Wyclif Hitherto Unprinted* (EETS 74 1880, 2nd revd. edn., 1902).

Monumenta Franciscana, ed. Richard Howlett (RS 1882), 2 vols.

Mum and the Sothsegger, edd. M. Day and R. Steele (EETS 199 1936).

The Parlement of the Thre Ages, ed. M.Y. Offord (EETS 246 1959).

Pearl, ed. E.V. Gordon (Oxford, 1953).

Pearsall, D., ed., *Piers Plowman by William Langland: An Edition of the 'C' Text* (London, 1978).

Pecock, R., *Donet*, ed. E.V. Hitchcock (EETS 156 1921).

Pierce the Ploughman's Crede, ed. W.W. Skeat (EETS 30 1867).

Puttenham, G., *The Arte of English Poesie* quoted from *Elizabethan Critical Essays*, ed. G.G. Smith (Oxford, 1937)

edd. A.G. Rigg and Charlotte Brewer, *Piers Plowman: The Z Version* (Toronto, 1983).

Robbins, R.H. ed., *Historical Poems of the XIVth and XVth Centuries* (New York, 1959).

A.V.C. Schmidt, ed., *The Vision of Piers Plowman: A Complete Edition of the 'B' Text*, 2nd ed. (London, 1987).

Scott, S.P., ed., *The Civil Law* (Cincinatti, 1932), 17 vols.

Selections from English Wycliffite Writings, ed. A. Hudson (Cambridge, 1978).

The Siege of Jerusalem, edd. E. Kolbing and M. Day (EETS 188 1932).

The Simonie, ed. D. Embree and E. Urquhart (Heidelberg, 1991).

Skeat, W.W., ed., *Langland's Vision of Piers the Plowman, Text C, together with Richard the Redeless and The Crowned King* (EETS 54 1873).

——, *Piers Plowman and Richard the Redeless* (London, 1886), 2 vols.

——, *Chaucerian and Other Pieces, The Complete Works of Geoffrey Chaucer* (Oxford, 1897).

Steele, R., ed., *Earliest English Arithmetics* (EETS ES 118 1922).

The Tale of Beryn, ed. John M. Bowers in *The Canterbury Tales: Fifteenth Century Continuations and Additions* (TEAMS 1992).

Thirty Seven Conclusions, = *Remonstrance against Romish Corruptions*, ed. J. Forshall (London, 1851).

Chronique de la Traison et Mort du Richart Deux Roy Dengleterre, ed. B. Williams (London, 1846).

Registrum Johannis Trefnant, ed. W.W. Capes (Canterbury and York Society, 1916).

Johannis de Trokelowe et Henrici de Blaneforde, *Chronica et Annales*, ed. H.T. Riley (London, 1886). (*Annales*)

Chronicon Adae de Usk, ed. and trans. E.M. Thompson (London, 1904).

Walsingham, T., *Historia Anglicana*, ed. H.T. Riley (RS 1864), 2 vols.

Wimbledon's Sermon, ed. I.K. Knight (Pittsburgh, 1967).

Wright, T., ed., *Political Poems and Songs* (RS 1859-61), 2 vols.

Wynnere and Wastoure ed. S. Trigg (EETS 297 1990).

SECONDARY SOURCES

Abraham, D.H., ' "Cosyn and Cosynage": Pun and Structure in the *Shipman's Tale'*, *ChauR*, 11 (1977), 319-27.

Adams, R., 'Mede and Mercede': The Evolution of the Economics of Grace in the *Piers Plowman* B and C Versions' in *MESGK*, pp.217-32.

Aers, D., *Piers Plowman and Christian Allegory* (London, 1975).

Alford, J.A., 'Literature and Law in Medieval England', *PMLA*, 92 (1977), 941-51.

——, *Piers Plowman: A Glossary of Legal Diction* (Cambridge, 1988).

——, 'The Idea of Reason in *Piers Plowman*', in *MESGK*, pp.199-215.

Allen, J.B. 'Langland's Reading and Writing: Detractor and the Pardon Passus', *Speculum* 59 (1984), 342-59.

Allen, R.J., 'A Recurring Motif in Chaucer's *House of Fame*', *JEGP*, 55 (1956), 393-405.

Amassian M., and Sadowsky, J., 'Mede and Mercede: A Study of the Grammatical Metaphor in *Piers Plowman* C IV 335-409', *NM*, 72 (1971), 457-76.

Ashley, K.M., 'Renaming the Sins: A Homiletic Topos of Linguistic Instability in the *Canterbury Tales*', in *Sign, Sentence, Discourse*, edd. Julian Wasserman and Lois Roney (New York, 1989), 272-293.

Aston, M., *Lollards and Reformers: Images and Literacy in Late Medieval Religion* (London, 1984).

——, ' "Caim's Castles": Poverty, Politics and Disendowment', in R.B. Dobson, ed., *The Church, Politics and Patronage in the Fifteenth Century* (Gloucester, 1984), 45-81.

Axton, R.A., 'Chaucer's Heir' in *Chaucer Traditions*, edd. Ruth Morse and B. Windeatt (Cambridge, 1990), 21-38.

Baldwin, A., *The Theme of Government in Piers Plowman* (Cambridge, 1981).

——, 'The Historical Context' in *A Companion to Piers Plowman*, ed. J. Alford (Berkeley, 1988), 67-86.

Barfield, O., 'Poetic Diction and Legal Fiction, in *Essays presented to Charles Williams*, ed. C.S. Lewis (London, 1947), 106-27.

Barnie, J., *War in Medieval Society* (London, 1974).

Barr, H., 'The Use of Latin Quotations in *Piers Plowman* with special reference to Passus XVIII', *N&Q*, 231 (1986), 441-8.

——, *A Study of Mum and the Sothsegger in its Literary and Political Contexts* (unpublished Oxford D.Phil thesis 1989).

——, 'The Dates of *Richard the Redeless* and *Mum and the Sothsegger*', *N&Q*, 235 (1990), 270-5. (1990[1])

——, 'The Relationship of *Richard the Redeless* and *Mum and the Sothsegger*', *YLS*, 4 (1990), 105-33. (1990[2])

——, 'The Treatment of Natural Law in *Richard the Redeless* and *Mum and the Sothsegger*', *LSE*, 23 (1992), 49-80.

Barthes, R., 'The Death of the Author', in *Image, Music, Text*, ed. and trans. Stephen Heath (London, 1977), 142-48.

Bennett, J.A.W., 'Chaucer's Contemporary', in *Piers Plowman: Critical Approaches*, ed. S.S. Hussey (London, 1969), 310-24,

——, ' "Nosce te ipsum": Some Medieval Interpretations', in *J.R.R. Tolkein: Scholar and Storyteller*, edd. Mary Salu and Robert T. Farrell (Ithaca, New York, 1979), 138-58.

——, *Middle English Literature*, ed. and completed by D. Gray (Oxford, 1986).

Bestul, T.H., *Satire and Allegory in Winner and Waster* (Nebraska, 1974).

Birnes, W.J., 'Christ as Advocate: the Legal Metaphor of *Piers Plowman*', *Annuale Medievale*, 16 (1975), 71-93.

Blake, N.F., *The English Language in Medieval Literature* (London, 1979).

Blamires, A, '*Mum and the Sothsegger* and Langlandian Idiom', *NM*, 76 (1975), 583-604.

——, 'The Wife of Bath and Lollardy', *Medium Aevum*, 58 (1989), 224-42.

Blanch, R.J.and Wasserman, J.N., 'Medieval Contracts and Covenants: The Legal Colouring of *Sir Gawain and the Green Knight*,' *Neophilologus*, 68 (1984), 598-610.

Bloom, H., *The Anxiety of Influence* (New York, 1973).

Boitani, P., 'Chaucer's Labyrinth: Fourteenth Century Literature and Language', *ChauR*, 17 (1983), 197-220

——, *Chaucer and the Imaginary World of Fame* (Cambridge, 1984).

Bowers, J.M., '*Piers Plowman* and the Police: Notes Toward a History of the Wycliffite Langland', *YLS*, 6 (1992), 1-50.

Burnley, D., 'Langland's Lunatik Clergial' in *Langland, The Mystics and the Medieval English Religious Tradition*, ed. Helen Phillips (Cambridge, 1990), 31-8.

J.A. Burrow, 'The Audience of *Piers Plowman*', *Anglia*, 75 (1957), 373-84.

——, *Ricardian Poetry* (London, 1971).

——, 'Two Notes on *Sir Gawain and the Green Knight*', *N&Q*, N.S. 19 (1972), 43-5.

——, 'Hoccleve and Chaucer' in *Chaucer Traditions*, edd. Ruth Morse and B. Windeatt (Cambridge, 1990), 54-61.

Cavanaugh, S.H., *A Study of Books Privately Owned in England 1300-1450* (unpublished PhD thesis, University of Pennsylvania, 1980).

Colish, M.L., *The Mirror of Language* (Nebraska, 1983).

Cooper, H., 'Langland's and Chaucer's Prologues', *YLS*, 1 (1987), 71-81.

——, 'Generic Variations on the Theme of Poetic and Civil Authority' in *Poetics: Theory and Practice in Middle English Literature*, edd. P. Boitani and A. Torti (Cambridge, 1991), 83-103.

Crane, S., 'The Writing Lesson of 1381' in *Chaucer's England*, ed. B. Hanawalt (Minnesota, 1992), 201-221.

Crowley, T., *The Politics of Discourse* (London, 1989).

Curley, M.J., 'The Cloak of Anonymity and *The Prophecy of John of Bridlington*, *MP*, 77 (1980), 361-9.

Curzon, L.B., *English Legal History* (Plymouth, 1979).

Davie, D., *The Purity of Diction in English Verse* (London, 1967).

Davlin, M.C., *The Game of Heuene* (Cambridge, 1989).

Delaney, S., *Chaucer's House of Fame: The Poetics of Skeptical Fideism* (Chicago, 1972).

Derrida, J., *Of Grammatology*, trans. Gayatri Chakravorty Spivak (Baltimore, 1976).

——, *Dissemination*, trans. Barbara Johnson (Chicago, 1981).

Dillon, J., '*Piers Plowman*: A Particular Example of Wordplay and its Structural Significance', *Medium Aevum*, 50 (1981), 40-8.

Donaldson, E.T., *Piers Plowman: The C Text and its Poet* (New Haven, 1949)

——, 'The Texts of *Piers Plowman*: Scribes and Poets', *MP*, 1 (1952), 269-73.

——, 'MSS R and F in the B Tradition of *Piers Plowman*', *TCAAS*, 39 (1955), 177-212.

Doyle, A.I., 'An Unrecognised Piece of *Pierce the Ploughman's Crede* and other Work by its Scribe', *Speculum*, 34 (1959), 428-36.

——, 'The Manuscripts' in Lawton (1982), 88-100.

Duggan, H., 'Langland's Meter', *YLS*, 1 (1987), 41-71.

Eckhardt, C., 'Another Historical Allusion in *Mum and the Sothsegger*', *N&Q*, 225 (1980), 495-7.

Edwards, A.S.G., 'Chaucer and the Poetics of Utterance' in *Poetics: Theory and Practice in Middle English Literature*, ed. P. Boitani and A. Torti (Cambridge, 1991), 57-67.

Elliott, T.J., 'Middle English Complaints Against the Times: To Contemn the World or to Reform it?', *Annuale Mediaevale*, 14 (1973), 22-35.

Embree, D., '*Richard the Redeless* and *Mum and the Sothsegger*: A Case of Mistaken Identity', *N&Q*, 220 (1975), 4-12.

——, 'The King's Ignorance: A Topos for Evil Times', *Medium Aevum*, 54 (1985), 121-26.

Everett D., and Hurnard, N.D., 'Legal Phraseology in a Passage in *Pearl*', *Medium Aevum*, 16 (1947), 9-15.

Fairclough, N., *Language and Power* (London, 1989).

Foucault, M., *The Archaeology of Knowledge*, trans. A.M. Sheridan Smith (London, 1972).

——, *The History of Sexuality. Volume 1: An Introduction* (1976), trans. Robert Hurley (Harmondsworth, 1979).

——, 'What is an Author?' in *Textual Strategies*, ed. J.Harari (London, 1979), pp.141-60.

Frank, R.W., 'The Pardon Scene in *Piers Plowman*', *Speculum*, 26 (1951), 317-31.

Fry, D.K., 'The Authority of "Elde" in *The Parlement of the Thre Ages*', in *Hermeneutics and Medieval Culture*, edd. Patrick J. Gallacher and Helen Damico (New York, 1989), 213-24.

Gellrich, J.M., *The Idea of the Book in the Middle Ages* (Cornell, 1985).

Godden, M., *The Making of Piers Plowman* (London, 1990).

Gradon, P., 'Langland and the Ideology of Dissent', *PBA*, 66 (1980), 179-20.

Green, R.F., 'John Ball's Letters: Literary History and Historical Literature' in *Chaucer's England: Literature in Historical Context*, ed. Barbara A. Hanawalt (Minnesota, 1992), 176-200.

Gwynn, A., *The English Austin Friars in the Time of Wyclif* (Oxford, 1940).

Haines, R.M., 'Our Master Mariner, Our Sovereign Lord: A Contemporary Preacher's View of Henry V', *Medieval Studies*, 38 (1976), 85-96.

Hanna III, Ralph, *William Langland* (Aldershot, 1993).

Heffernan, T.J., 'Aspects of the Chaucerian apocrypha: animadversions on William Thynne's edition of *The Plowman's Tale*', in *Chaucer Traditions*, edd. Ruth Morse and B.A. Windeatt (Cambridge, 1990), 155-67.

Hudson, A., *Lollards and their Books* (London, 1985).

——, 'Wycliffism in Oxford', in *Wyclif in his Times*, ed. A.J.P. Kenny (Oxford, 1986), 67-84.

——, *The Premature Reformation* (Oxford, 1988). (1988[1])

——, 'The Legacy of *Piers Plowman*', in *A Companion to Piers Plowman*, ed. J.A. Alford (Berkeley, 1988), 251-66. (19882)

——, 'The King and Erring Clergy: A Wycliffite Contribution' in *SCH*, Subsidia 9 (1991), 269-78.

——, '*Piers Plowman* and the Peasants' Revolt: A Problem Revisited' (forthcoming *YLS*, 8 1994).

——, and Spencer, H.L., 'Old Author, New Work: The Sermons of MS Longleat 4', *Medium Aevum*, 53 (1984), 220-38.

Huppé, B.F., 'Petrus id est Christus': Wordplay in *Piers Plowman* the B Text', *ELH* 17 (1950), 163-70.

Hussey, S.S., 'Langland's Reading of Alliterative Poetry', *MLR*, 60 (1965), 163-70.

Jacobs, N., 'Alliterative Storms: A Topos in Middle English', *Speculum*, 47 (1972), 695-719.

S.L. Jansen, 'Politics, Protest and a New *Piers Plowman* Fragment', *RES*, 40 (1989), 93-99.

Jordan, R.M., 'Lost in the Funhouse of Fame: Chaucer and Postmodernism', *ChauR*, 18 (1983), 100-15.

Justice, S., 'The Genres of *Piers Plowman*', *Viator*, 19 (1988), 291-306.

Kane, G., *The Evidence for Authorship* (London, 1965).

——, 'Music Neither Unpleasant nor Monotonous' in *Medieval Studies for J.A.W.Bennett*, ed. P.L. Heyworth (Oxford, 1981), pp.43-63.

——, 'The "Z version" of *Piers Plowman*', *Speculum*, 60 (1985), 910-30.

——, 'Some Fourteenth Century "Political" Poems', in *Medieval English and Ethical Literature: Essays in Honour of G.H. Russell*, ed. G. Kratzmann and J. Simpson (Cambridge, 1986), 82-91.

——, 'The Text', in *A Companion to Piers Plowman*, ed. J.A. Alford (Berkeley, 1988), 175-200.

Kean, P.M., *Pearl: An Interpretation* (London, 1967).

Kendall, R.D., *The Drama of Dissent: The Radical Poetry of Nonconformity 1380-1590* (North Carolina, 1986).

Kenny, A., *Wyclif* (Oxford, 1985).

Khinoy, S.A., 'Inside Chaucer's Pardoner', *ChauR*, 6 (1972), 255-67.

Kirby, J.L., *Henry IV of England* (London, 1970).

Kress, G., *Linguistic Processes in Sociocultural Practices* (Oxford, 1985).

Kuhn, T.S., *The Structure of Scientific Revolutions* (Chicago, 1962).

Lampe, D., 'The Satiric Strategy of *Pierce the Ploughmans Crede*', in *The Alliterative Tradition in the Fourteenth Century*, edd. B.S. Levy and P.S. Szarmach (Ohio, 1981).

Lawton, D., '*Scottish Fielde*: Alliterative Verse and Stanley Encomium in the Percy Folio', *LSE*, 10 (1978), 42-57.

——, 'Lollardy and the *Piers Plowman Tradition*', *MLR*, 76 (1981), 780-93.

——, ed. *Middle English Alliterative Poetry and its Literary Background*, (Cambridge, 1982).

——, 'The Unity of Middle English Alliterative Poetry', *Speculum*, 58 (1983), 72-94.

——, 'The Subject of *Piers Plowman*', *YLS*, 1 (1987), 1-30.

——, 'Alliterative Style,' in *A Companion to Piers Plowman*, ed. J. Alford (Berkeley, 1988), 223-50.

——, 'The Diversity of Middle English Alliterative Poetry', *LSE*, 20 (1989), 143-72.

Lee, D., *Competing Discourses* (London, 1992).

Leech, G., *A Linguistic Guide to English Poetry* (London, 1969).

——, *Semantics* (Harmondsworth, 1981).

——, and Short, M., *Style in Fiction* (London, 1981).

Leff, G., *Heresy in the Later Middle Ages* (Manchester, 1967).

Lerner, R.E., 'Medieval Prophecy and Religious Dissent', *Past and Present*, 72 (1976), 3-24.

McDonald, C., 'The Perversion of Law in Robert Henryson's Fable of "The Fox, the Wolf and the Husbandman" ', *Medium Aevum*, 49 (1980), 244-53.

Macdonnell, D., *Theories of Discourse: An Introduction* (Oxford, 1986).

McNiven, P., *Heresy and Politics in the Reign of Henry IV: The Burning of John Badby* (Cambridge, 1987).

Mann. J., *Chaucer and Medieval Estates Satire* (Cambridge, 1973).

——, 'Eating and Drinking in *Piers Plowman*', *E&S*, 32 (1979), 26-43.

——, 'The Tyranny of the Alphabet: The Relationship of the A and B Versions of *Piers Plowman*' (forthcoming *YLS*, 8 1994).

Martin, P., *Piers Plowman: The Field and the Tower* (London, 1979).

Middleton, A., 'The Idea of Public Poetry in the Reign of Richard II', *Speculum*, 53 (1978), 94-114.

——, 'The Audience and Public of *Piers Plowman*' in Lawton (1982), 101-23.

——, 'Making a Good Ende: John But as a Reader of *Piers Plowman*', in *MESGK*, pp.243-266.

——, 'William Langland's "Kynde Name": Authorial Signature and Social Identity in Late Fourteenth-Century England', in *Literary Practice and Social Change in Britain, 1380-1530*, ed. Lee Patterson (Berkeley, 1990), 15-82.

Miller, P., 'John Gower: Satiric Poet', in *Gower's Confessio Amantis: Responses and Reassessments*, ed. A.J. Minnis (Cambridge, 1983), 79-105.

Minnis, A., ' "Authorial Intention" and "Literal Sense" in the Exegetical Theories of Richard Fitzralph and John Wyclif', *PRIA*, 75 (1975), 1-31.

——, 'Chaucer's Pardoner and the Office of Preacher', in *Intellectuals and Writers in Fourteenth Century Europe*, edd. P. Boitani and A. Torti (Cambridge, 1986), 88-119.

——, *The Medieval Theory of Authorship*, 2nd edn. (Aldershot, 1988).

Bibliography

——, 'John Gower: "Sapiens" in Ethics and Politics', in *Gower's Confessio Amantis: A Critical Anthology*, ed. P. Nicholson (Cambridge, 1991), 158-76.

Muscatine, C., 'The Locus of Action in Medieval Narrative', *Romance Philology*, 17 (1963), 115-22.

Oakden, J.P., *Alliterative Poetry in Middle English: The Dialectal and Metrical Survey* (Manchester, 1968), 2 vols.

Ong, W.J., *Orality and Literacy* (London, 1982).

Overstreet, S., ' "Grammaticus Ludens": Theological Aspects of Langland's Grammatical Allegory', *Traditio*, 40 (1984), 251-96.

Patterson, L, *Chaucer and the Subject of History* (London, 1991).

Pearsall, D., *Old and Middle English Poetry* (London, 1977)

——, 'The "Ilchester" Manuscript of *Piers Plowman*', *NM*, 82 (1981), 181-93.

——, 'The Alliterative Revival: Origins and Social Backgrounds' in *Middle English Alliterative Poetry*, ed. David Lawton (Cambridge, 1982), 34-53.

Pecheux, M., *Language, Semantics and Ideology: Stating the Obvious* (1975), trans. H. Nagpal (London, 1982).

Peter, J.D., *Complaint and Satire in Early English Literature* (Oxford, 1956).

Purdon, L.O., 'Chaucer's *Lak of Stedfastnesse*: A Revalorisation of the Word', in *Sign, Sentence and Discourse*, edd. Julian Wasserman and Lois Roney (New York, 1989), 144-52.

Reisner, T.A. 'The "Cortaysye" sequence in *Pearl*', *MP*, 72 (1975), 400-03.

Reiss, E., 'Ambiguous Signs and Authorial Deceptions in Fourteenth Century Fictions', in *Sign, Sentence and Discourse*, edd. Julian Wasserman and Lois Roney (New York, 1989), 113-140.

Revard, C., 'The Tow on Absolon's Distaff and the Punishment of Lechers in Medieval London', *ELN*, 17 (1980), 168-70.

Ricks, C., 'Metamorphosis in Other Words', in *Gower's Confessio Amantis: Responses and Reassessments*, ed. A.J. Minnis (Cambridge, 1983), pp.25-49.

Rigg, A.G., '*John of Bridlington's Prophecy*: A New Look', *Speculum*, 63 (1988), 596-613.

Robbins, R.H., 'Middle English Poems of Protest', *Anglia*, 78 (1960), 193-203.

Robson, J.A., *Wyclif and the Oxford Schools* (Cambridge, 1961).

Ronan, N., '1381: Writing in Revolt: Signs of Confederacy in the Chronicle Accounts of the English Rising', *Forum for Modern Language Studies*, 25 (1989), 304-14.

Russell, G.H., 'Some Early Responses to the C Version of *Piers Plowman*', *Viator*, 15 (1984), 276-91.

——, and Venetia Nathan, 'A *Piers Plowman* Manuscript in the Huntingdon Library', *HLQ*, 26 (1963), 119-30.

E.Salter, '*Piers Plowman* and *The Simonie*', *Archiv*, 203 (1967), 241-54.

——, 'Alliterative Modes and Affiliations in the Fourteenth Century', *NM*, 79 (1978), 25-35.

——, 'Langland and the Contexts of *Piers Plowman*', *E&S*, 32 (1979), 19-25.

Scase, W., 'Two *Piers Plowman* C Text Interpolations: Evidence for a Second Textual Tradition', *N&Q*, 232 (1987), 453-63.

——, *Piers Plowman and the New Anticlericalism* (Cambridge, 1989).

Scattergood, V.J., *Politics and Poetry in the Fifteenth Century* (London, 1971).

Schmidt, A.V.C., 'Langland's Structural Imagery', *EIC*, 30 (1980), 311-25.

——, ' "Lele Wordes" and "Bele Paroles": Some Aspects of Langland's Wordplay', *RES*, 34 (1983), 137-50.

——, 'The Authenticity of the Z Text of *Piers Plowman*: Further Notes on Metrical Evidence', *Medium Aevum*, 56 (1987), 25-45.

——, *The Clerkly Maker: Langland's Poetic Art* (Cambridge, 1987).

Schmitz, G, 'Rhetoric and Fiction: Gower's Comments on Eloquence and Courtly Fiction', in *Gower's Confessio Amantis: A Critical Anthology*, ed. P. Nicholson (Cambridge, 1991), 117-142.

Schoeck, R.J., 'A Legal Reading of Chaucer's *Hous of Fame*', *UTQ*, 23 (1954), 185-92.

Shepherd, G., 'The Nature of Alliterative Poetry in Medieval England', *PBA*, 41 (1970), 57-76.

Shoaf, R.A., 'Speche þat Spire is of Grace': A Note on *Piers Plowman* B IX 104', *YLS*, 1 (1987), 128-33.

——, 'The Play of Puns in Late Middle English Poetry: Concerning Juxtology', in *On Puns: The Foundation of Letters*, ed. Jonathan Culler (Oxford, 1988), 44-61.

Simpson, J., 'The Transformation of Meaning: A Figure of Thought in *Piers Plowman*', *RES*, 37 (1986), 161-83.

——, *Piers Plowman: An Introduction to the B-Text* (London, 1990).

——, 'The Constraints of Satire in *Piers Plowman* and *Mum and the Sothsegger*', in *Langland, the Mystics and the Medieval English Religious Tradition*, ed. H. Phillips (Cambridge, 1990), 11-30.

Southern, R., *The Making of the Middle Ages* (London, 1967).

——, 'Aspects of the European Tradition of Historical Writing: History as Prophecy', *TRHS*, 22 (1972), 159-60.

Spearing, A.C., *Medieval to Renaissance in English Poetry* (Cambridge, 1985).

Steel, A. *Richard II* (Cambridge, 1962).

Stokes, M., *Justice and Mercy in Piers Plowman* (London, 1984).

Strohm, P., 'Chaucer's Fifteenth Century Audience and the Narrowing of the ''Chaucer tradition'' ', *SAC*, 4 (1982), 3-32.

Szittya, P., *The Antifraternal Tradition in Medieval England* (Princeton, 1986).

Tavers, J.K., 'The Abbess's ABC', *YLS*, 2 (1988), 137-42.

Taylor, P.B., ' ''Peynteyd Confessiouns''; Boccaccio and Chaucer', *Comparative Literature*, 34 (1982), 116-29.

Taylor, R., *The Political Prophecy in England* (New York, 1911).

Traugott, E.C., and Pratt, M.L., *Linguistics for Students of Literature* (New York, 1980).

Trigg, S., 'Israel Gollancz's *Wynnere and Wastoure*: Political Satire or Editorial Politics', in *Medieval English Religious and Ethical Literature: Essays in Honour of G.H. Russell*, ed. G. Kratzmann and J. Simpson (Cambridge, 1986), pp.115-27.

Tuck, A., *Richard II and the English Nobility* (London, 1973).

Turville-Petre, T., *The Alliterative Revival* (Cambridge, 1977).

Uhart, M-L., *The Early Reception of Piers Plowman* (unpublished Leicester PhD thesis, 1986).

Vickers, B., *In Defence of Rhetoric* (Oxford, 1988).

Von Nolcken, C., '*Piers Plowman*, the Wycliffites and *Pierce the Ploughman's Crede*', *YLS*, 2 (1988), 71-102.

Wawn, A., 'The Genesis of *The Plowman's Tale*', *YES*, 2 (1972), 21- 40.

——, 'Truth-Telling and the Tradition of *Mum and the Sothsegger*', *YES*, 13 (1983), 270-87.

Wenzel, S., '*Mum and the Sothsegger*, lines 421-22', *ELN*, 14 (1976), 87-90.

Wimsatt W.K. and Beardsley, M.C., 'The Intentional Fallacy' in *The Verbal Icon* (Kentucky, 1954), 3-18.

Windeatt, B.A., 'The Scribes as Chaucer's Earliest Critics', *SAC*, 1 (1979), 119-42.

——, 'Chaucer Traditions' in *Chaucer Traditions*, edd. Ruth Morse and B. Windeatt (Cambridge, 1990), 1-20.

——, 'Chaucer and Fifteenth Century Romance: *Partonope of Blois*' in *Chaucer Traditions*, 62-80.

Woolf, R., 'The Tearing of the Pardon' in *Piers Plowman: Critical Approaches*, ed. S.S. Hussey (London, 1969), 50-75.

York, E.C., 'The Duel of Chivalry in Malory's Book XIX', *PQ*, 48 (1969), 181-91.

——, 'Legal Punishment in Malory's *Le Morte D'Arthur*, *ELN*, 1 (1973), 14-21.

Index